A Midsummer Night's Dream

GW00480609

Continuum Renaissance Drama

Series editors: Andrew Hiscock, University of Wales Bangor, UK and Lisa Hopkins, Sheffield Hallam University, UK

Continuum Renaissance Drama offers practical and accessible introductions to the critical and performative contexts of key Elizabethan and Jacobean plays. Each guide introduces the text's critical and performance history but also provides students with an invaluable insight into the landscape of current scholarly research through a keynote essay on the state of the art and newly commissioned essays of fresh research from different critical perspectives.

Current titles:

Doctor Faustus, ed. Sara Munson Deats

'Tis Pity She's A Whore, ed. Lisa Hopkins

Forthcoming titles:

1 Henry IV, ed. Stephen Longstaffe

The Duchess of Malfi, ed. Christina Luckyj

King Lear, ed. Andrew Hiscock and Lisa Hopkins

Volpone, ed. Matthew Steggle

Women Beware Women, ed. Andrew Hiscock

A MIDSUMMER NIGHT'S DREAM

A Critical Guide

Edited by Regina Buccola

continuum

Continuum
The Tower Building
11 York Road
London SE1 7NX

80 Maiden Lane, Suite 704
New York
NY 10038

www.continuumbooks.com

British Library Cataloguing-in-Publication Data
A catalogue record for this book is available from the British Library.

ISBN: 978-1-8470-6135-5 (Hardback)
         978-1-8470-6136-2 (paperback)

Library of Congress Cataloging-in-Publication Data
A catalog record for this book is available from the Library of Congress.

Typeset by BookEns Ltd, Royston, Hertfordshire
Printed and bound in Great Britain by
CPI Antony Rowe, Chippenham, Wiltshire

Contents

Series Introduction

The drama of Shakespeare and his contemporaries has remained at the very heart of English curricula internationally and the pedagogic needs surrounding this body of literature have grown increasingly complex as more sophisticated resources become available to scholars, tutors and students. This series aims to offer a clear picture of the critical and performative contexts of a range of chosen texts. In addition, each volume furnishes readers with invaluable insights into the landscape of current scholarly research as well as including new pieces of research by leading critics.

This series is designed to respond to the clearly identified needs of scholars, tutors and students for volumes which will bridge the gap between accounts of previous critical developments and performance history and an acquaintance with new research initiatives related to the chosen plays. Thus, our ambition is to offer innovative and challenging guides which will provide practical, accessible and thought-provoking analyses of Renaissance drama. Each volume is organized according to a progressive reading strategy involving introductory discussion, critical review and cutting-edge scholarly debate. It has been an enormous pleasure to work with so many dedicated scholars of Renaissance drama and we are sure that this series will encourage you to read 400-year old playtexts with fresh eyes.

Andrew Hiscock and Lisa Hopkins

Timeline

Late 1380s: Geoffrey Chaucer composes 'The Knight's Tale' for *The Canterbury Tales* (one source for the Theseus/Hippolyta plotline in *A Midsummer Night's Dream*) and 'The Merchant's Tale', which features a quarrel between the king and queen of fairies over a pair of mortal lovers.

1534: Sir John Bourchier, Lord Berners, translates the French *Huon de Burdeux* into English, providing a source for Shakespeare's Oberon.

1566: William Adlington translates Apuleius's *The Golden Ass* into English; the tale features a love affair between a young woman and a man completely transformed into an ass.

1567: Ovid's *Metamorphoses* translated into English by Arthur Golding (source for the *Pyramus and Thisbe* material in *Dream*).

1575: Queen Elizabeth I greeted by the fairy queen in a courtly entertainment at Woodstock.

1578: Boys dressed as fairies dance before Queen Elizabeth I at Norwich in an entertainment by Thomas Churchyard combining fairy belief with classical myth.

1579: Sir Thomas North translates Plutarch's *The Lives of the Noble Grecians and Romans* into English, providing a source in 'The Life of Theseus'.

1584: Reginald Scot writes *The Discoverie of Witchcraft*, which derides fairy belief and witchcraft accusations.

c.1590: Robert Greene writes *The Scottish History of James IV*, featuring Oberon as a character – a likely influence on Shakespeare's portrait of the fairy king.

1591: Queen Elizabeth I cast as the favourite of the fairy queen in a courtly entertainment at the Earl of Hertford's estate, Elvetham.

1590, 1596: Edmund Spenser completes two sets of three books each of *The Faerie Queene*, in which homage is paid to Elizabeth I in the person of the title character.

1595–96: Probable date of composition of *A Midsummer Night's Dream* (Shakespeare's lyric period, which also includes the history *Richard II* and the tragedy *Romeo and Juliet*).

1597: Shakespeare writes *The Merry Wives of Windsor*, featuring a sub-plot in which Windsor youth disguised as fairies seek playful revenge against a would-be adulterer.

1598: Francis Meres's *Palladis Tamia* credits Shakespeare with authorship of *A Midsummer Night's Dream*, establishing the date by which the play must have been completed.

1600: Publication of *A Midsummer Night's Dream* in quarto (small, single-volume publication analogous to a small paperback book of today). Publication of the ballad *The Mad Merry Pranks of Robin Good-fellow*, which reprises many elements from Puck's II.i speech of self-introduction from *A Midsummer Night's Dream*.

1610: Ben Jonson writes *The Alchemist*, featuring a London con artist disguised as the fairy queen.

1611: Ben Jonson writes the court masque *Oberon, The Fairy Prince*.

1619: Publication of second quarto edition of *A Midsummer Night's Dream*, clearly derived from the first quarto.

1623: Publication of the *First Folio*, the first collected works of Shakespeare's plays, including a slightly expanded version of *A Midsummer Night's Dream* (i.e. more detailed stage directions).

1634: John Ford's *Perkin Warbeck* presents the fairy king and queen on the Caroline stage.

1638: Continuing the vogue for plays about the king and queen of fairyland, Thomas Randolph incorporates the pair into *Amyntas, or The Impossible Dowry*.

1655: Even with the theatres closed during the Interregnum, James

Shirley finds a reading audience for another play featuring the fairy king and queen, *The Gentleman of Venice*.

1662: Restoration diarist Samuel Pepys attends perhaps the first production of *Dream* with actresses appearing in the women's roles, but scoffs at the play as 'ridiculous'. Hinting at adaptation, the production Pepys saw was entitled *The Merry Conceited Humours of Bottom the Weaver*.

1692: Elkanah Settle premieres an operatic version of *Dream* called *The Fairy Queen* with music by Henry Purcell at Dorset Gardens Theatre in London.

1754: David Garrick mounts the popular production *The Fairies*, *A Midsummer Night's Dream* redux focused on the fairies, retaining only about a quarter of the play's original text, but beefed up with 28 songs.

1827: Felix Mendelssohn composes the incidental music for a Prussian production of *A Midsummer Night's Dream*, which has since graced countless stage and film productions.

1840: Madame Vestris combines Shakespeare's full text with Mendelssohn's full score for a production of *A Midsummer Night's Dream* at Covent Garden, London.

1909: Charles Kent and J. Stuart Blackton direct the first film version of *Dream*.

1914: Harley Granville-Barker stages *A Midsummer Night's Dream* at the Savoy Theatre in London on a brightly-lit thrust stage intended to mimic original performance conditions.

1934: Maximillian Reinhardt directs *A Midsummer Night's Dream* at the Hollywood Bowl in California.

1935: Maximillian Reinhardt commits his lavish production of *Dream* to film, starring Olivia de Havilland, James Cagney, Victor Jory and Mickey Rooney, and set to Mendelssohn's music.

1937: Vivien Leigh stars in Tyrone Guthrie's fanciful Victorian vision of *A Midsummer Night's Dream* at the Old Vic in London.

1954: Michael Benthall returns *Dream* to the Old Vic in a production combining high-profile actors like Moira Shearer with the dancing talents of the Sadler's Wells Ballet, performing to the music of Mendelssohn.

1959, 1962: Peter Hall directs *A Midsummer Night's Dream* for the

Royal Shakespeare Company in Stratford-upon-Avon, in productions determined to return the play to its roots.

1964: Jan Kott publishes his controversial essay about the pervasive darkness and bestial sexuality of *Dream* that powerfully influences subsequent productions and critical interpretations of the play.

1967: Peter Hall's successful stage production of *Dream* is committed to film, setting the action in a wet, muddy countryside with actors that become proportionately less clothed as they get dirtier.

1970: Peter Brook directs his landmark production of *Dream* for the Royal Shakespeare Company, with a cast perched on trapezes in a white box space.

1989: *A Midsummer Night's Dream* returns to the Royal Shakespeare Company in Stratford under the direction of John Caird, with trashy-chic fairies frolicking on piles of rubbish in combat boots.

1999: Michael Hoffman sets *Dream* in the Victorian era for his film starring Michelle Pfeiffer, Rupert Everett, Christian Bale, Calista Flockhart and Kevin Kline.

2006: Tim Supple premieres his multi-lingual production of *Dream* in New Delhi, India, with actors speaking in English and seven South Asian dialects.

Introduction

Regina Buccola

A Midsummer Night's Dream: An Overview

In many ways, *A Midsummer Night's Dream* stands as the most conventional of comedies. Indeed, one can study an array of comic conventions in the course of studying this play. To begin at the ending, the play concludes with the joyous celebration of a triple wedding; happy marriages, either planned or celebrated, are characteristic of the final scenes of comedies even in today's favourite entertainment genre, film. In Shakespeare's era, the classical tradition of new comedy featured the generational conflict that figures so prominently in *A Midsummer Night's Dream*, in which the elder generation has to be coaxed and cajoled into agreement with the desires of the younger generation, often with respect to their romantic choices. In the formulations of Northrop Frye and C. L. Barber, the excursion of the four young lovers of *A Midsummer Night's Dream* into the fairy wood also marks the play out as a 'green world' comedy in which the central characters resolve crises in their lives by leaving the environment where the trouble originated for a remote, 'green' location like the fairy wood outside Athens, where resolution is achieved – sometimes, as in *Dream*, with supernatural assistance of some kind. Such oscillation between the city and its troubles and an idyllic rural space is also, as Helen Hackett points out, an element of pastoral: 'a narrative in which characters leave their customary abode of civilization, whether the court or the city, and experience either a voluntary or forced exile in a natural space, where they learn a better understanding of themselves', which they take with them back to the court.[1] The glee that Puck takes in causing trouble for the fairy queen and the four young lovers on the run in his woodland stomping grounds can be situated in the context of Mikhail Bakhtin's formulations of the carnivalesque, a period of misrule that serves a cathartic function both within the world of the fictional narrative and, as scholars applying Bakhtin's theories to dramatic texts have argued, for the watching audience, so that all are prepared for the restoration of order ushered in during the final act.[2]

Some scholars of *A Midsummer Night's Dream* have found it to be the obverse of Shakespeare's great tragedy of young love, *Romeo and Juliet*.[3] As when one turns a piece of printed fabric inside out, the tragic pattern of *Romeo and Juliet* remains visible, in a residual way, in *Dream*'s narrative of captive women (Hippolyta), potential forced marriage (Hermia and Demetrius) and a terrifying night in a fairy wood that leaves Demetrius under the influence of Oberon's love drug at the end of the play. It is hard to fully embrace Demetrius's drugged marriage to Helena, a woman he had repudiated, as a happy one.[4] Then again, as Peter Hollindale points out, since Demetrius has reportedly vacillated once, before the action of the play begins, shifting from loving Helena to loving Hermia, 'The play's convention of sudden and magically-induced transfers of allegiance is not an aberration confined to the wood. It has its prototype in the "real" world'.[5] Indeed, as I completed work on this introduction, Tom Clayton sent me an article describing how modern science might make the love potions of popular culture a reality by manipulating oxytocin levels in women, and vasopressin levels in men.[6] Perhaps a future production of *A Midsummer Night's Dream* will find a way to make Demetrius a vasopressin junkie. As the numerous productions and adaptations over the years have demonstrated, the play is flexible enough to support a wide array of interpretations: 'it can be a lightweight family entertainment, or an orgiastic adult fantasy; a joyous celebration of love and marriage, or a near-tragedy haunted by infidelity and mortality'.[7]

R. A. Foakes finds *Dream*'s strength to lie

> in the way its delightful fictions and charming poetry [...] continually reverberate with profundities that are in the end as far beyond our grasp as Bottom's dream. No doubt further significances will continue to be found in it, for like other great plays by Shakespeare, it appears to be inexhaustible'.[8]

The myriad responses *Dream* has inspired notwithstanding, some reactions to the play are cited repeatedly in the essays collected here, indicating their wide impact upon the study of *A Midsummer Night's Dream*. The most widely cited responses include those of: Samuel Pepys (hated it); Felix Mendelssohn (unforgettably scored it); Minor White Latham (questioned the origins of the play's minuscule fairies); Peter Brook and Jan Kott (looked at it through a darker lens); David P. Young (analysed *Dream*'s artistry); Marjorie Garber (explored the implications of the dreams named in the play's title); Louis Montrose (found in Titania a cathartic release for early modern male anxieties about an ageing, heirless queen on the English throne); Ania Loomba (considered the colonialist implications of Oberon's desired henchman, the Indian boy); and Valerie Traub (thoughtfully interrogated the dual presence of Helena and Hermia's homoerotic attachment to one another and the captive Amazonian queen, Hippolyta). Students who have studied literary theory will recognize a number of theoretical approaches in the works discussed in this volume and employed in the essays within it. Among the critical perspectives that have been most frequently and fruitfully applied to *A Midsummer Night's Dream* are: psychoanalytic criticism; new historicism/cultural materialism; gender criticism; postcolonial criticism; and performance studies criticism.

All of the many scholarly editions of *A Midsummer Night's Dream* currently available offer introductory overviews of the play's critical and performance history. A number of commonalities emerge when one reads even a sampling of these introductions to the play.[9] One of the views most frequently expressed is that those who regard *A Midsummer Night's Dream* as merely a whimsical bit of fairy fluff are sorely mistaken, and liable to be caught off guard by the complexity and emotional depth of the play.[10] Indeed, *Dream* reflects some of Shakespeare's habitual fixations across generic borders, including gender relations, folk customs and beliefs, and the status of patriarchal/monarchical authority.

A Midsummer Night's Dream features a number of vexed gender relationships: Hippolyta is Theseus's prisoner as well as his fiancée; Hermia is required by two patriarchal authority figures – her literal father and her political father, Duke Theseus – to accept Demetrius as her spouse when she has chosen Lysander for herself; Helena betrays her longstanding friendship to Hermia in a heartbeat when she sees an opportunity to gain even a modicum of ground with the cruel Demetrius by revealing her friend's secrets; and even in the fairy world, Puck and Oberon collude in using potent drugs to overcome Titania and wrest a young Indian boy that she has adopted from her. Moreover, while Theseus does finally relent and permit Hermia to marry Lysander, he seems to do so largely because the still-drugged Demetrius of *Dream*'s fifth act has switched his allegiance back from Hermia to Helena. Oberon, the king of the fairy wood, engineered that switch. Therefore, *Dream*'s audience is potentially left with the uncomfortable sense that male political leaders call the shots on everything from warfare, to distribution of children, to marital pairings.

Since Peter Brook's landmark production of *Dream* at the Royal Shakespeare Theatre in 1970 in which he doubled the roles of Theseus and Hippolyta with those of Oberon and Titania, the pairing has become de rigueur in modern productions and may, as Helen Hackett has pointed out, reflect theatrical practice in Shakespeare's own era, when individual actors routinely played multiple roles in the same play. Such doubling, as Hackett notes, contributes to the dream elements of the play's plot since

> it creates a sense that the fairy action of the play is related to and a reflection of the action in the outer Athenian frame; that Oberon and Titania are the dream-personae of Theseus and Hippolyta through which the Athenian couple can enact their secret desires and work out their buried resentments.[11]

Doubling these parts also underscores the extent to which the paired rulers of Athens and the fairy wood comment upon one another's leadership styles and, perhaps, political leadership broadly defined. Hippolyta, as an Amazon, has been a formidable opponent of Theseus prior to the beginning of the play's action, as Titania has been to her fairy spouse, Oberon. However, over the course of the play, this power dynamic shifts, placing the two male figures in the ascendant. Notice that in the end, however, the presence of the fairies in Athens corroborates Hippolyta's view that the story told by the four lovers should be countenanced whereas Theseus dismisses it, and Titania calls for the fairy benediction that Oberon performs in the final scene.

Folk beliefs regarding fairies and witches abound in Shakespeare's plays; *A Midsummer Night's Dream* joins the tragedy *Macbeth* and the late comedy (or 'romance') *The Tempest* in placing supernatural figures at the forefront of the dramatis personae and the movement of the plot. Macbeth would probably never aspire to kingship if it were not for the equivocating prophecies of the weird sisters, and how potent would Prospero's magic really be if he did not use it primarily to harness the energies of the sylph Ariel? Such beliefs have risen to a new prominence in scholarly work of the past few decades, and are explored in detail here in the essays of Matthew Woodcock and Annaliese Connolly.

Modern readers sometimes balk at what seems a hiccup in the seasonal setting of the play. The title places it in 'midsummer', but at the end Theseus suggests that the four lovers discovered sleeping on the ground rose early 'to observe | The rite of May' (IV. i. 131–32). In fact, Shakespeare mixes and matches popular rituals associated with two different holidays, May Day and Midsummer's Eve, in *Dream*, which, 'though six weeks apart, were not distinct occasions [...] Instead, Maygames were celebrated throughout the months of May and June, and the two holidays overlapped, encompassing the whole season' of fertility.[12] May Day also had associations with fairies, as guardian spirits of the king and queen of the May who were crowned as part of the festivities.[13]

Despite its festive aspects, at the centre of *A Midsummer Night's Dream* are bitter conflicts over marital arrangements in the human realm and, in the fairy realm, over guardianship of a changeling child, the son of a woman who served Titania in India as a votaress.[14] The dramatis personae does not call for a changeling child, and there are no speech prefixes or stage directions that allude to him, either. However, many productions choose to represent the boy (as do many film productions, including Michael Hoffman's [1999] and Maximilian Reinhardt's [1935]). One does not need an onstage representation of the contested boy to see changelings in *A Midsummer Night's Dream*, though. Many of the characters in the play could, at some point, be understood to be changelings, if you use the broadest definition of that term – one substituted for another. So, in the opening scene of the play, one could construe Demetrius as a forced changeling for Lysander in Hermia's romantic life. Once the two young men are drugged in the forest, Helena becomes a changeling for Hermia as the besotted men pursue Helena under the influence of Puck's misapplied love potion. Finally, Titania substitutes the ass-headed Bottom for her husband in her bower, a distraction which permits Oberon to substitute himself for Titania as the guardian of the changeling child.[15]

Shakespeare's depiction of a pair of fairy monarchs in *A Midsummer Night's Dream* is fascinating to scholars of today for a wide array of reasons. As Matthew Woodcock argues, the fairy queen came to Shakespeare's stage with a great deal of baggage in terms of cultural associations, not all of them positive. Since *Dream* was originally staged during the reign of Queen Elizabeth I – a single woman with over three decades on the throne who had been popularly associated with the fairy queen prior to Shakespeare's play – scholars have long argued over the import of the fairy queen's appearance in this play, with a spouse who tricks and manipulates her into tacit obedience. Some, including Woodcock, have argued that Shakespeare's audience perceived the double valence of the fairy queen just as well as modern scholars do.[16]

Both Dorothea Kehler and Paul Menzer address the textual issues associated with the three different published versions of *Dream* in their essays for this collection. At just over 2,000 lines, *A Midsummer Night's Dream* is one of the shortest plays in the Shakespeare canon. That is curious, since there are three different versions of it, whereas one of the other of the shortest major plays in the canon, *Macbeth*, exists in only one text, the *First Folio*. In other cases in which multiple, competing texts of Shakespeare's plays survive – such as *King Lear* and *Hamlet* – multiplicity leads to multiplication: sometimes entire scenes or at least substantive speeches exist in one version but not another. Such sharp differences do not exist among the three extant texts of *Dream*.

All three different published versions of *A Midsummer Night's Dream* date from the seventeenth century: two quartos (1600 and 1619) and the *Folio* text (1623). The terms 'quarto' and 'folio' refer to the size of the book. When printers prepared a folio, they ran a sheet of paper through the press that would be folded in half and then bound into the finished book. 'Quartos' were smaller, a result of the same size sheet of paper run through the press but folded twice, to produce four different pages. A quarto was roughly the size of a small paperback book today, and often contained only a single playtext, which is the case with the two quartos of *Dream*. Given their larger format (and greater expense), folios often contained multiple texts; the *First Folio* of Shakespeare's work, assembled posthumously by his colleagues from the theatre world, contained most – though not all – of the plays that are currently ascribed to him, divided into the categories of comedy, history and tragedy.

R. A. Foakes sums up the three texts as follows: the 1600 quarto (Q1) is typically the text that editors use to produce modern editions, combined with the expanded stage directions of the *First Folio*, as well as the expansion of Theseus's speech about the lover, the poet and the madman from Act V. The second quarto (Q2), printed in 1619 with the erroneous title page claim that it was published in 1600, derives from Q1, but corrects some of Q1's printing errors, at least. The *First Folio* text (F) constitutes another degree of derivation, since it seems to have been prepared using Q2. However, F includes 'some important substantive changes, and adds or expands some thirty or so stage directions'.[17] Foakes concludes,

'Q1 gives us as near a sense of what Shakespeare wrote as a printed text is likely to get'.[18]

There is relatively little that can give us a sense of how Shakespeare intended for this play to be staged. How were the fairies attired, for example, and did the four lovers appear via costume as interchangeable as they can come to seem as they chase one another through the fairies' wood? As in so many of his other works, Shakespeare embeds metatheatrical performance cues in *Dream*. So, for example, like *Hamlet*, *A Midsummer Night's Dream* famously contains a play-within-the-play, *Pyramus and Thisbe*. In his Penguin Critical Guide to *A Midsummer Night's Dream*, Peter Hollindale points out that the lovers are also unwitting actors in a comedy scripted by Puck and Oberon, largely for the entertainment of the impish Puck. By Act V, the lovers have metamorphosed from actors to audience, as they snigger their way through the tedious brief scene of *Pyramus and Thisbe*, rendered unintentional tragical mirth. The lovers may get the last laugh, but as Hollindale observes, they also 'have performed a doleful story of unfortunate and suffering love, made comic and tolerable by the presence of a "contributory audience" in the persons, part mischievous and part benevolent, of Oberon and Puck'.[19]

Hollindale makes an interesting point about the hierarchy of watching set up in the play: the character-groups are presented in a hierarchy of status which is identified with their relationship to audiences. The lowest status belongs to Bottom and the mechanicals; they are observed by all the other character-groups, either in rehearsal or performance, and also by ourselves, the theatre audience. The lovers have higher status and are observed by Oberon and Puck, and by the theatre audience. Theseus and Hippolyta are 'watched', and watched over, by Oberon and the fairies, though not cast as theatrical by them, and they are observed by the theatre audience. Titania is observed by Oberon and Puck, and by us. Only Oberon and Puck are audiences who themselves at no time have an audience, except in the theatre itself.[20]

Notice that, in the play's final speech, Puck is watching the audience – anxiously – for their response to the play that they have just seen. In Peter Brook's celebrated 1970 production of *Dream* for the Royal Shakespeare Company, Puck actually entered the audience on the lines, 'Give me your hands, if we be friends' (v. i. 428), completely blurring the line between the watcher and the watched, and between the dream world of the fairies, the 'real' world of the Athenian theatregoers, and the actual theatregoers. The community established at the end of the play via the Athenian marriages and the restored amity between Oberon and Titania in the fairy world ultimately expanded in Brook's production to include the audience in a ritual that has symbolized peaceful accord through the centuries: a handshake.

The Guide

The best place to begin study of *A Midsummer Night's Dream* is with a scholarly edition of the play supported by explanatory notes and a substantive introduction to the play, its sources and its textual history. The authors of this collection have used Peter Holland's Oxford Classic edition of the play, but there are many fine editions available, including those in the Oxford and Norton anthologies of Shakespeare's collected works, and individual paperbacks, such as the Arden edition of *Dream*. Adrienne Eastwood's bibliographic essay will orient you to the available critical editions of *Dream*, along with other research materials that you will find helpful as you embark on deeper study of the play. Two significant predecessors to this collection are Dorothea Kehler's indispensable *A Midsummer Night's Dream: Critical Essays*, and Jay L. Halio's *A Midsummer Night's Dream: A Guide to the Play*.[21] Kehler's collection offers essays by a variety of scholars, and you will see work from her book cited widely here; however, that collection is already a decade old. Anchoring this collection, Kehler offers a thorough update to new trends in the study of *A Midsummer Night's Dream* since the publication of her collection in the paired essays 'The Critical Backstory and The State of the Art', which survey the main critical trends of the recent past. Both Kehler's evaluative essay and Adrienne Eastwood's source review are helpfully divided into sections which will allow students to 'browse', reading the sections that are most relevant to the work that they are doing with *Dream*. Moreover, each section of Eastwood's essay concludes with a works cited, and the entire essay culminates in an extensive annotated bibliography to guide your research. Eastwood's essay also discusses the various editions of *Dream* that are available and their relative merits.

Kehler's and Eastwood's survey essays appear in the company of five 'New Directions' essays commissioned specifically for this collection that provide exciting new perspectives on and interpretations of aspects of the play such as its unique mix of verse forms (Tom Clayton's essay) and the fascinating glimpse *Dream* affords us of both theatrical and printing practices of the era (Paul Menzer's essay). The authors gathered here have been chosen with care, providing a judicious mix of longstanding scholars in the field who have been working with *Dream* provocatively for years (Dorothea Kehler and Tom Clayton), along with a group of scholars that are more junior in their careers (Jeremy Lopez, Paul Menzer, Matthew Woodcock, Adrienne Eastwood, Annaliese Connolly, Tripthi Pillai and me).

Jeremy Lopez's essay on the theatrical history of *A Midsummer Night's Dream* provides a brief overview of the best and most recent sources on the play's performance history in the section entitled 'Interlude: Introduction'. Jay Halio has written about *A Midsummer Night's Dream* repeatedly over the course of his distinguished career, and is, as you will see when you read Lopez's performance history, the starting point for the study of *Dream* in performance. *Dream* offers particularly fruitful ground for performance-based analysis for several reasons. First, as Lopez's essay makes clear, *Dream* is one of the most frequently performed and adapted of Shakespeare's plays. Second, as Paul Menzer's essay points out, the play contains some of the most self-conscious exploration of theatrical practice in the Shakespeare canon with the rehearsal for and staging of the play-within-the-play, *Pyramus and Thisbe*. Finally, the play calls for an astonishing ensemble performance from its actors since, rather than a few central characters surrounded by supporting cast, the play features nine central roles (Theseus, Hippolyta, Oberon, Titania, the four young lovers and Puck).[22]

Tom Clayton's name comes up many times in this collection. He has turned repeatedly to *A Midsummer Night's Dream*, interrogating its bawdry,[23] and the curious role that is not one, that of the Indian 'changeling boy' who serves as a prime mover of the action in the plot without ever being directed to be physically present,[24] among other things. For this collection, he turns his attention to the incredibly pliant verse structure of *A Midsummer Night's Dream*, at times so lyrical that it has found a comfortable home in the opera house for centuries, and at other times so whimsically earthy in its prose passages that it has spawned freestanding drolls, and vaudevillian routines.[25]

Clayton's essay joins a rich ongoing conversation about the play's amazing range of verse styles and effects. Jay Halio, for example, discusses the different planes of reality represented by the various verse styles in the play. So, for example, while both Theseus and Oberon speak in verse, as befitting their rank as rulers, the quality of the verse that each speaks differs markedly, revealing details of not only their respective characters to the audience, but also of the kingdoms where they reign: Athens and the fairy wood, respectively.[26] Clayton's essay analyses the varied verse effects that Shakespeare employs in A *Midsummer Night's Dream*, considering their impact upon characterization, mood and the overall movement of the play's action. Just as the weird sisters of *Macbeth* are differentiated from the rest of the characters by the tetrameter verse that they repeatedly speak, Clayton demonstrates that *Dream's* fairies have their own poetic language, too. Characterization is conveyed by Shakespeare's sonorous verse.

Paul Menzer discusses the way in which A *Midsummer Night's Dream* offers a unique perspective upon both early modern printing practices – because of the rather methodical progression of the playtext from the first quarto to the second and then on to its slightly expanded form in the *First Folio* – and upon rehearsal and performance practices in the era. The expanded stage directions in the *Folio* are of interest in this respect, but so are the scenes of assignment of parts, rehearsal and performance by Bottom, Quince, Snug and Flute before the court. As Menzer argues, these scenes are illustrative of unique aspects of the theatre for which Shakespeare wrote. So, for example, Francis Flute the bellows-mender must play the woman's part of Thisbe. The actors are not given the full text of the play, but only their parts, with cue lines. In Act III, the distribution of parts becomes a source of humour when Flute reads every line given to him at once, as well as his cue lines, failing to understand the give and take that the script requires with other actors. The actors' concern over the potential response of the royal wedding party to their performance, and their fear lest they inadvertently do something to give offence, is rendered humorous in *Dream*, but reflects very real concerns in Shakespeare's era about staying under the radar of the Master of the Revels, who could refuse to license a play for performance, or demand that potentially problematic material be altered, or left out entirely. Finally, the minimal props and costume pieces available for the performance are indicative of performance conventions on the stage at Shakespeare's Globe.[27]

Matthew Woodcock and Annaliese Connolly address the characters that drive (and frustrate) the action of A *Midsummer Night's Dream*, the fairies. Over the course of her 45-year reign, Queen Elizabeth I repeatedly went on progresses through her kingdom during the summer months. The members of the nobility with whom Elizabeth stayed during her travels treated their monarch to lavish entertainments during her visits. Woodcock discusses the repeated invocation of the character of the fairy queen in these entertainments, noting the potential problems inherent in linking 'the Virgin Queen' Elizabeth to a figure of popular lore notorious for abducting young men to her subterranean kingdom in order to sate her lust. In his book, *Fairy in 'The Faerie Queene': Renaissance Elf-Fashioning and Elizabethan Myth-Making*, Woodcock notes the uneasy similarity between aspects of fairy belief and beliefs associated with witchcraft, relating it to 'the essential doubleness of the figure of the fairy queen in the romance and popular traditions: her capacity to both reward and punish, and to occupy an uneasy liminal space between heaven and hell'.[28] Woodcock's essay here invites us to dispel our Disneyfied notions of what Shakespeare's fairies are like, in favour of a more complicated portrait offering new ways of interpreting the fairies and the significant actions that they take in the plot of *A Midsummer Night's Dream*.

Given the ambiguity surrounding the status of fairies in early modern culture, one of the areas of most fruitful debate with respect to *Dream* in the past decade or so has concerned the precise nature of the relationship between Oberon and Titania. For years, the patriarchal political order encouraged scholars and audience members to assume that Titania's refusal to surrender the Indian boy to Oberon constituted intransigence on her part to her fairy lord and master that is squelched after Oberon drugs her.[29] More recently, scholars such as Diane Purkiss, Wendy Wall, Matthew Woodcock and I have begun to challenge that assumption by placing the events of *Dream* in the context of fairy beliefs current in Shakespeare's day, which were a bit more ambiguous about who, exactly, ruled the fairy roost.[30]

In her essay, Annaliese Connolly discusses the complex romance history of Oberon which underlies Shakespeare's portrayal of the fairy king, but from which Shakespeare also sharply deviated in depicting Oberon as the consort of a fairy queen. Connolly points out that, just as it was unusual to see Titania with a spouse when Shakespeare wrote *A Midsummer Night's Dream*, so, too, was his presentation of a married Oberon. She connects the vexed fairy genealogies provided for the fairy analogues to Henry VIII and Elizabeth I in Edmund Spenser's *Faerie Queene* to the equally vexed genealogical trajectories that lead from each real-life Tudor monarch to his or her successor. Henry VIII famously required several wives to get the male heir that he desired (Edward VI), while Elizabeth, as the celebrated Virgin Queen, had no heir of her body of either gender, and therefore had to 'adopt' one, as Connolly points out that Oberon does in the prose romance *Huon of Burdeux*, a likely influence on Shakespeare's portrait of the fairy king. While other scholars have argued that *Huon of Burdeux* and *The Faerie Queene* exerted influence on Shakespeare's portrait of Oberon (including Woodcock, in his essay here), Connolly expands these discussions by carefully tracing the literary lineage of Oberon from *Huon of Burdeux* through other neglected plays from Shakespeare's time which also featured Oberon as a character, such as Robert Greene's *The Scottish History of James IV*. Situating Shakespeare's Oberon in the context of other works from the period – both epic verse and verse drama – offers a more nuanced view of what Shakespeare appropriated and what he invented in his own depiction of the fairy monarchs.

Finally, the collection concludes with an essay by Tripthi Pillai which looks to the future of scholarship on *A Midsummer Night's Dream*. Using a metaphor that links her essay to Paul Menzer's, Pillai argues that while no theoretical perspective (like the new historicism of the latter decades of the twentieth century) has risen to prominence as of yet in the decade-old 'new' millennium, scholars can weave extant theories together, creating hybrid theoretical approaches. Her essay focuses on the conjunction of temporal and spatial logics to trace 'the complex intersections between desire and spatio-temporal relations' in *Dream* as manifested in characters 'who strive to construct alternative futures and identities for themselves or others'. In particular, Pillai employs the theory of becoming articulated by Gilles Deleuze and Félix Guattari, in which subjects are not bound by history, politics or any other circumstances but are, rather, free to access many different modes of being. Pillai combines the theory of becoming with the Deleuzian formulation of 'deterritorialization', the state of flux that creates the conditions for becoming.

It seems fitting to end an essay collection devoted to *A Midsummer Night's Dream* with an essay concerned not with what is, but with what could be. By its title alone, the play signals that it traffics in fantasy and magic; by the end of the first scene, Shakespeare adds to that the volatile alchemy of romantic love. The authors gathered here have offered new visions of *Dream* on the page and the stage, as it strikes the ear and moulds the 'I'. From this point forward, as Helena enjoins, *Dream*'s 'story shall be changed' (II. i. 130).

Notes

1   William Shakespeare, *A Midsummer Night's Dream*, ed. Helen Hackett
    (Plymouth: Northcote, 1997), p. 70.
2   See Mikhail Bakhtin, *Rabelais and His World*, trans. H. Iswolsky (Cambridge,
    MA: MIT Press, 1968) and Peter Stallybrass and Allon White, 'Introduction',
    The Politics and Poetics of Transgression (Ithaca, NY: Cornell University Press,
    1986), pp. 6–26.
3   Among the scholars who discuss this are Jay L. Halio, *A Midsummer Night's
    Dream: A Guide to the Play*, Greenwood Guides to Shakespeare (London:
    Greenwood Press, 2003), pp. 46–47 and R. A. Foakes, 'Introduction', *A
    Midsummer Night's Dream*, The New Cambridge Shakespeare (Cambridge:
    Cambridge University Press, 1984), p. 2.
4   For an alternative view of Demetrius's drug-induced love for Helena, see *Dream*,
    ed. Hackett, pp. 42–43.
5   Peter Hollindale, *Shakespeare: A Midsummer Night's Dream* (Harmondsworth:
    Penguin, 1992), p. 61.
6   John Tierney, 'Anti-Love Drug may be Ticket to Bliss', *New York Times*,
    online: www.nytimes.com/2009/01/13/science/13tier.html?emc=eta1.
7   *Dream*, ed. Hackett, p. 56.
8   *Dream*, ed. Foakes, p. 41.
9   The sampling to which I refer here included William Shakespeare, *A
    Midsummer Night's Dream*, ed. Mario DiGangi, Barnes & Noble Shakespeare
    (New York: Barnes & Noble, 2007); R. A. Foakes (William Shakespeare, *A
    Midsummer Night's Dream*, ed. R. A. Foakes [1984] [Cambridge: Cambridge
    University Press, 1987]); Helen Hackett; Peter Holland (William Shakespeare, *A
    Midsummer Night's Dream*, ed. Peter Holland [Oxford: Oxford University
    Press, 1994]); Burton Raffel (William Shakespeare, *A Midsummer Night's
    Dream*, ed. Burton Raffel [New Haven, CT: Yale University Press, 2005]); and
    Gail Kern Paster and Skiles Howard (*A Midsummer Night's Dream: Texts and
    Contexts*, ed. Gail Kern Paster and Skiles Howard, [New York: Bedford/St
    Martin's Press, 1999]).
10 See, for example, 'Introduction', *A Midsummer Night's Dream*, ed. Raffel, pp.
    xix–xx, and *A Midsummer Night's Dream*, ed. Foakes, pp. 27–28.
11 *Dream*, ed. Hackett, p. 53.
12 Paster and Howard, *A Midsummer Night's Dream: Texts and Contexts*, p. 91.
13 *Dream*, ed. Hackett, p. 36.
14 Both Woodcock and Connolly discuss the significance of India for early modern
    fairy beliefs in their essays.
15 I offer an expanded argument along these lines in *Fairies, Fractious Women, and
    the Old Faith: Fairy Lore in Early Modern British Drama and Culture*
    (Selinsgrove, PA: Susquehanna University Press, 2006), pp. 73–79.
16 Among these scholars are Louis Adrian Montrose, ' "Shaping Fantasies":
    Figurations of Gender and Power in Elizabethan Culture', in *Representing the
    English Renaissance*, ed. Stephen Greenblatt (Berkeley, CA: University of
    California Press, 1988), pp. 31–64 and Diane Purkiss, 'Old Wives' Tales Retold:
    The Mutations of the Fairy Queen', in *'This Double Voice': Gendered Writing
    in Early Modern England*, ed. Danielle Clarke and Elizabeth Clarke, (New
    York: St Martin's Press, 2000), pp. 103–22.
17 *Dream*, ed. Foakes, p. 42.
18 *Dream*, ed. Foakes, p. 136.
19 *Dream*, ed. Hollindale, p. 21.
20 *Dream*, ed. Hollindale, p. 69.
21 Dorothea Kehler, ed., *A Midsummer Night's Dream: Critical Essays* (New
    York: Garland, 1999); Jay L. Halio, *A Midsummer Night's Dream: A Guide to
    the Play* (Westport, CT: Greenwood Press, 2003).

22 *Dream*, ed. Raffel, p. xxi.

23 Thomas Clayton, '"Fie what a question's that if thou wert near a lewd interpreter": The Wall Scene in *A Midsummer Night's Dream*', *Shakespeare Studies* 7 (1974), pp. 101–13.

24 Thomas Clayton, '"So quick bright things come to confusion"; or, What Else is *A Midsummer Night's Dream* About?', in *Shakespeare: Text and Theater: Essays in Honor of Jay L. Halio*, ed. Lois Potter and Arthur F. Kinney (Newark, DE: University of Delaware Press, 1999), pp. 62–91.

25 Peter Hollindale also discusses the play's 'exceptional range of styles' (p. 42).

26 *Shakespeare in Performance: A Midsummer Night's Dream*, ed. Jay L. Halio, 2nd edn (Manchester: Manchester University Press, 2003), pp. 34–36.

27 Gail Paster and Skiles Howard make similar observations in the Bedford Texts and Contexts edition of the play (p. 125).

28 Matthew Woodcock, *Fairy in 'The Faerie Queene': Renaissance Elf-Fashioning and Elizabethan Myth-Making* (Aldershot: Ashgate, 2004), p. 106.

29 Halio, *Shakespeare in Performance*, pp. 56–57.

30 Diane Purkiss, *At the Bottom of the Garden: A Dark History of Fairies, Hobgoblins, and Other Troublesome Things* (New York: New York University Press, 2000).

31 Wendy Wall, 'Why Does Puck Sweep?: Fairylore, Merry Wives, and Social Struggle', *Shakespeare Quarterly* 52.1 (2001), pp. 67–106; Woodcock, *Fairy in The Faerie Queene*; Buccola, *Fairies, Fractious Women, and the Old Faith*.

CHAPTER ONE

The Critical Backstory and The State of the Art

Dorothea Kehler

A play as rich as *Dream* necessarily elicits complex criticism; thus, many, perhaps most, of the essays I cite overlap categories. Nevertheless, since taxonomy is crucial for research, I can only hope that my reader will pardon classifications that may seem arbitrary. Omitted are pedagogical and performance essays, foreign-language essays, annotated student editions and most journal articles only partly devoted to *Dream*.[1] Unless substantially revised or more easily accessible in a collection, reprints of listed essays are also omitted. When reprints *are* cited, however, the original date of publication appears in brackets.

Among bibliographies I have found especially useful are James Harner's annual online *World Shakespeare Bibliography* for *Shakespeare Quarterly*, Dorothea Kehler's 'A Midsummer Night's Dream: A Bibliographic Survey of the Criticism',[2] and Judith M. Kennedy's 'A Midsummer Night's Dream in the 1990s' (1999).[3] Even so, despite vast resources, this bibliography is far from exhaustive.

Beginnings

Through their concerns and approaches, literary critics paint a portrait of their eras while revealing their own predilections and prejudices. Many themes of interest to later critics were first treated by the pre-twentieth-century *literati* (almost exclusively male). A brief survey of their work uncovers a host of subjects. For example, John Dryden believed that Shakespeare's right to depict the supernatural was in question and required his vigorous defence against neo-classicists whose respect for a revitalized science had mistaken its target.[4] Some two centuries later in 1895–96, the Dane George Brandes understood *Dream*'s fairies far more broadly; they symbolized the erotic impulse rooted in the unconscious,[5] a view that prepared for Jan Kott's landmark psycho-sexual reading.[6]

Political issues were raised by the Anglo-Irish critic Edmond Malone, a luminary among eighteenth-century Shakespeareans, who tempered his praise of *Dream* by deprecating its lack of decorum: Shakespeare had ignored, nay, even reversed, the hierarchy of social class.[7] Writing in 1849, in the wake of Europe's failed class insurrections, Charles Knight took issue with Malone, insisting on the play's decorum and on Bottom as the essence of humanity.[8] In 1904, G. K. Chesterton echoed Knight.[9] During the first half of the twentieth century, following Chesterton's lead were such notables as J. B. Priestley, H. B. Charlton and John Palmer.[10] At the end of the century a slew of politically progressive critics from Elliott Krieger to Louis A. Montrose focused on class issues.[11] Even so conservative a critic as Harold Bloom helped to keep this tradition alive, calling Bottom 'a wise clown' and 'Shakespeare's Everyman'.[12]

Prior to the nineteenth century, plot and structure were at the centre of critical attention. Over the years, these continued to attract commentators. August Wilhelm Schlegel, Shakespeare's German translator, defended *Dream* by replying to earlier criticism of the various story lines.[13] Schlegel's contemporary, William Hazlitt, also delighted in the text but was an early spokesman for the nineteenth-century prejudice against Shakespeare in performance.[14] Such a bias was not surprising in view of the altered 'improved' versions then dominating the stage. In contrast, our own time has given birth to performance criticism. Among its more radical exponents is Charles Marowitz, who asserts the primacy of the director as *auteur* and of the Shakespeare spin-off over Shakespeare's text – in effect, a return to 'improved' versions.[15]

Philosophy and its Victorian offspring, sociology, also provided approaches to *Dream*. The romantic poet Samuel Taylor Coleridge may be regarded as the father of *Dream*'s Platonist criticism, in so far as his belief that Shakespeare intended the play to be 'a *dream* throughout' was widely influential.[16] For the German philosopher Hermann Ulrici, Shakespeare's Platonic dream world foreshadowed a Christian paradise, a perspective that (generally in more secular form) has been expounded from the 1960s on.[17] Less happily, Coleridge introduced a note of misogyny; he explains Helena's sharing her friend's confidences with Demetrius as grounded in the nature of women: 'they feel less abhorrence of moral evil in itself and more for its outward consequence, as detection, loss of character, etc.'.[18] Coleridge's literary stature could well have given subsequent *Dream* critics permission to indulge misogynistic biases, but those canards evoked an early proto-feminist response. Julia Wedgwood is impressed by Titania's goddess-like qualities, by her fidelity to her friend's memory and by the inadequacy of Theseus's refutation of the supernatural. In light of these aspects of *Dream*, to which Wedgwood adds love's vicissitudes, she asks, 'Did Shakespeare mean to imply that "the imperial votaress" had chosen the better part?'.[19] Since the last quarter of the twentieth century, a spate of feminist Shakespeare criticism has drowned out misogynous voices.

Today, nineteenth-century Shakespeare criticism is best known for its focus on character. In particular, Theseus and Bottom have been singled out as embodying Shakespeare's own views. William Maginn, like Malone an Anglo-Irishman, regarded Theseus as Shakespeare's authentic voice pleading for receptive imaginative spectators.[20] German critic G. G. Gervinus called Theseus a profound thinker and therefore the only estimable character in *Dream*. For Gervinus the play is ethical in purpose, pitting rationality against sensuality.[21] In contrast, Frederick S. Boas, describing Theseus as an Elizabethan aristocrat, initiated a line of historicist criticism very much in vogue today.[22]

Since 1900

Which text?

Because three versions of *Dream*, distinguished mostly by the quantity of stage directions, have come down to us, modern criticism is first of all anxious to establish a valid text. Textual scholarship involves chronology (e.g., did *Dream* precede or follow *Romeo and Juliet*? Was it written for a noble wedding?). John Dover Wilson authored a generally accepted theory in which he explained the multiple texts by claiming that Shakespeare began *Dream* in 1592 and then revised it around 1595 and again in 1598. 'The poet' was a later addition to Theseus's speech about 'the lunatic' and 'the lover'. More controversial is Wilson's claim that the final revision was intended for the wedding of the Earl of Southampton, dedicatee of Shakespeare's early erotic poetry and perhaps the 'young man' of Shakespeare's sonnets.[23] Marion Colthorpe, who considers this and various other occasions, argues that *if Dream* was written for a wedding, Queen Elizabeth I was probably *not* present.[24] Addressing the occasion of *Dream*'s composition, David Wiles plumps for the wedding of Elizabeth Carey, granddaughter of the lord chamberlain, the patron of Shakespeare's acting company.[25] Among a number of subjects treating female sexuality, Helen Hackett, too, discusses Elizabeth Carey's wedding.[26]

In his variant of Wilson's theory, the poet Walter de la Mare suggested that Shakespeare may have written *Dream* at various times, perhaps revising portions of another playwright's work. This method would explain lines De la Mare finds unworthy of Shakespeare.[27] Returning to Wilson's proposals, Janis Lull focuses on Theseus and finds two dukes, one who learns to value imagination, another who remains insensitive.[28] The director can choose between them. Similarly drawn to the theatrical implications of textual theory, both Barbara Hodgdon and Philip C. McGuire point out that only in the *Folio* text does Egeus appear at the wedding.[29] At play's end, therefore, relations within his family and between family and state are strained in the quarto but conciliatory in the *Folio*. Claiming that *Dream* was written for weddings two years apart, William B. Hunter classifies the *Folio* version as a memorial performance text, whereas Roger Prior believes that *Dream* was written expressly for the second wedding of Mary, Countess of Southampton and mother of the young Earl.[30] Hunter augments this thesis. He holds that *Dream*, with the addition of Act I's first 15 lines, was performed for Elizabeth Carey's 1596 wedding as well.[31] Editors of standard editions – Harold F. Brooks, R. A. Foakes and especially Peter Holland – also deal at some length with textual questions.

The stories behind the story

Standard editions provide summaries of Shakespeare's sources, but the classic starting place for source study is Geoffrey Bullough's *Narrative and Dramatic Sources of Shakespeare*.[32] Another key work is T. Walter Herbert's book on received ideas and new theories embedded in *Dream*, as they would have been understood by an educated Elizabethan.[33] *Dream*'s blurred classical allusions interest Thomas Moisan, who observes that such intertextuality is not without danger; similarly bringing to bear a wide range of classical sources, Laurie E. Maguire finds that Shakespeare's efforts free his Helens from an 'associative onomastic straitjacket'.[34] Among more specialized classical source studies is Mihoko Suzuki's on Seneca's play about Hippolytus, Theseus's son by Hippolyta.[35] Many scholars have written about Shakespeare's use of Ovid, including J. W. Robinson, Mary Ellen Lamb, Leonard Barkan, Clifford Davidson, Anthony Brian Taylor, Kerry Lynne Thomsen and

Jonathan Bate.[36] Kenneth Muir, Madeleine Doran, and Niall Rudd focus on the play-within-the-play of *Pyramus and Thisbe*.[37] Whereas feminist D'Orsay W. Pearson's study of the mythological Theseus reveals his overall literary reputation as a bounder, Douglas Freake traces the relationship between the Athenian rulers who were Theseus's ancestors and male dominance in early modern England.[38] A. D. Nuttall, reflecting on myths about Theseus and others, views the entirety of *Dream* as an *apotrope*, a ritual to avert misfortune.[39] The relevance of the Bible, particularly 1 Corinthians, to Shakespeare's delineation of Bottom has been discussed by Thomas B. Stroup, Jan Kott and Louis Adrian Montrose.[40]

Scholars have also unearthed a host of medieval and Renaissance literary sources for *Dream*. One of Shakespeare's favourites was Chaucer. E. Talbot Donaldson compares Chaucer and Shakespeare's Theseus, dubbing the latter a 'male chauvinist'.[41] Barbara A. Mowat points to diverse, even conflicting, sources shaping Theseus.[42] Thomas Moisan, comparing Chaucer's depiction of 'Solempnytee' in 'The Knight's Tale' with Shakespeare's in *Dream* and *Romeo and Juliet,* discovers similar ironies.[43] Although Frank Kermode examines the influence of the ancients – Macrobius and Apuleius – he also discusses the Italian philosopher-scientist, Giordano Bruno.[44] Recently, in a chapter on *Dream,* Robert H. F. Carver re-evaluates affinities between Shakespeare and Apuleius.[45] Among sources fairly contemporaneous with Shakespeare, A. B. Taylor points to similarities between Gower's *Confessio Amantis* and Shakespeare's *Pyramus and Thisbe*, while Thelma N. Greenfield singles out the writings of the Dutch humanist Erasmus.[46] Hugh M. Richmond identifies Cinthio's *Hecatommithi*, a collection of stories from the Italian Renaissance, as a source, Richard Andrews sees an Italian influence in Shakespeare's depiction of Fairyland, and Louise George Clubb catalogues elements of the Italian pastoral, which she locates in *Dream*. Clubb argues that Shakespeare was familiar not only with Italian plays but also with Italian genre theory.[47] As for English Renaissance writers, Robert L. Reid looks to Spenser's *Faerie Queene,* Lisa Hopkins calls attention to the influence of Mary Sidney's *Tragedy of Antony,* and Wolfgang Riehle recognizes Lysander (Bottom's 'Limander') as Marlowe's Leander, ordered to '[l]ie further off'.[48]

Source studies treating historical subjects continue to attract critics. Edith Rickert, Maurice Hunt and J. P. Conlan detect topical allusions to Shakespeare's aristocratic contemporaries, Conlan claiming that Shakespeare intended *Dream* as a compliment to Elizabeth.[49] Lisa Hopkins, on the other hand, holds that Shakespeare takes pains here, as in all his comedies, to duck even mention of Elizabeth.[50] Following Boas, G. K. Chesterton and B. Ifor Evans write about the Englishness of *Dream*, of Bottom and his band as English workers, and of Theseus as an English country squire.[51] Rejecting Maginn's view,[52] A. B. Taylor argues that Theseus is not Shakespeare's alter-ego; artisan Peter Quince is.[53]

Plot and structure

Aesthetic and formalist approaches embracing *Dream*'s intricate plot and structure have long appealed to critics from August Wilhelm Schlegel to twenty-first century writers. Bertrand Evans attributes the play's structural success to dramatic irony; the audience knows far more than the characters, with the possible exception of Hippolyta.[54] More important, writes Sheldon P. Zitner, is the characters' ability to elude disaster.[55] G. K. Hunter believes that *Dream* is designed to contrast various forms of love, while for Larry S. Champion the play's structure derives from plot lines disposed so as to create an ideal comic perspective.[56]

Observing the violence and animal imagery, the Thesean surface text and Hippolytan subtext, anthropologically oriented René Girard concludes that, like the canon as a whole, structurally *Dream* is based on myth.[57] Also employing structuralist theory, Mark Rose sees the bi-fold settings of city and wood unified when Titania falls in love with Bottom.[58] M. E. Comtois adumbrates eight actions including marriage that the four couples must accomplish.[59] Based on her analysis of *Dream*'s impediments to resolution and the overcoming of those impediments, Ruth Nevo argues that the play's structure illuminates the workings of imagination itself.[60] John Baxter studies structure through the lens of mimesis; through *Dream*'s tragic undercurrents, Shakespeare teaches that dramatic fiction offers a path to truth.[61] Susan Baker analyses *Dream*'s structure in accordance with theorist Mikhail Bakhtin's concept of chronotopes that determine the behaviour of characters, chronotopes being a function of when and where the characters live and of the genre they occupy.[62] Because Shakespeare borrows from others and from himself, Mark Taylor emphasizes the importance of imitation to *Dream*'s structure.[63] Students may find Andy Mousley's pedagogically orientated volume especially valuable; Mousley illustrates his survey of current theoretical methods with a poststructuralist analysis of *Dream*.[64]

Mood: language, dance and music

Few modern critics have subscribed to Hazlitt's nineteenth-century anti-theatrical credo: that dramatization transforms *Dream* 'from a delightful fiction into a dull pantomime'.[65] Yet even so celebrated a man-of-the-theatre as Harley Granville-Barker asserted the primacy of *Dream*'s poetry over the play in performance. Analysing *Pyramus and Thisbe* semiotically, Michael J. Sidnell agrees that in light of its overmastering verbal signs, visual signs are redundant.[66] Anticipating Jan Kott's controversial essay in *Shakespeare Our Contemporary*, G. Wilson Knight contends that 'darkness and fear' constitute the atmosphere of *Dream*.[67] Taking a sunnier view, Mark Van Doren, Harold Brooks (in his edition), and David Young discuss the play's lyrical iterative imagery of water, moon, flora and forest sounds.[68] Writing over half a century after Van Doren, Stuart M. Tave expands on the former's celebration of *Dream*'s Mozartian perfection of language, plot and character.[69] Young concentrates not only on *Dream*'s imagery but on each character group's individualized versification. Various critics focus on the language of specific character groups: Stephen Fender and Joan Stansbury on the lovers, Brian Vickers and Wolfgang Franke on the mechanicals.[70] Ralph Berry studies the play's imagery as a facet of Shakespeare's themes of reality, illusion and imagination.[71] Stephen Booth locates various poetic images − moon, dogs and 'the incessant hum of "part" references' such as a role, a section, to divide, to leave − that unify the play. Arpad Szakolczai proposes that *Dream* is an early example of how images can manipulate behaviour; Puck's 'image-magic' leads characters to believe they are behaving rationally when, in fact, they are mostly controlled.[72] Milton Crane examines Shakespeare's intermingling of verse with prose.[73] James E. Robinson also notes two kinds of language, one belonging to Athens (societal), the other to the wood (natural), a binarism that is ultimately reconciled.[74] According to Madeleine Forey, Shakespeare is amused that Ovid's *Metamorphoses* makes its Puritan translator Arthur Golding uncomfortable, inspiring him to burlesque Golding's inept style.[75] Rhetorician Christy Desmet investigates *Dream* as a study in hypallage, 'the rhetorical figure by which a symmetrical exchange of parts creates nonsense'. She demonstrates how the female characters use language to render patriarchal control nonsensical.[76]

A major critical debate pits realism against rhetoric. Jan Kott avers that literal onstage bestiality takes place between Titania and Bottom in scenes designed to 'rouse rapture and disgust, terror and abhorrence'.[77] But if, as Deborah Baker Wyrick argues, Bottom is not merely an ass of a character but 'an animated metaphor' encapsulating *Dream*'s Apollonian/Dionysian structural binarism, then his love affair with Titania is a metaphor, too.[78] For Bruce Boehrer, allusions to bestiality and same-sex attachments are significant in so far as they constitute alternative erotic modes against which to measure *Dream*'s unconvincing heterosexual marriages.[79] More playfully, Cedric Watts, Thomas Clayton and Patricia Parker enjoy explicating Shakespeare's verbal bawdry. Watts asks, 'Does Bottom Cuckold Oberon?' and answers that he does, having been 'purge[d]' of his 'mortal grossness'.[80] Inclined to the negative, Stanley Wells emphasizes the spiritual dimensions of Bottom's efforts to fathom his metamorphosis once restored to himself. Wells addresses these issues further in his *Looking for Sex in Shakespeare*.[81]

Such pithy controversies would have carried no weight with *Dream*'s first written evaluator, Samuel Pepys, the Restoration diarist who confided to his famous journal that although it was a 'ridiculous' play, it was partly redeemed by 'some good dancing and some handsome women'.[82] Dance is an important aspect of *Dream* to Enid Welsford, who finds the play informed by the Elizabethan court masque.[83] John H. Long, one of the pioneer scholars of Shakespeare's music, asserts that the play's poetic ambience derives above all from its songs and dances, a thesis developed by Alan Brissenden and Skiles Howard.[84] Maurice Hunt broadens the rubric 'music' to include all the sounds heard in the play; these comprise its tonality.[85] Aligned to these studies is Wes Folkerth's valuable *The Sound of Shakespeare*, in which a chapter is devoted to Bottom's Bakhtinian ears and mouth – his many voices, personal syntax and blurring of the senses.[86]

Philosophic underpinnings

The school of philosophy most closely associated with *Dream* is Platonism inflected by religious faith: neoplatonism. Although deriving from sixteenth-century thinkers, nineteenth-century commentators – among them Coleridge in England, Hermann Ulrici in Germany and H. N. Hudson in America[87] – prepared the ground for more recent neoplatonic literary criticism. As John Vyvyan explains, correspondences exist between emotional states and conditions in the 'real' world. When characters experience love, they see the divine in each other and create an ordered world.[88] A critical debate has arisen over whether or not this is true of all the characters in *Dream*. Jane K. Brown claims that the kind of love each of the four couples feels serves the neoplatonic search for truth.[89] Exclusionary critics are divided over which characters are most commendable. Peter G. Phialas believes that only Theseus and Hippolyta embody the mystery of ideal love, a step on the way to faith, but Sidney Homan regards fairyland as an imaginative reality beyond 'the mundane world' of Theseus's Athens and thus closer to the Platonic ideal.[90] No, farther, asserts David Ormerod, harkening back to Maginn and Gervinus; Ormerod reads *Dream* as a neoplatonic allegory in which the labyrinthine woods harbour moral misprision, a higher reality being located in Theseus's Athens.[91]

Examining *Dream*'s Platonic elements alongside those of the pastoral and Orphic traditions, Richard Cody observes a celebration of art and a drive toward oneness.[92] For Andrew D. Weiner, imagination, whether interpreted within a Platonic or Christian framework, is proof of God's love for mankind.[93] Those other-worldly beings, Shakespeare's fairies, lead Ronald F. Miller to reflect on the mysteriousness of our place in the universe.[94] Stuart Sillars focuses on Hippolyta. He aligns her belief in the lovers' account of their night in the wood with the notion of visionary moments grounded in instinct, feeling and faith that transcend reason: *via stultitiae*, the way of the foolish. Educated spectators familiar with syncretic neoplatonism as expounded by Erasmus, Ficino and della Mirandola would accordingly interpret *Dream* as a refutation of social hierarchy.[95] Neoplatonism is one of the subjects ranging from astrology to modern science that the celebrated William Empson devotes himself to in a recently recovered typescript on Elizabethan attitudes towards spirits.[96] But whatever most Elizabethans may have believed, Colin McGinn argues that in *Dream* Shakespeare writes as a sceptic for whom identity is unstable and imagination irrational, albeit our only bridge between the senses and the intellect; 'love is a waking dream' and the wood a 'Cartesian nightmare', where illusion and reality are inseparable.[97]

Issues and Themes

Imagination and dream

In the world of Shakespeare's fantasy, dream appears to represent imagination. Peter Holland's survey of dream theory from ancient times through the Renaissance provides an appropriate context for that association. It may be, as Coleridge suggested, that the play is itself a dream, the product of Shakespeare's vivid imagination.[98] Or perhaps, as Ernest Schanzer claims, imagination merely creates the love-madness that allies the lover with the lunatic and the poet.[99] Harold C. Goddard, himself one of the most imaginative of 1950s critics, argues for imagination as a spiritual force that can harmonize disparate and contradictory entities.[100] Not so, writes conservative critic George A. Bonnard, his position an unpleasant variant within the neoplatonist debate. Assuring us of 'Shakespeare's Purpose',

Bonnard equates imagination with amoral sensuality (that of the fairies), then contrasts the reprehensible Titania with the admirable Hippolyta, whose silence regarding Egeus's mandate signifies her wifely submission.[101] Peter F. Fisher, who also associates imagination with fairies, subordinates them to Theseus's court, which represents reason.[102] Not unexpectedly, Howard Nemerov, an erstwhile Poet Laureate, takes the opposite position. Nemerov demonstrates the superiority of Hippolyta's views on imagination and art over Theseus's insensitivity to both.[103]

C. L. Barber is noted for his study of the holidays and customs that served Shakespeare as a Saturnalian source (Saturnalia was a Roman holiday during which the breaching of hierarchy was allowed). While equating the fairies with imagination, Barber sees them as symbolic; the night in the wood is 'a release of shaping fantasy which brings clarification about the tricks of strong imagination'.[104] R. W. Dent takes issue with such readings. Imagination engenders love no less fine for being irrational, although uncontrolled love – when unrequited like Demetrius's for Hermia or inappropriate like Titania's for Bottom – is problematic. Because imagination engenders art, which proves Theseus himself to be an 'antique fable', he is mistaken in his lunatic/lover/poet speech.[105] Philip Edwards generally follows Dent's view of *Dream* as a paean to imagination and art.[106] In her study of the interactions between aesthetic creativity and nature, and between 'nature, mind, and language', Elizabeth Sewell anticipated later ecological criticism; the mechanicals' names suggest the oneness of natural history and art. She concludes that within *Dream* rationality is enriched by encompassing imagination.[107] Looking backward, Kathryn L. Lynch sees a parallel between the ways in which Chaucer and Shakespeare treat imagination, with Shakespeare following and burlesquing Chaucer, who draws on the medieval dream-vision.[108] In *Dream*, claims David Schalkwyk, imagination creates a world in which to love is to serve and thus to attain perfect freedom; embodying that freedom is the actor serving his public.[109]

Known for his work on metadrama (how the text metaphorically reflects on its own construction), James Calderwood employs this approach to *Dream*.[110] The lovers appeal to Calderwood because they resemble actors in so far as their identities become unstable. Oberon is their director/*auteur*, and *Dream*'s subjects are art, reason and imagination. Stephen Fender, A. P. Riemer, and J. Dennis Huston follow in Calderwood's wake. Fender holds that the fairies control events and that all the explanations of the midsummer night contain some truth; *Dream* teaches that fiction can never be reduced

to a single meaning.[111] Riemer proposes that physical transformation in *Dream* stands for the playwright's ability to transform his
world through art,[112] and Huston suggests that despite its parodies,
this imaginative self-reflexive comedy and art itself are 'both illusion
and revealed truth'.[113] Looking back to C. L. Barber's work, Kevin
Pask sees the central issue in *Dream* as imagination with its relation
to chaotic longings and, like Barber, finds its genealogy in the
culture of the English countryside.[114] David Mikics shifts the
discussion from imagination in the play to Shakespeare's own
literary imagination, then demonstrates the supremacy of art over
politics, to the disadvantage of new historicism.[115]

Perhaps the most controversial *Dream* critic is Jan Kott, a Polish
émigré professor whose work prepares for Boehrer's. In his
Shakespeare Our Contemporary, Kott describes imagination as
sexually violent, bestial and wanton.[116] Titania and the young lovers
spend an orgiastic night in the wood. Although some critics
disregard Kott (e.g. David Young,[117] being largely concerned with
Shakespeare's attitude toward art) and others like Michael
MacOwan attempt to refute Kott,[118] he remains significant. Herbert
S. Weil likens aspects of *Dream* to the plays of Jean Genet,[119] and
Hugh M. Richmond locates a 'sadomaschostic type of sexuality' in
Dream.[120] In contrast, Marjorie B. Garber contends that for
Shakespeare's characters to dream is to release the imagination,
which opens new perspectives and insights inaccessible to reason.[121]
Such insights need not be a gathering of Freudian symbols, argues
Thelma Greenfield. Dreams have their own validity. Whereas in the
waking world Bottom is metaphorically an ass, in the dream world
he is literally an ass. Shakespeare's spectator, like the dreamer,
participates and watches the imaginative illusion.[122] Striking a
compromise in the Kott debate, both Alexander Leggatt and David
Bevington acknowledge *Dream*'s darker aspects but assert their
subordination to a benign imagination, to a comic perspective and
romantic love.[123]

Magic and the supernatural

From the seventeenth century, when Dryden first defended
Shakespeare's right to depict 'things which really exist not, if they
are founded on popular belief', Shakespeare's fairies have been
understood as an integral part of *Dream*.[124] Brandes proposed that
the fairies were a psychic symbol for sexuality.[125] They initially
evoked a blander commentary; Frank Sidgwick discussed Shakespeare's miniaturization of supernatural beings.[126] However,
Katharine M. Briggs observed that belief in tiny fairies had preceded

Dream.[127] In 1930 Minor White Latham pointed out that prior to *Dream*, good-natured, congenial fairies had not been imagined.[128] Ernest Schanzer discussed Shakespeare's differentiation of the various fairy characters, Bonnard their amorality. Titania and Oberon, states H. B. Charlton, are rash and foolish mates.[129] C. L. Barber understands otherwise; drawn from folklore and pastoral, they are symbolic of the imagination, beyond judgement.[130] Kenneth Burke's insightful political essay, composed in 1972 and demonstrating that the fairies are vital to the class structure of *Dream*, was published posthumously (see Chapter 8).

In recent years, the fairies have attracted considerable attention. Marjorie Swann traces how Shakespeare's version of the supernatural displaced folklore and courtly fairies in Stuart poetry.[131] More broadly, Diane Purkiss remarks on the persistent influence of *Dream*'s fairies throughout all literature (see Chapter 8). Mary Ellen Lamb and Wendy Wall, among others, study the social uses of the supernatural. Using popular belief as the context for Shakespeare's supernatural beings, Lamb claims that Shakespeare allows the audience to reconsider the superiority of high, urban, literate, male culture to the popular, illiterate, rural culture of women.[132] Wall asks, 'Why Does Puck Sweep?' and replies by presenting links between domestic labour, class and popular beliefs about fairies. The supernatural is relevant not only to the home but also to the nation (see Chapter 8). Regina Buccola discerns the relation of fairies to witchcraft, Catholicism and healing powers. Titania may be an 'unruly' woman, but Oberon serves Helena. Both she and Hermia wed the men they desire, and female characters triumph over patriarchally mandated social and religious behaviour (see Chapter 8). Laurel Moffatt sees the wood as a displacement of Athens, where the fairies establish what the characters and playgoers consider real, and R. W. Maslen suggests that another displacement, Puck's, from English folklore and early modern satirical pamphlet literature to classical Greece, works to defuse the anti-theatrical prejudice.[133]

Love and marriage

At the turn of the twentieth century, E. K. Chambers accounted for the darkness Kott was to find some half century later by explaining young lovers' passion, their whimsical action, infidelity, and contempt for law and reason as inherent in the traditional comic perspective; misbehaviour was standard behaviour.[134] The supernatural in *Dream* was no more than a symbolic representation of young love. E. C. Pettet concurs; *Dream* is about romantic love and wooing, not marital relations. The 'truth' that lovers find in each other's beauty cannot be judged by the out-of-love rationalist.[135] Terry Eagleton, one such rationalist, argues deconstructively that romantic love is no more than reciprocally shared illusions, however inescapable a social exigence.[136]

Even so, it surpasses marriage, depicted by the old guard as an idyllic hierarchical relationship, shamefully disrupted by wives like Titania. Donald C. Miller explains that Titania may be motivated by a poorly repressed desire for the changeling boy.[137] For Gerald F. Jacobson she is guilty of 'feminiz[ing] the male child' because she is a 'castrating woman [with] claims to possess the penis'.[138] R. A. Zimbardo damns her as a sensualist given to obsessive mothering,[139] but her chief sin is disobedience, for which Oberon justly humiliates her. Bonnard blames the victim: 'on awaking from her delusion, she feels no regret, no shame; and there is no scene of reconciliation with her husband [...] there is no trace of a real feeling in her'.[140] Titania should take lessons from Hippolyta, writes Paul A. Olson; the captive Amazon is a model wife, who subjugates herself to her husband, her marriage being based on reason rather than passion.[141] Germaine Greer counters these readings with her own: *Dream* offers a formula for an egalitarian reconciliation of passion and societal demands: marriages should be based on mutual respect (like that shared by Quince's actors) and by parenthood, to which the epithalamion looks forward.[142] A. B. Taylor writes perceptively that the opposition between a male-dominant marriage and an emergent semi-egalitarian model, figured by the behaviour of Theseus and Hippolyta in Act V, anticipates the relationships in Shakespeare's future comedies.[143]

Angles of Vision

Psychological, anthropological, scientific

Dream first attracted extended psychoanalytic study in the mid-twentieth century when beating up on Titania was acceptable. Writing in the early 1970s, M. D. Faber is noteworthy for a thought-provoking essay in which he explains Hermia's dream as representing the distance between the conscious and unconscious sides of the mind (the socialized versus the primordial). Theseus can negotiate that distance thanks to his sexual experiences, but in a patriarchal society that circumscribes gender roles, repressed desires create anxiety, albeit masked by Oberon's love juice. Finding one's sexual identity remains a challenge highlighted by the 'homosexual overtones' of the changeling's situation.[144] Aaron Aronson, a

Jungian, positions Theseus and Puck (a trickster figure) as a binary opposition of conscious/unconscious. The forest and Bottom as ass are fertility symbols; they stand for the transgressive desire the lovers experience.[145] Norman Holland goes further in his analysis of Hermia's dream. For Holland it mirrors the young woman's conflict between her wish for and fear of sex. The play is concerned with separation and fusion, the separations being 'both loving and cruel'. Transactively, Holland then relates those subjects to his own life.[146] Mordecai Marcus takes another tack. Analysing the characters' unwitting use of sexual language, he argues against Kott and Richmond, who hold that *Dream* is informed by the opposition between the life instinct and the death instinct. Rather, writes Marcus, the two go hand in hand: 'love requires the risk of death, and achieves force and direction from the interweaving of the life impulse with the deathward-release of sexual tension'.[147] In an important and wide-ranging essay, Catherine Belsey couples the hope that Peter Quince will make a ballad of Bottom's dream to the search for identity.[148]

Two Lacanian-based works are significant. Allen Dunn studies male fear of Oedipal vengeance; sexual clashes, he believes, are at the heart of *Dream*'s plot strands, clashes figuring the father's 'enabling death sentence which forces the son into the social world', in Lacanian terms 'the symbolic order'.[149] James Calderwood also relies heavily on Lacanian theory in his book on *Dream*.[150] Among psychoanalytic essays treating the play's social implications is that by Jan Lawson Hinely, who claims that the characters' dreams alleviate their sexual fears. Societal concord is established, and patriarchy is modified by the trust and respect the men offer the female characters.[151] Invoking the Renaissance notion that the mind microcosmically reflects the great chain of being, Barbara Freedman employs Freudian and Lacanian theory to argue that *Dream*'s metaphors of authority are in fact a kind of censorship supporting the ideology of absolute monarchy, though with considerable transparency. Freedman avails herself of anthropological, visual, gender and theatrical theories as well as psychoanalytic premises.[152] Katharine Eisaman Maus juxtaposes the theatrical and the psycho-analytic in her study of sorcery debates and subjectivity in *Dream*. Maus detects a blurring between Shakespeare's portrayal of the fairies as theatrical characters and as coherent selves.[153]

In related work, Richard Scholar attempts to pin down the 'strange and admirable', or *je ne sais quoi*, a quality not unlike Sillars's Christian *via stultitiae*, the way of the foolish.[154] Those who experience this uncanny phenomenon (e.g., Bottom's dream), find

themselves thinking in new ways. Other critics take their lead from
the work of cultural anthropologist Victor Turner, who studied the
modes in which societies and individuals are transformed by
traditional rites of passage. Florence Falk submits that the lovers
flee from Theseus's unaccommodating Athens (structure severed
from myth) to the *communitas* of the wood. This transitory liminal
phase (in which they are in flux) enables their self-knowledge and
the renewal of Athens.[155] William C. Carroll argues that for *Dream*'s
lovers to ready themselves for marriage they must first pass through
a liminal stage in the process of metamorphosis; therein 'the
monstrous' (sexuality, violence and death) undergoes 'comic
detoxification'.[156] Frank Nicholas Clary uses Turner's theories of
liminality to argue that ritual reassures the anxious bridegroom.[157]
Here as elsewhere, René Girard reads anthropologically; he notes
that in all of Philostrates's offered entertainments a poet is
victimized, and that only through scapegoating does Puck avert
the death of Demetrius and/or Lysander.[158] Henry S. Turner is
notable for a new and productive approach: he reconciles literature
and science by showing how *Dream* deconstructs the modernist
settlement that reserves the creative use of language to the former,
its factual use to the latter. The form of Turner's book is no less
original than its content.[159]

Historical

Whether as background or foreground, historicism has long been a
popular approach to Shakespeare's plays. The early modern court,
town, nation, social classes, sexual politics, domestic practices,
economic issues, religious conflicts, colonialism, postcolonialism –
all such rubrics fall under the aegis of historical criticism. From
Malone to Montrose, social hierarchy is a major focus of *Dream*.
George A. Bonnard comes down hard on the mechanicals for daring
to act before the duke – 'they have lost their common sense'.[160] But
the great preponderance of critics ignore or reject elitism; indeed,
Bottom has become the darling of the left, appreciated for his
literary gifts by G. K. Chesterton, for his theatrical passion by J. B.
Priestley, for his realism by H. B. Charlton and for his 'courtesy or
apprehension' by John Palmer.[161] To Richard H. Cox, who draws
parallels between classical Greece and Elizabethan England, Bottom
is the hero and saviour of Athens.[162] For Michael D. Bristol, Bottom
is a semiotic device that challenges restricted roles and 'social
discrimination', while *Pyramus and Thisbe* challenges the patriarchal social structure, if unintentionally.[163] Michael Schneider finds
that challenge not only in the interlude but in Bottom's affair with

Titania.[164] Theodore B. Leinwand argues that the mechanicals have roots in reality. He identifies them as analogues to Shakespeare's fellow actors, no less eager for the nobility's approval.[165] Louis A. Montrose, too, reminds us that, like Bottom, Shakespeare was an artisan and that Bottom's dream speech from 1 Corinthians exalts the lowly over their betters.[166] In an investigation of art and the state, Richard Wilson draws on Marx and René Girard; Wilson aligns the mechanicals' need to placate the ruling class through self-censorship with Foucault's contention that the state's punitive ability to curtail artistic resistance to its power initiates the concept of authorship.[167] Annabel Patterson lauds Bottom and the class he represents; society runs smoothly and cheerfully thanks to them.[168] Less sanguine, Marcia McDonald compares Bottom to Shakespeare's theatre as an institution, independent yet troubling and marginalized.[169] Is the net result of *Dream* subversion or containment of privilege? Containment, say Elliott Krieger, James H. Kavanagh and Wilson; subversion, say Bristol, Schneider, Montrose and Patricia Parker.[170] Or does *Dream* offer only an entrée to the court?[171]

Social history provides an equally important context for understanding *Dream*. Parents frequently died before their children had come of age, and guardianship, when commodified, could be fraught with peril for orphans. Both Heather Dubrow and Alan Sinfield maintain that, appropriate or not, custody of the changeling assures Oberon's male dominance.[172] Though Shakespeare does not specify the changeling's age, Tom Clayton, in a comprehensive, traditionally-minded essay, argues for the appropriateness of the changeling's joining Oberon's henchmen – 'in the patriarchal fairy culture' the Indian boy is ready to be 'Fairy barmitzvahed'.[173] Anne E. Witte explains *Dream*'s numerous allusions to weaving and its associated subjects of marriage and magic as a function of the economic crisis of the 1590s that made a target of immigrant workers.[174] Frederick Turner takes a liberal humanist view of where *Dream* stands on Elizabethan gender theory and individualist economics. In 'The Seal and the Wax in *A Midsummer Night's Dream*', Turner argues that because Hermia, the wax, rejects a patriarchal seal ill-befitting her nature, she demonstrates that subjectivity is not socially constructed. The plea for autonomy in love is joined to an endorsement of communal connection in financial dealings.[175]

For nations as well as for individuals, under capitalism what you own determines who you are. Postcolonialist studies, another recent mode of analysis, has illuminated the connection between the changeling and Elizabethan England's economic spheres of influence. Viewing a production of *Dream* at the University of California, Santa Cruz, Margo Hendricks was disappointed by the representation of the changeling as 'a rich oriental "trifle"' appropriated by Oberon and unwittingly mirroring the racial and imperialist undertones of the play.[176] Foreigners – 'Indians, Tartars, and "Ethiops"' – live in the forest, a space linked to threatening female sexuality, states Kim Hall.[177] Ania Loomba sees the Indian changeling as a colonial commodity whose ownership is 'represented in terms of a gendered familial battle' that determines not only dominance or subservience but the very identity of the contestants (see Chapter 8).[178] Whereas Raman Shankar offers a psychoanalytic exploration of *Dream*'s patriarchal marriage trope as a means of validating colonialism, R. W. Desai reads the play as a political allegory in which the European powers struggle for control of the spice trade. In this allegory Oberon is Elizabeth, Titania Portugal/Spain and the changeling India (see Chapter 8).

Gender Studies

Initially Shakespearean gender studies took the form of misogynous outpourings by conservative male critics. Following Coleridge, fully persuaded of the 'lax holds that principles have on the female heart', the German critic G. G. Gervinus, writing in the last third of the nineteenth century, faults Hermia and Thisbe for not accepting their fathers' authority (and faults their young lovers for defying patriarchal rule). Titania is to blame for disobeying her husband. Like the other fairies, she loves superficially and sensually.[179] Attention to Shakespeare's female characters on the part of female critics, albeit sometimes critical, also prepared for a full-scale, late-twentieth-century feminist movement in the arts. Writing in the tradition of the Victorian lady, Agnes Mure MacKenzie took exception to Shakespeare's delineation of Titania as 'shrill', Helena as 'abject', Hippolyta (in Act V) as 'self-consciously superior', and more generally to 'moments of unintentional vulgarity' prone to mar the women's representation.[180] Although more sympathetic critics sporadically addressed themselves to the female characters, not until the mid-1970s did feminist Shakespearean criticism find its voice. Like D'Orsay Pearson, Ruth Nevo views Theseus sceptically. According to Nevo, Titania's attachment to the pregnant votary and the changeling was caused by Oberon's inability or refusal to give her a child.[181] Shirley Nelson Garner believes that patriarchal power triumphs in *Dream* but adds that heterosexuality is destabilized and same-sex love between women evoked: 'men fear that if women join with each other, they will not need men, will possibly exclude them or prefer the friendship and love of women'.[182] David Marshall also makes an important point: in the theatre we are prone to accept what we are apt to query in the study. *Dream*'s viewers are manipulated into accepting the notion that Hippolyta enjoys surrendering her independence, that Titania will not miss the child she loves, that the play ends happily for all the characters. In fact, says Marshall, spectators and characters alike are manipulated to consent to patriarchal power.[183] Why this design?

Louis Adrian Montrose, in 'Shaping Fantasies', suggests that *Dream* provides a strategic narrative for dealing with the threat a female ruler poses to male power. In the play, an Amazon is defeated, 'a barren sister' is wretched and the changeling is not abducted but liberated by Oberon. However, although Theseus functions as a stand-in for Elizabeth, power being in essence masculine, that Shakespeare controls this world intimates the playwright's claim to 'cultural authorship and social authority'.[184] Montrose further elaborates his views on gender issues in *The Purpose of Playing*. Patriarchal power is no guarantor of concord, observes D'Orsay Pearson, adumbrating its various other causal factors,[185] and Terence Hawkes illuminates the play, Ovid and patriarchal practices by reading *Dream* from the perspective of its female characters.[186] Other critics who see *Dream*'s female characters as victims include Jeffrey D. Frame and Dympna C. Callaghan. Frame discusses Puck and Oberon as invisible voyeurs who deploy scopophilia to achieve male control of Titania, enslaving her to Bottom.[187] Callaghan writes on the association between males playing women's roles and the powerlessness of women characters in *Dream*; she understands the brutish obliviousness of Bottom to his transformation as signifying that he stands in for 'woman'; furthermore, she takes the play's subject to be the humiliation of aristocratic women.[188]

As Garner observed in 1981, *Dream* has proven a rewarding subject for queer theory thanks to Hippolyta's Amazonian identity, the relationship between Hermia and Helena, and the bond between Titania and her votary. Celebrating Puck as a queer hero, Douglas E. Green locates the play's queer moments despite the attempted exclusion of same-sex desire. Green also proposes ways of queering the canon for students.[189] Attending to Hermia's and Helena's homoerotic language, Valerie Traub explains why lesbian desire, seldom taken seriously, was suitable for theatrical performance.[190] In a later essay, 'Setting the Stage', she rehearses legal and religious responses to lesbianism. Traub discusses Titania and to a lesser extent Hippolyta as sexually independent.[191] Invoking Derridean theory and the mythology of Amazon women, Kathryn Schwarz claims that Theseus's victory over Hippolyta comes to signify violence against all the female characters. At the same time, Hippolyta's delineation intimates how slight are the gendered distinctions on which patriarchal hegemony rests.[192]

Disturbing as such insights may be to some, we need not worry on Shakespeare's account. At the turn of the twenty-first century, aptly on Valentine's Day, Cardiff's *Western Mail* reported that the perfumery Quest International had manufactured 'Puck's Potion', a veritable replica of Oberon's amorous stimulant.[193] What better proof that not only the critics but the general public remain engaged with *A Midsummer Night's Dream*?

Notes

1   See Chapter 8 in this volume for a brief discussion of pedagogical essays and annotated student editions, and the performance history in Chapter 2 for a discussion of these materials. Cross-references are to Eastwood's annotated bibliography in Chapter 8.

2   Dorothea Kehler, '*A Midsummer Night's Dream*: A Bibliographic Survey of the Criticism', in *A Midsummer Night's Dream: Critical Essays*, ed. Dorothea Kehler (New York: Garland, 1998), pp. 3–76.

3   Judith M. Kennedy, '*A Midsummer Night's Dream* in the 1990s', in *Where Are We Now in Shakespearean Studies*, ed. W. R. Elton and John M. Mucciolo (Aldershot: Ashgate, 1999), pp. 287–301.

4   John Dryden, 'The Authors Apology for Heroique Poetry; and Poetique Licence', in *The State of Innocence, and Fall of Man. The Complete Works of John Dryden*, ed. Vinton A. Dearing, 16 vols (Berkeley, CA: University of California Press 1994), XII, pp. 86–97.

5   George Brandes, '*A Midsummer Night's Dream* – Its Historical Circumstances – Its Aristocratic, Popular, Comic, and Supernatural Elements', in *William Shakespeare*, trans. William Archer, Mary Morison and Diana White (New York: Macmillan, 1924), pp. 63–71.

6   Jan Kott, 'Titania and the Ass's Head', in *Shakespeare Our Contemporary*, trans. Boleslaw Taborski (1964) (New York: Norton, 1974), pp. 213–36.

7   Edmond Malone, 'An Attempt to Ascertain the Order in Which the Plays of Shakspeare Were Written: *A Midsummer-Night's Dream*' (1778), in Edmond Malone, *The Plays and Poems of William Shakspeare*, 15 vols (1821) (New York: AMS Press, 1966), II, pp. 333–40.

8   Charles Knight, '*A Midsummer Night's Dream*', in *Studies of Shakspere: Forming a Companion Volume* (London: 1849), pp. 207–13.

9   G. K. Chesterton, '*A Midsummer Night's Dream*' [1904], reprinted in *The Common Man* (London: Sheed and Ward, 1950), pp. 10–21.

10   J. B. Priestley, 'Bully Bottom', in *The English Comic Characters* (London: The Bodley Head, 1925), pp. 1–17; H. B. Charlton, '*A Midsummer Night's Dream*' (1933), in *Shakespearian Comedy* (London: Methuen, 1938), pp. 100–22; and John Palmer, 'Bottom', in *Comic Characters of Shakespeare* (London: Macmillan, 1946), pp. 92–109.

11   Elliot Krieger, '*A Midsummer Night's Dream*', in *A Marxist Study of Shakespeare's Comedies* (New York: Barnes & Noble, 1979); Louis A. Montrose, '"Shaping Fantasies": Figurations of Gender and Power in Elizabethan Culture', *Representations* 1.2 (1983), pp. 61–94, 'A Kingdom of

Shadows', in *The Theatrical City: Culture, Theatre, and Politics in London 1576–1649*, ed. David L. Smith, Richard Strier and David Bevington (Cambridge: Cambridge University Press, 1995), pp. 68–86, and *The Purpose of Playing: Shakespeare and the Cultural Politics of the Elizabethan Theatre* (Chicago: University of Chicago Press, 1996).

12 Harold Bloom, 'A *Midsummer Night's Dream*', in *Shakespeare: The Invention of the Human* (New York: Riverhead Books, 1988).

13 August Wilhelm Schlegel, 'Criticisms on Shakspeare's Comedies', in *A Course of Lectures on Dramatic Art and Literature*, ed. A. J. W. Morrison, trans. John Black, revised edition (London: Henry G. Bohn, 1846), pp. 379–99.

14 William Hazlitt, 'The *Midsummer Night's Dream*', in *Characters of Shakespeare's Plays* (1817) (London: Oxford University Press, 1916), pp. 103–9.

15 Charles Marowitz, 'Seeds of "*Verfremdung*" in *A Midsummer Night's Dream*', in *Recycling Shakespeare* (New York: Applause/Theatre Book, 1991).

16 Samuel Taylor Coleridge, 'Notes on the Comedies of Shakespeare: *Midsummer Night's Dream*' (1818) reprinted in *Shakespearean Criticism*, ed. Thomas Middleton Raysor, 2nd edn, 2 vols (New York: Dutton, 1960), I, pp. 90–92.

17 Hermann Ulrici, '*Midsummer Night's Dream*', in *Shakspeare's Dramatic Art: And His Relation to Calderon and Goethe*, trans. A. J. W. Morrison (London: Chapman Brothers, 1846), pp. 270–75.

18 Coleridge, 'Notes on the Comedies of Shakespeare'.

19 Julia Wedgwood, '*The Midsummer Night's Dream*', *Contemporary Review* (April, 1890), pp. 580–87, reprinted in *Women Reading Shakespeare 1660–1900: An Anthology of Criticism*, ed. Ann Thompson and Sasha Roberts (Manchester: Manchester University Press, 1997), pp. 214–16.

20 William Maginn, 'Characters in the Plays – Bottom, the Weaver', in *The Shakespeare Papers of the Late William Maginn, LL.D.*, ed. Shelton Mackenzie (New York: Redfield, 1856), pp. 85–104.

21 G. G. Gervinus, 'Second Period of Shakspeare's Dramatic Poetry: *Midsummer-Night's Dream*', in *Shakespeare Commentaries* (1849), trans. F. E. Bunnett, revised edn (1877) (New York: AMS Press, 1971), pp. 187–203.

22 Frederick S. Boas, 'Shakespere's Poems: The Early Period of Comedy', in *Shakespere and His Predecessors* (New York: Scribner, 1896), pp. 185–96.

23 John Dover Wilson, 'The Copy for *A Midsummer Night's Dream*', in *A Midsummer-Night's Dream*, ed. Arthur Quiller-Couch and John Dover Wilson (Cambridge: Cambridge University Press, 1924), pp. 77–100.

24 Marion Colthorpe, 'Queen Elizabeth I and *A Midsummer Night's Dream*', *Notes and Queries* 34.2 (232) (June, 1987), pp. 205–7.

25 David Wiles, *Shakespeare's Almanac: 'A Midsummer Night's Dream', Marriage, and the Elizabethan Calendar* (Cambridge: D.S. Brewer, 1993).

26 Helen Hackett, '*A Midsummer Night's Dream*', in *A Companion to Shakespeare's Works*, ed. Richard Dutton and Jean E. Howard, 3 vols (Oxford: Blackwell 2003), III, pp. 338–57.

27 Walter De la Mare, 'Introduction', *A Midsummer Night's Dream*, ed. C. Aldred (London: Macmillan [1935]); reprinted as '*The Dream*', in *Pleasures & Speculations* (London: Faber and Faber, 1940), pp. 270–305.

28 Janis Lull, 'Textual Theory, Literary Interpretation, and the Last Act of *A Midsummer Night's Dream*', in *A Midsummer Night's Dream: Critical Essays*, ed. Dorothea Kehler (New York: Garland, 1998), pp. 241–58.

29 Barbara Hodgdon, 'Gaining a Father: The Role of Egeus in the Quarto and the Folio', *Review of English Studies* n. s. 37 (1986), pp. 534–42.

30 William B. Hunter, 'New Readings of *A Midsummer Night's Dream*', *ANQ* 15 (2002), pp. 3-10; Roger Prior, 'The Occasion of *A Midsummer Night's Dream*', *Library Record* 17 (2000), pp. 56–64.

31 William B. Hunter, 'Performance and Text: The Evidence of *A Midsummer Night's Dream*', *ANQ* 11 (1998), pp. 7–11.

32 Geoffrey Bullough, 'Introduction to *A Midsummer Night's Dream*', in

Narrative and Dramatic Sources of Shakespeare, 7 vols (London: Routledge & Kegan Paul, 1957), III, pp. 367–76.

33   T. Walter Herbert, *Oberon's Mazéd World: A Judicious Young Elizabethan Contemplates 'A Midsummer Night's Dream' with a Mind Shaped by the Learning of Christendom Modified by the New Naturalist Philosophy and Excited by the Vision of a Rich, Powerful England* (Baton Rouge, LA: Louisiana State University Press, 1977).

34   Thomas Moisan, 'Antique Fables, Fairy Toys: Elisions, Allusion, and Translation in *A Midsummer Night's Dream*', in *A Midsummer Night's Dream: Critical Essays*, ed. Dorothea Kehler (New York: Garland, 1998), pp. 275–98; Laurie E. Maguire, *Shakespeare's Names* (Oxford: Oxford University Press, 2007), p. 119. Also see pp. 74–119, especially pp. 82–91.

35   Mihoko Suzuki,'The Dismemberment of Hippolytus: Humanist Imitation, Shakespeare's Translation', *Classical and Modern Literature* 10 (1990), pp. 103–12.

36   J. W. Robinson, 'Palpable Hot Ice: Dramatic Burlesque in *A Midsummer Night's Dream*', *Studies in Philology* 61 (1964), pp. 192–204; Mary Ellen Lamb, '*A Midsummer Night's Dream*: The Myth of Theseus and the Minotaur', *Texas Studies in Literature and Language* 21 (1979), pp. 478–91; Leonard Barkan, 'Ovid "Translated" ', in *The Gods Made Flesh: Metamorphosis and the Pursuit of Paganism* (New Haven, CT: Yale University Press, 1986), pp. 251–70; Clifford Davidson, ' "What hempen home-spuns have we swagg'ring here?": Amateur Actors in *A Midsummer Night's Dream* and the Coventry Civic Plays and Pageants', *Shakespeare Studies* 19 (1987), pp. 87–99; Anthony Brian Taylor, 'Golding's Ovid, Shakespeare's "Small Latin" and the Real Object of Mockery in *Pyramus and Thisbe*', *Shakespeare Survey* 42 (1990), pp. 53–64; Kerri Lynne Thomsen, 'Melting Vows: *A Midsummer Night's Dream* and Ovid's *Heroycall Epistles*', *English Language Notes* 40.4 (2003), pp. 25–33; and Jonathan Bate, 'Comedy and Metamorphosis', in *Shakespeare and Ovid* (Oxford: Clarendon Press, 1993), pp. 118–70, especially pp. 129–44.

37   Kenneth Muir, '*A Midsummer Night's Dream*', in *Shakespeare's Sources* (London: Methuen, 1961), pp. 31–47; Madeleine Doran, (1962) 'Pyramus and Thisbe Once More', in *Essays on Shakespeare and Elizabethan Drama in Honor of Hardin Craig*, ed. Richard Hosley (Columbia, MO: University of Missouri Press, 1962), pp. 149–61; and Niall Rudd, 'Pyramus and Thisbe in Shakespeare and Ovid', in *Shakespeare's Ovid: The Metamorphoses in the Plays and Poems*, ed. A. B. Taylor (Cambridge: Cambridge University Press, 2000), pp. 113–125.

38   W. D'Orsay Pearson, ' "Unkinde" Theseus: A Study in Renaissance Mythography', *English Literary Renaissance* 4.2 (1974), pp. 276–98, and Douglas Freake, '*A Midsummer Night's Dream* as a Comic Version of the Theseus Myth', in *A Midsummer Night's Dream: Critical Essays*, ed. Dorothea Kehler (New York: Garland, 1998), pp. 259–74.

39   A. D. Nuttall, '*A Midsummer Night's Dream*: Comedy as Apotrope of Myth', *Shakespeare Survey* 53 (2000), pp. 49–59.

40   Thomas B. Stroup, 'Bottom's Name and His Epiphany', *Shakespeare Quarterly* 29 (1978), pp. 79–82; Jan Kott, 'The Bottom Translation', trans. Daniela Miedzyrzecka, in *Assays: Critical Approaches to Medieval and Renaissance Texts*, ed. Peggy A. Knapp and Michael A. Stugrin (Pittsburgh, PA: University of Pittsburgh Press, 1981), I, pp. 117–149; and Montrose, 'A Kingdom of Shadows' and *The Purpose of Playing*.

41   E. Talbot Donaldson, 'The Lunacy of Lovers: *The Knight's Tale, The Merchant's Tale, and A Midsummer Night's Dream*', in *The Swan at the Well: Shakespeare Reading Chaucer* (New Haven, CT: Yale University Press, 1985), pp. 30–49.

42   Barbara A. Mowat, ' "A Local Habitation and a Name": Shakespeare's Text as Construct', *Style* 23 (1989), pp. 335–51.

43   Thomas Moisan, 'Chaucerian *Solempnytee* and the Illusion of Order in Shakespeare's Athens and Verona', *Upstart Crow* 7 (1987), pp. 36–49.

44 Frank Kermode, 'The Mature Comedies', *Early Shakespeare*, Stratford-upon-Avon Studies 3, ed. John Russell Brown and Bernard Harris (London: Edward Arnold, 1961), pp. 211–27.

45 Robert H. F. Carver, 'Shakespeare's Bottom and Apuleius' Ass', in *The Protean Ass: The Metamorphoses of Apuleius from Antiquity to the Renaissance* (Oxford: Oxford University Press, 2007), pp. 429–45.

46 A. B. Taylor, 'John Gower and "Pyramus and Thisbe" ', *Notes and Queries* 54 (2007), pp. 282–83; and Thelma N. Greenfield, '*A Midsummer Night's Dream* and *The Praise of Folly*', *Comparative Literature* 20 (1968), pp. 236–44.

47 Hugh M. Richmond, 'Shaping a Dream', *Shakespeare Studies* 17 (1985), pp. 49–60; Richard Andrews, '*A Midsummer Night's Dream* and Italian Pastoral', in *Transnational Exchange in Early Modern Theatre*, ed. Robert Henke and Eric Nicholson (Aldershot: Ashgate, 2008), pp. 49–62; and Louise George Clubb, 'Pastoral Jazz from the Writ to the Liberty', in *Italian Culture in the Drama of Shakespere and His Contemporaries: Rewriting, Remaking, Refashioning*, ed. Michele Marrapodi (Aldershot: Ashgate, 2007), pp. 15–26.

48 Robert L. Reid, 'The Fairy Queen: Gloriana or Titania?', *Upstart Crow* 13 (1993), pp. 16–32; Lisa Hopkins, '*A Midsummer Night's Dream* and Mary Sidney', *English Language Notes* 41.4 (2004), pp. 23–28; and Wolfgang Riehle, 'What's in Lysander's Name?' *Notes and Queries* 54 (2007), pp. 274–75.

49 Edith Rickert, 'Political Propaganda and Satire in *A Midsummer Night's Dream*', *Modern Philology* 21 (1923–24), pp. 133–54; Maurice Hunt, 'A Speculative Political Allegory in *A Midsummer Night's Dream*', *Comparative Drama* 34 (2000–01), pp. 423–53; J. P. Conlan, 'The Fey Beauty of *A Midsummer Night's Dream*: A Shakespearean Comedy in Its Courtly Context', *Shakespeare Studies* 32 (2004), pp. 118–72.

50 Lisa Hopkins, *Writing Renaissance Queens: Texts by and about Elizabeth I and Mary, Queen of Scots* (Newark, DE: University of Delaware Press, 2002), pp. 105–7.

51 G. K. Chesterton, '*A Midsummer Night's Dream*' (1904), reprinted in *The Common Man* (London: Sheed and Ward, 1950); B. Ifor Evans, '*A Midsummer-Night's Dream*', in *The Language of Shakespeare's Plays* (London: Methuen, 1952), pp. 70–77.

52 Maginn, 'Characters in the Plays'.

53 Anthony Brian Taylor, ' "When everything seems double": Peter Quince, the Other Playwright in *A Midsummer Night's Dream*', *Shakespeare Survey* 56 (2003), pp. 55–66.

54 Bertrand Evans, 'All shall be well: The Way Found: *A Midsummer Night's Dream*', in *Shakespeare's Comedies* (Oxford: The Clarendon Press, 1960), pp. 33–46.

55 Sheldon P. Zitner, 'The Worlds of *A Midsummer Night's Dream*', *South Atlantic Quarterly* 59 (1960), pp. 397–403.

56 G. K. Hunter, *Shakespeare: The Later Comedies*, Writers and Their Works 143, (London: Longmans, Green, 1962); Larry S. Champion, 'The Comedies of Action', in *The Evolution of Shakespeare's Comedy: A Study in Dramatic Perspective* (Cambridge, MA: Harvard University Press, 1970), pp. 12–59.

57 René Girard, 'Myth and Ritual in Shakespeare: *A Midsummer Night's Dream*', in Josué V. Harari, ed., *Textual Strategies: Perspectives in Post-Structuralist Criticism*, (Ithaca, NY: Cornell University Press, 1979), pp. 189–212.

58 Mark Rose, *Shakespearean Design* (Cambridge, MA: Belknap Press, 1972).

59 M. E. Comtois, 'The Hardiness of *A Midsummer Night's Dream*', *Theatre Journal* 32 (1980), pp. 305–11.

60 Ruth Nevo, 'Fancy's Images', *Comic Transformations in Shakespeare* (London: Methuen, 1980), pp. 96–114.

61 John Baxter, ' "Growing to a point": Mimesis in *A Midsummer Night's Dream*', *English Studies in Canada* 22 (1996), pp. 17–33.

62 Susan Baker, 'Chronotope and Repression in *A Midsummer Night's Dream*', in *A Midsummer Night's Dream: Critical Essays*, ed. Dorothea Kehler (New York: Garland, 1998), pp. 345–68.

63 Mark Taylor, 'A Midsummer Night's Dream: Imitation and Translation', in
    Shakespeare's Imitations (Newark, DE: University of Delaware Press, 2002), pp.
    34–65.
64 Andy Mousley, Renaissance Drama and Contemporary Literary Theory (New
    York: St Martin's Press, 2002), pp. 74–100.
65 William Hazlitt, 'The Midsummer Night's Dream', in Characters of Shake-
    speare's Plays (1817) (London: Oxford University Press, 1916), pp. 103–9.
66 Harley Granville-Barker, 'Preface to A Midsummer Night's Dream' [1924], in
    More Prefaces to Shakespeare, ed. Edward M. Moore (Princeton, NJ: Princeton
    University Press, 1972), pp. 94–134; and Michael J. Sidnell, 'Semiotic Arts of
    Theatre', Semiotica 168 (2008), pp. 11–43.
67 G. Wilson Knight, 'The Romantic Comedies', in The Shakespearian Tempest
    (Oxford: Oxford University Press, 1932), pp. 75–168.
68 Mark Van Doren, 'A Midsummer Night's Dream', in Shakespeare (New York:
    Henry Holt, 1939), pp. 76–83; and David P. Young, Something of Great
    Constancy: The Art of 'A Midsummer Night's Dream' (New Haven, CT: Yale
    University Press, 1996).
69 Stuart M. Tave, ' "A league without the town": A Midsummer Night's Dream',
    in Lovers, Clowns, and Fairies: An Essay on Comedies (Chicago: University of
    Chicago Press, 1993), pp. 1–25.
70 Stephen Fender, Shakespeare: 'A Midsummer Night's Dream' (London: Edward
    Arnold, 1968); Joan Stansbury, 'Characterization of the Four Young Lovers in A
    Midsummer Night's Dream', Shakespeare Survey 35 (1982), pp. 57–63; Brian
    Vickers, 'From Clown to Character', in The Artistry of Shakespeare's Prose
    (London: Methuen, 1968), pp. 52–88; Wolfgang Franke, 'The Logic of Double
    Entendre in A Midsummer Night's Dream', Philological Quarterly 58 (1979),
    pp. 282–97.
71 Ralph Berry, 'The Dream and the Play', in Shakespeare's Comedies:
    Explorations in Form (Princeton, NJ: Princeton University Press, 1972), pp.
    89–110.
72 See Eastwood's Annotated Bibliography on Booth, Chapter 8.
73 Milton Crane, Shakespeare's Prose (Chicago: University of Chicago Press,
    1951); and Arpad Szskolczai, 'Image-magic in A Midsummer Night's Dream:
    Power and Modernity from Weber to Shakespeare', History of the Human
    Sciences 20.4 (2007), pp. 1–26.
74 James E. Robinson, 'The Ritual and Rhetoric of A Midsummer Night's Dream',
    PMLA 83 (1968), pp. 380–91.
75 Madeleine Forey, ' "Bless thee, Bottom, bless thee! Thou art translated!": Ovid,
    Golding, and A Midsummer Night's Dream', Modern Language Review 93
    (1998), pp. 321–29.
76 Christy Desmet, 'Disfiguring Women with Masculine Tropes: A Rhetorical
    Reading of A Midsummer Night's Dream', in A Midsummer Night's Dream:
    Critical Essays, ed. Dorothea Kehler (New York: Garland, 1998), pp. 299–329.
77 Kott, 'Titania and the Ass's Head'.
78 Deborah Baker Wyrick, 'The Ass Motif in The Comedy of Errors and A
    Midsummer Night's Dream', Shakespeare Quarterly 33 (1982), pp. 432–48.
79 Bruce Thomas Boehrer, 'Bestial Buggery in A Midsummer Night's Dream', in
    The Production of English Renaissance Culture, ed. David Lee Miller, Sharon
    O'Dair and Harold Weber (Ithaca, NY: Cornell University Press, 1994) pp. 123–
    50; revised version printed in Shakespeare among the Animals: Nature and
    Society in the Drama of Early Modern England (New York: Palgrave, 2002).
80 Cedric Watts, 'Does Bottom Cuckold Oberon?', in Henry V, War Criminal? and
    Other Shakespeare Puzzles, ed. John Sutherland and Cedric Watts (Oxford:
    Oxford University Press, 2000), pp. 137–42; Thomas Clayton, ' "Fie what a
    question's that if thou wert near a lewd interpreter": The Wall Scene in A
    Midsummer Night's Dream', Shakespeare Studies 7 (1974), pp. 101–13; Patricia
    Parker, ' "Rude Mechanicals": A Midsummer Night's Dream and Shakespear-

ean Joinery', in *Shakespeare from the Margins: Language, Culture, Context* (Chicago: University of Chicago Press, 1996), pp. 83–115; '(Peter) Quince: Love Potions, Carpenter's Coigns, and Athenian Weddings', *Shakespeare Survey* 56 (2003), pp. 39–54; and 'The Name of Nick Bottom', in *Autour du Songe d'une nuit d'été de William Shakespeare*, ed. Claire Gheeraert-Graffeuille and Nathalie Vienne-Guerrin (Rouen: Publications de l'Université de Rouen), pp. 9–29.

81   Stanley Wells, Translation in *A Midsummer Night's Dream*', in *Translating Life: Studies in Transpositional Aesthetics*, ed. Shirley Chew and Alistair Stead (Liverpool: Liverpool University Press, 1999), pp. 15–32, and *Looking for Sex in Shakespeare* (Cambridge: Cambridge University Press, 2004), pp. 10–37.

82   Samuel Pepys, '29 September 1662', in *The Diary of Samuel Pepys* (1662), ed. Robert Latham and William Matthews, 11 vols (Berkeley, CA: University of California Press, 1970), III, p. 208.

83   Enid Welsford, 'The Masque Transmuted', in *The Court Masque: A Study in the Relationship Between Poetry & the Revels* (Cambridge: Cambridge University Press, 1927), pp. 324–49.

84   John H. Long, 'A Midsummer Night's Dream', in *Shakespeare's Use of Music: A Study of the Music and Its Performance in the Original Production of Seven Comedies* (Gainesville, FL: University of Florida Press, 1955), pp. 82–104; Alan Brissenden, 'The Comedies I', in *Shakespeare and the Dance* (Atlantic Highlands, NJ: Humanities Press, 1981), pp. 34-48; Skiles Howard, 'Hands, Feet, and Bottoms: Decentering the Cosmic Dance in *A Midsummer Night's Dream*', *Shakespeare Quarterly* 44 (1993), pp. 325–42.

85   Maurice Hunt, 'The Voices of *A Midsummer Night's Dream*', *Texas Studies in Literature and Language* 34 (1992), pp. 18–38.

86   Wes Folkerth, 'Transformation and Continuity', in *The Sound of Shakespeare* (London: Routledge, 2002), pp. 87–104.

87   H. N. Hudson, 'Shakespeare's Characters: *A Midsummer Night's Dream*', in *Shakespeare: His Life, Art, and Characters* (revised edn, vol. 1, 1872) (New York: Haskell House, 1970), pp. 259–75.

88   John Vyvyan, *Shakespeare and Platonic Beauty* (London: Chatto & Windus, 1961), pp. 77–91.

89   Jane K. Brown, '*Discordia Concors*: On the Order of *A Midsummer Night's Dream*', *Modern Language Quarterly* 48 (1987), pp. 20–41.

90   Peter G. Phialas, '*A Midsummer Night's Dream*', *Shakespeare's Romantic Comedies: The Development of Their Form and Meaning* (Chapel Hill, NC: University of North Carolina Press, 1966), pp. 102–33; Sidney R. Homan, 'The Single World of *A Midsummer Night's Dream*', *Bucknell Review* 17.1 (1969), pp. 72–84.

91   Maginn, 'Characters in the Plays'; G. G. Gervinus, 'Second Period of Shakspeare's Dramatic Poetry: *Midsummer-Night's Dream*', in *Shakespeare Commentaries* (1849), trans. F. E. Bunnètt, revised edition (1877) (New York: AMS Press, 1971), pp. 187–203; and David Ormerod, '*A Midsummer Night's Dream*: The Monster in the Labyrinth', *Shakespeare Studies* 11 (1978), pp. 39–52.

92   Richard Cody, '*A Midsummer Night's Dream*: Bottom Translated', in *The Landscape of the Mind: Pastoralism and Platonic Theory in Tasso's 'Aminta' and Shakespeare's Early Comedies* (Oxford: Clarendon Press, 1969), pp. 127–50.

93   Andrew D. Weiner, '"Multiformitie Uniforme": *A Midsummer Night's Dream*', *ELH* 38 (1971), pp. 329–49.

94   Ronald F. Miller, '*A Midsummer Night's Dream*: The Fairies, Bottom, and the Mystery of Things', *Shakespeare Quarterly* 26 (1975), pp. 254–68.

95   Stuart Sillars, '"Howsoever, strange and admirable:" *A Midsummer Night's Dream* as via stultitiae', *Archiv für das Studium der neueren Sprachen und Literaturen* 244 (2007), pp. 27–39.

96   William Empson, 'The Spirits of the "Dream"', in *Essays on Renaissance*

Literature, ed. John Haffenden, vol. 2 (Cambridge: Cambridge University Press, 1994), pp. 170–248.

97 Colin McGinn, *Shakespeare's Philosophy: Discovering the Meaning behind the Plays* (New York: HarperCollins, 2006), pp. 17–34.

98 Coleridge, 'Notes on the Comedies of Shakespeare'.

99 Ernest Schanzer, 'The Central Theme of *A Midsummer Night's Dream*', *University of Toronto Quarterly* 20 (1951), pp. 233–38.

100 Harold C. Goddard, '*A Midsummer-Night's Dream*', in *The Meaning of Shakespeare*, vol. 1 (Chicago: University of Chicago Press, 1951), pp. 74–80.

101 George A. Bonnard, 'Shakespeare's Purpose in *A Midsummer Night's Dream*', *Shakespeare Jahrbuch* 92 (1956), pp. 268–79.

102 Peter F. Fisher, 'The Argument of *A Midsummer Night's Dream*', *Shakespeare Quarterly* 8 (1957), pp. 307–10.

103 Howard Nemerov, 'The Marriage of Theseus and Hippolyta', *Kenyon Review* 18 (1956), pp. 633–41.

104 C. L. Barber, 'May Games and Metamorphoses on a Midsummer Night', in *Shakespeare's Festive Comedy: A Study of Dramatic Form and its Relation to Social Custom* (Princeton, NJ: Princeton University Press, 1959), pp. 119–62.

105 R. W. Dent, 'Imagination in *A Midsummer Night's Dream*', *Shakespeare Quarterly* 15.2 (1964), pp. 115–29.

106 Philip Edwards, 'The Abandon'd Cave', in *Shakespeare and the Confines of Art* (London: Methuen, 1968), pp. 49–70.

107 Elizabeth Sewell, *The Orphic Voice: Poetry and Natural History* (New Haven, CT: Yale University Press, 1960-1), pp. 53–168.

108 Kathryn L. Lynch, 'Baring Bottom: Shakespeare and the Chaucerian Dream Vision', in *Reading Dreams: The Interpretation of Dreams from Chaucer to Shakespeare*, ed. Peter Brown (Oxford: Oxford University Press, 1999), pp. 99–124.

109 David Schalkwyk, 'Performance and Imagination', in *Shakespeare, Love, and Service* (Cambridge: Cambridge University Press, 2008), pp. 57–79, especially pp. 69–79.

110 James L. Calderwood, *A Midsummer Night's Dream* (New York: Twayne, 1992), pp. 120–48.

111 Stephen Fender, *Shakespeare: 'A Midsummer Night's Dream'* (London: Edward Arnold, 1968).

112 A. P. Riemer, 'Emblems of Art', in *Antic Fables: Patterns of Evasion in Shakespeare's Comedies* (New York: St Martin's Press, 1980), pp. 193–228.

113 J. Dennis Huston, 'Parody and Play in *A Midsummer Night's Dream*', in *Shakespeare's Comedies of Play* (New York: Columbia University Press, 1981), pp. 94–121.

114 Kevin Pask, 'Engrossing Imagination: *A Midsummer Night's Dream*', *Shakespearean International Yearbook* 3 (2003), pp. 172–92.

115 David Mikics, 'Poetry and Politics in *A Midsummer Night's Dream*', *Raritan* 18.2 (1998), pp. 99–119.

116 Kott, 'Titania and the Ass's Head'.

117 Young, *Something of Great Constancy*.

118 Michael MacOwan, 'The Sad Case of Professor Kott', *Drama* 88 (spring, 1968), pp. 30–37.

119 Herbert S. Weil, 'Comic Structure and Tonal Manipulation in Shakespeare and Some Modern Plays', *Shakespeare Survey* 22 (1969), pp. 27–33.

120 Hugh M. Richmond, 'Bottom as Romeo', in *Shakespeare's Sexual Comedy: A Mirror for Lovers* (Indianapolis, IN: Bobbs-Merrill, 1971), pp. 102–22.

121 Marjorie B. Garber, 'Spirits of Another Sort: *A Midsummer Night's Dream*', in *Dream in Shakespeare: From Metaphor to Metamorphosis* (New Haven, CT: Yale University Press, 1974), pp. 59–87.

122 Thelma N. Greenfield, 'Our Nightly Madness: Shakespeare's *Dream* without *The Interpretation of Dreams*', in *A Midsummer Night's Dream: Critical Essays*, ed. Dorothea Kehler (New York: Garland, 1998), pp. 331–44.

123   Alexander Leggatt, 'A Midsummer Night's Dream', in Shakespeare's Comedy of Love (London: Methuen, 1974), pp. 89–115; and David Bevington, ' "But we are spirits of another sort": The Dark Side of Love and Magic in A Midsummer Night's Dream', Medieval and Renaissance Studies 7 (1975), pp. 80–92.

124   Dryden, 'The Authors Apology for Heroique Poetry; and Poetique Licence'.

125   Brandes, 'A Midsummer Night's Dream'.

126   Frank Sidgwick, 'Introduction', in The Sources and Analogues of 'A Midsummer Night's Dream' (London: Chatto and Windus, 1908), pp. 1–68.

127   Katherine. M. Briggs, 'Shakespeare's Fairies', in The Anatomy of Puck: An Examination of Fairy Beliefs among Shakespeare's Contemporaries and Successors (London: Routledge & Kegan Paul, 1959), pp. 44–55.

128   Minor White Latham, The Elizabethan Fairies: The Fairies of Folklore and the Fairies of Shakespeare (1930) (New York: Octagon, 1972).

129   Charlton, 'A Midsummer Night's Dream'.

130   Barber, 'May Games and Metamorphoses on a Midsummer Night'.

131   Marjorie Swann, 'The Politics of Fairylore in Early Modern English Literature, Renaissance Quarterly 53 (2003), pp. 449–73.

132   Lamb, 'A Midsummer Night's Dream: The Myth of Theseus and the Minotaur'.

133   Laurel Moffatt, 'The Woods as Heterotopia in A Midsummer Night's Dream', Studia Neophilologica 76 (2004), pp. 182–87; R. W. Maslen, 'Dream, Freedom of Speech, and the Demonic Affiliations of Robin Goodfellow', Journal of Northern Renaissance 1 (2009), online: www.northernrenaissance.org/issues/The-Idea-of-North/1.

134   E. K. Chambers, 'A Midsummer Night's Dream' (1905), in Shakespeare: A Survey (London: Sidgwick & Jackson, 1958), pp. 77–87.

135   E. C. Pettet, 'Shakespeare's Detachment from Romance', in Shakespeare and the Romance Tradition (London: Staples, 1949), pp. 101–35.

136   Terry Eagleton, 'Desire: A Midsummer Night's Dream, Twelfth Night', in William Shakespeare (Oxford: Blackwell, 1986), pp. 18–34.

137   Donald C. Miller, 'Titania and the Changeling', English Studies 22 (1940), pp. 66–70.

138   Gerald F. Jacobson, 'A Note on Shakespeare's Midsummer Night's Dream', American Imago 19 (1962), pp. 21–26, p. 23.

139   R. A. Zimbardo, 'Regeneration and Reconciliation in A Midsummer Night's Dream', Shakespeare Studies 6 (1970), pp. 35–50.

140   Bonnard, 'Shakespeare's Purpose in A Midsummer Night's Dream', p. 271.

141   Paul A. Olson, 'A Midsummer Night's Dream and the Meaning of Court Marriage', ELH 24 (1957), pp. 95–119.

142   Germaine Greer, 'Love and the Law', in Politics, Power, and Shakespeare, ed. Frances McNeely Leonard (Arlington, TX: Texas Humanities Research Center, 1981), pp. 29–45.

143   A.B. Taylor, 'Ovid's Myths and the Unsmooth Course of Love in A Midsummer Night's Dream', in Shakespeare and the Classics, ed. Charles Martindale and A. B. Taylor (Cambridge: Cambridge University Press, 2004), pp. 49–65.

144   M. D. Faber, 'Hermia's Dream: Royal Road to A Midsummer Night's Dream', Literature and Psychology 22 (1972), pp. 179–90.

145   Aaron Aronson, 'Eros: Sons and Mothers: III', in Psyche & Symbol in Shakespeare (Bloomington, IN: Indiana University Press, 1972), pp. 204–12.

146   Norman Holland, 'Hermia's Dream', in Representing Shakespeare: New Psychoanalytic Essays, ed. Murray M. Schwartz and Coppélia Kahn (Baltimore, MD: Johns Hopkins University Press, 1980), pp. 1–20.

147   Mordecai Marcus, 'A Midsummer Night's Dream: The Dialectic of Eros-Thanatos', American Imago 38.3 (1981), pp. 269–78, , p. 277.

148   Catherine Belsey, 'Peter Quince's Ballad: Shakespeare, Psychoanalysis, History', Deutsche Shakespeare-Gesellschaft/Deutsche Shakespeare-Gesellschaft West Jahrbuch 1994 (1994), pp. 65–82.

149   Allen Dunn, 'The Indian Boy's Dream Wherein Every Mother's Son Rehearses

His Part: Shakespeare's *A Midsummer Night's Dream*', *Shakespeare Studies* 20 (1988), pp. 15–32, p. 22.

150 Calderwood, *A Midsummer Night's Dream*.

151 Jan Lawson Hinely, 'Expounding the Dream: Shaping Fantasies in *A Midsummer Night's Dream*', in *Psychoanalytic Approaches to Literature and Film*, ed. Maurice Charney and Joseph Reppen (Rutherford, NJ: Fairleigh Dickinson University Press, 1987), pp. 120–38.

152 Barbara Freedman, 'Dis/Figuring Power: Censorship and Representation in *A Midsummer Night's Dream*', in *Staging the Gaze: Postmodernism, Psychoanalysis, and Shakespearean Comedy* (Ithaca: Cornell University Press, 1991), pp. 154–91.

153 Katharine Eisaman Maus, 'Sorcery and Subjectivity in Early Modern Discourses of Witchcraft', in *Historicism, Psychoanalysis, and Early Modern Culture*, ed. Carla Mazzio and Douglas Trevor (New York: Routledge, 2000), pp. 325–48.

154 Richard Scholar, 'Bottom's Dream', in *The je-ne-sais-quoi in Early Modern Europe: Encounters with a Certain Something* (Oxford: Oxford University Press, 2005), pp. 282–88.

155 Florence Falk, 'Dream and Ritual Process in *A Midsummer Night's Dream*', *Comparative Drama* 14 (1980), pp. 263–79.

156 William C. Carroll, '*A Midsummer Night's Dream*: Monsters and Marriage', in *The Metamorphoses of Shakespearean Comedy* (Princeton, NJ: Princeton University Press, 1985), pp. 141–77.

157 Frank Nicholas Clary, ' "Imagine no worse of them": Hippolyta on the Ritual Threshold in Shakespeare's *A Midsummer Night's Dream*', in *Ceremony and Text in the Renaissance*, ed. Douglas F. Rutledge (Newark, DE: University of Delaware Press, 1996), pp. 155–66.

158 René Girard, 'Sweet Puck: Sacrificial Resolution in *A Midsummer Night's Dream*', in *A Theatre of Envy: William Shakespeare* (Oxford: Oxford University Press, 1991), pp. 234–42.

159 Henry S. Turner, *Shakespeare's Double Helix* (London: Continuum, 2007).

160 Bonnard, 'Shakespeare's Purpose in *A Midsummer Night's Dream*', p. 271.

161 Palmer, 'Bottom'.

162 Richard H. Cox, 'Shakespeare: Poetic Understanding and Comic Action (A Weaver's Dream)', in *The Artist and Political Vision*, ed. Benjamin R. Barber and Michael J. Gargas McGrath (New Brunswick, NJ: Transaction Books, 1982), pp. 165–92.

163 Michael D. Bristol, 'Wedding Feast and Charivari', in *Carnival and Theater: Plebeian Culture and the Structure of Authority in Renaissance England* (New York: Methuen, 1985), pp. 162–78.

164 Michael Schneider, 'Bottom's Dream, the Lion's Roar, and Hostility of Class Difference in *A Midsummer Night's Dream*', in *From the Bard to Broadway*, ed. Karelisa V. Hartigan (Lanham, MD: University Press of America, 1987), pp. 191–212.

165 Theodore B. Leinwand, ' "I Believe We Must Leave the Killing Out": Deference and Accommodation in *A Midsummer Night's Dream*', *Renaissance Papers* (1986), pp. 11–30.

166 Montrose, 'A Kingdom of Shadows'.

167 Richard Wilson, 'The Kindly Ones: The Death of the Author in Shakespearean Athens', in *Shakespeare in French Theory: King of Shadows* (London: Routledge, 2007), pp. 143–62.

168 Annabel Patterson, 'Bottoms Up: Festive Theory in *A Midsummer Night's Dream*', *Renaissance Papers* (1988), pp. 25–39.

169 Marcia McDonald, 'Bottom's Space: Historicizing Comic Theory and Practice in *A Midsummer Night's Dream*', in *Acting Funny: Comic Theory and Practice in Shakespeare's Plays*, ed. Frances Teague (Rutherford, NJ: Fairleigh Dickinson University Press, 1994), pp. 85–108.

170 Krieger, '*A Midsummer Night's Dream*'; James H. Kavanagh, 'Shakespeare in

Ideology', in *Alternative Shakespeares*, ed. John Drakakis (London: Methuen, 1985), pp. 144–65; Wilson, 'The Kindly Ones'; (2007: 143–62); Bristol, 'Wedding Feast and Charivari'; Schneider, 'Bottom's Dream'; Montrose, 'A Kingdom of Shadows'; and Patricia Parker, '"Rude Mechanicals"'.

171   Penry Williams, 'Shakespeare's *A Midsummer Night's Dream*: Social Tensions Contained', in *The Theatrical City: Culture, Theatre and Politics in London 1576–1649*, ed. David L. Smith, Richard Strier, and David Bevington (Cambridge: Cambridge University Press, 1995), pp. 55–67.

172   Heather Dubrow, *Shakespeare and Domestic Loss: Forms of Deprivation, Mourning, and Recuperation* (Cambridge: Cambridge University Press, 1999), pp. 144–56; and Alan Sinfield, 'Cultural Materialism and Intertextuality: The Limits of Queer Reading in *A Midsummer Night's Dream* and *The Two Noble Kinsmen*', *Shakespeare Survey* 56 (2003), pp. 67–78.

173   Tom Clayton, ' "So quick bright things come to confusion"; or, What Else is *A Midsummer Night's Dream* About?', in *Shakespeare: Text and Theater: Essays in Honor of Jay L. Halio*, ed. Lois Potter and Arthur F. Kinney (Newark, DE: University of Delaware Press, 1999), pp. 62–91, p. 71.

174   Anne E. Witte, 'Bottom's Tangled Web: Texts and Textiles in *A Midsummer Night's Dream*', *Cahiers Élisabéthains* 56 (1999), pp. 25–39.

175   Frederick Turner, 'The Seal and the Wax in *A Midsummer Night's Dream*, in *Shakespeare's Twenty-First Century Economics: The Morality of Love and Money* (Oxford: Oxford University Press, 1999), pp. 95–103.

176   Margo Hendricks, ' "Obscured by Dreams": Race, Empire, and Shakespeare's *A Midsummer Night's Dream*', *Shakespeare Quarterly* 47 (1996), pp. 37–60.

177   Kim F. Hall, *Things of Darkness: Economies of Race and Gender in Early Modern England* (Ithaca, NY: Cornell University Press, 1995), pp. 1–24, especially pp. 22–24.

178   Ania Loomba, 'The Great Indian Vanishing Trick: Colonialism, Property, and the Family in *A Midsummer Night's Dream*', in *A Feminist Companion to Shakespeare*, ed. Dympna C. Callaghan (Oxford: Blackwell, 2000), pp. 163–87.

179   Coleridge, 'Notes on the Comedies of Shakespeare'; and Gervinus, 'Second Period of Shakspeare's Dramatic Poetry'.

180   Agnes Mure MacKenzie, *The Women of Shakespeare's Plays: A Critical Study from the Dramatic and the Psychological Points of View and in Relation to the Development of Shakespeare's Art* (Garden City, NY: Doubleday, Page, 1924), pp. 28–34.

181   Nevo, 'Fancy's Images'.

182   Shirley Nelson Garner, '*A Midsummer Night's Dream*: "Jack shall have Jill: / Nought shall go ill" ', *Women's Studies* 9 (1981), pp. 47–63, p. 61.

183   David Marshall, 'Exchanging Visions: Reading *A Midsummer Night's Dream*', *ELH* 49 (1982), pp. 543–75.

184   Montrose, 'Shaping Fantasies'.

185   Pearson, ' "Unkinde" Theseus: A Study in Renaissance Mythography'.

186   Terence Hawkes, 'Or', in *Meaning by Shakespeare* (London: Routledge, 1992), pp. 11–41.

187   Jeffrey D. Frame, ' "Now will I to the chink,/To spy ... "': Scopophilia as Gender Sport in *A Midsummer Night's Dream*', *Upstart Crow* 19 (1999), pp. 50–61.

188   Dympna C. Callaghan, *Shakespeare without Women: Representing Gender and Race on the Renaissance Stage* (London: Routledge, 2000), pp. 141–57.

189   Douglas E. Green, 'Preposterous Pleasures: Queer Theories and *A Midsummer Night's Dream*', in *A Midsummer Night's Dream: Critical Essays*, ed. Dorothea Kehler (New York: Garland, 1998), pp. 369–97.

190   Valerie Traub, 'The (In)Significance of "Lesbian" Desire in Early Modern England', in *Erotic Politics: Desire on the Renaissance Stage*, ed. Susan Zimmerman (New York: Routledge, 1992), pp. 150–69.

191   Valerie Traub, 'Setting the Stage behind the Seen: Performing Lesbian History', in

The Queerest Art: Essays on Lesbian and Gay Theater, ed. Alisa Solomon and Framji Minwalla (New York: New York University Press, 2002), pp. 55–105.

192 Kathryn Schwarz, 'Tragical Mirth: Framing Shakespeare's Hippolyta', in *Tough Love: Amazon Encounters in the English Renaissance* (Durham, NC: Duke University Press, 2000), pp. 203–35.

193 Anon., 'Bard's Love Potion Brewed', *Western Mail* 14 February 2002, p. 10.

CHAPTER TWO

Dream: The Performance History

Jeremy Lopez

Prologue: The Music of Mendelssohn and the Rhetoric of Performance Criticism

Little could Felix Mendelssohn have imagined the integral place he would come to occupy in twentieth- and twenty-first-century North American and British Shakespeare criticism when, in 1843, he wrote incidental music for Ludwig Tieck's production of *A Midsummer Night's Dream*. Commissioned by King Friedrich Wilhelm IV of Prussia, Tieck's production was first performed in Potsdam's court theatre. It transferred thereafter to Berlin, where it was performed 'a total of 169 times before being abandoned in 1885'.[1] Mendelssohn had actually written his famous overture for incidental music to *Dream* 16 years earlier: it premiered in the Prussian city of Stettin in 1827, in London in 1829 and became associated with Shakespeare's play when it was used at the beginning of a production at Covent Garden (produced by Lucia Elizabeth Vestris, discussed below) in 1840. The complete score was featured in Williams Evans Burton's 1854 production in New York and in Samuel Phelps's 1861 production at Sadler's Wells Theatre in London's Covent Garden.[2] Selections from the score accompanied the dance sequences in Charles Kean's spectacular and balletic 1856 production at the Princess's Theatre. Perhaps most famously, Mendelssohn provided the musical backdrop for Herbert Beerbohm Tree's lavish production at Her Majesty's Theatre in 1900.

In a review of Peter Brook's extremely influential 1970 production of *Dream* for the Royal Shakespeare Company, Robert Speaight expressed a characteristic twentieth-century critical opinion of the effect Mendelssohn's score has had on productions of Shakespeare's play:

> A *Midsummer Night's Dream* used to come to us through many thicknesses of muslin and Mendelssohn until Granville-Barker, who didn't, I think, hold very much with fairies, turned these ones into gilded sprites [and made] the whole thing a little more folksy. Norman Wilkinson put the lovers into doublet and hose, and Bridges-Adams sent them to bed in any Jacobean mansion that came to mind. [...] Peter Hall [...] did not read the play very differently, and it seemed as if the only way you could give a new look to the *Dream* was to turn it into a nightmare. [Jan Kott, in his 1961 book *Shakespeare Our Contemporary*] had already worked this transformation with his customary disregard of any evidence to the contrary; and since the admiration of Peter Brook and Professor Kott for one another was mutual and declared, I awaited Mr. Brook's interpretation of the play with a curiosity not unmixed with apprehension.[3]

In a way that is representative of and consistent with almost all modern critical narratives of the play's performance history, Speaight uses Mendelssohn as the starting point for a narrative of progress, where productions move gradually away from gauzy, nostalgic romanticism, through a newly historicized sense of the play's Elizabethan identity, and toward fresh, contemporary experience – in this case, Peter Brook's acrobatic, circus-inspired *Dream* performed on a bright-white, nearly bare stage. In Speaight's derisively alliterative formulation, *muslin and Mendelssohn*, he abstracts the composer and his score out of a particular historical moment (the production at Potsdam, commissioned as part of a programmatic endeavour to express German national identity in terms of high art)[4] and makes them stand for a trans-historical and trans-national style of production.

The style of production critics have attributed to Mendelssohn-accompanied *Dreams* is one in which production values – in particular music, visual spectacle and non-textual 'business' – seem to supercede the thematic or poetic values that critics understand to reside in Shakespeare's text. Gary Jay Williams says that Mendelssohn's score is 'as programmatic as nineteenth-century pictorial scenery was in general illustrative'.[5] The productions most famous for using Mendelssohn – Kean's and Tree's – were also famous, and have since become notorious, for their extravagant visual spectacles: at the end of Act III in Kean's production, 'forty fairies danced a Maypole ballet around a palm tree that sprang from beneath the stage and rained down garlands of flowers'.[6] The costume chart for Tree's production

> listed ten 'special flying fairies, 4 fireflies, 9 imps, 4 sea urchins, 8 wood elves, [and] 2 wood fairies.' Some fairies could switch on battery-operated glow lamps which they wore at such moments as Puck's incantation over the sleeping lovers [. . .] Oberon wore an electrically lighted breastplate and crown'.[7]

As Williams explains, 6 of the 13 numbers in Mendelssohn's score are 'melodramas – music coordinated with specific passages in the play';[8] such programmatic music would seem amenable to a mode of staging that seeks to leave very little to a spectator's imagination, awing him or her with a highly choreographed, symphonic spectacle.

Robert Speaight's claim that Harley Granville-Barker's production of *Dream* marked a significant break from the spectacular, Mendelssohnian tradition of staging is typical of twentieth- and twenty-first-century criticism's conflation of heavy-handed, spectacular Shakespearean staging with a bygone, pre-modern era. Granville-Barker's production debuted in February 1914, just a few months before the onset of World War I, and this somewhat grim coincidence might seem to make his explicit repudiation of Victorian dramaturgy all the more significant: on the eve of the most horrific armed conflict it had ever seen, the world was about to change forever, and the mode of Shakespearean staging that would be characteristic of this historical moment was one that rejected the voluptuous and dreamlike pictorialism of the antebellum age. Insisting upon absolute faith in Shakespeare's text (only three lines were cut, and about five words altered),[9] Granville-Barker was also in step with the developing modernist tradition in literature and literary criticism, where an author's text was seen as totally coherent in itself; in such a cultural and intellectual context, the addition of music such as Mendelssohn's, which seemed to impose an anachronistic coherence upon the play rather than arise organically from the text, could only seem superfluous or crass.

As I discuss further below, Granville-Barker's production was self-consciously modern, particularly in its rejection of 'the tradition of children with gauzy wings playing the fairies':[10] the fairies in this production were 'covered [. . .] with gold paint and, where possible, actual gold leaf. Some also wore masks, Indian head-dresses, or wigs of ravelled rope and metallic curls'.[11] Production photos of the forest scene reveal these elaborately costumed fairies ornately posed against a backdrop featuring a sparkling, gauzy curtain rather than real or simulated vegetation. But an examination of reviews of productions written both before and after Robert Speaight's 1970 review of the Brook production reveals that Granville-Barker's production hardly marked the performance tradition's decisive break with Mendelssohn. In spite of Speaight's dismissal, the word 'Mendelssohn' is a persistent refrain in critical discussions of the play in performance, and its persistence suggests that there is something more at stake in discussions of spectacular staging than simply defining the moment at which staging of *Dream* entered the modern (or left the Victorian) era.

Discussing the Oregon Shakespeare Festival's 1949 production of *Dream* as a characteristic example of that Festival's attempts to 'present the plays with as few cuts as [...] possible and as nearly after the Elizabethan manner as stage, staff, and actors could manage', James Sandoe noted happily that it was 'played without Mendelssohn and without tulle, without any of those unfortunate romantic musical settings which discover Peaseblossom vocalizing in half an acre of willowy fellows and Oberon describing the wild thyme on the musical scale'.[12]

Thirty-five years after Granville-Barker's revolutionary production, it was still both possible and necessary to refer to 'those unfortunate romantic musical settings' as though they continued predictably to plague contemporary productions. Confirmation of the persistence of unfortunate romantic productions is provided by A. C. Sprague's review of the 1954 Old Vic production touring in New York City:

> Here, once more, was Mendelssohn's music, with all its Victorian associations, played by a large orchestra; here, too, the ponderous scenery [...] As if to complete the impression that we were in the theater of Charles Kean, the fairies were presented by a numerous *corps de ballet*.[13]

According to Williams, 'the 1954 Old Vic production marks the end of the resort to Victorian stagings for the play. Mendelssohn's score went out of use in major productions of the play proper thereafter'.[14] Yet in the decades that followed the Old Vic production, the spectre of Mendelssohn continued to haunt – and occasionally to surprise and delight – productions and their reviewers. In a review of the 1960 Old Vic production, Robert Speaight suggested that the theatre had mended its ways: 'instead of Mendelssohn we had Miss Thea Musgrave's woodnotes tactfully assisting the marvellous poetry of the play and never attempting to replace it'.[15] Mildred Kuner described a 1967 New York Shakespeare Festival production's ill-advised, gimmicky attempts at modernization: 'in the background, Mendelssohn was ground out by a jukebox'.[16] Praising a 1971 production at the Old Globe Theatre in San Diego, Lynn K. Horobetz was relieved that the fairies 'were not insipid, lovable, saccharine sprites flitting from tree to tree and dutifully intoning Mendelssohn'.[17] Arthur Ganz was somewhat more equivocally complimentary of a 1982 production by the Public Theatre in New York's Central Park, where the incidental music 'managed to avoid sounding like Mendelssohn, but only at the cost of sounding like a cross between Debussy and easy-listening pop'.[18] In 1990 Alfred Weiss was delighted by a 'fast paced, playful' student production at the Edinburgh Fringe Festival which 'began with a few bars from the Mendelssohn score, but almost immediately the onstage band of nine musicians [...] asserted itself with its own modern score, declaring that this would not be an old-fashioned romantic *Dream*'.[19] This production may have been inspired by the John Caird's Royal Shakespeare Company production of 1989, which began

> with a performance of Mendelssohn's overture that [...] gradually progressed through an exhilarating desecration of its central section with rock rhythms and foot-tapping use of side drums, returning to Mendelssohn's cool, calm chords at the end.[20]

Very occasionally Mendelssohn strikes the right note for a critic, and that note is usually one of mystery or nostalgia, or both: Claire McGlinchee enjoyed the modern incidental music composed for the 1958 American Shakespeare Theatre production, but found that it lacked the 'perfect fairy quality of Mendelssohn's score for the play'.[21] A perfect fairy quality is what Shakespeare & Co. seemed to be after in their 1978 outdoor production in Lenox, Massachusetts where, according to Judy Salsbury, just before the show began, 'Mendelssohn's music [...] softly filled the air. [...] The pine woods below the audience became the fairies' domain. Actors entered from paths, through bushes, and sometimes swinging on ropes through the trees'.[22] Discussing what he called a 'distinctly unmodern' 1981 production in Berlin, Wilhelm Hortmann noted that its use of Mendelssohn's 'haunting fairy motif, first performed in Berlin on 14 October 1843 and rarely heard nowadays, created an atmosphere of harmony and peace in sharp contrast to the frequently disruptive and anti-illusionist styles of present day productions'.[23] In 2001, the City of London Sinfonia, celebrating its thirtieth anniversary, performed Mendelssohn's music at the Barbican, accompanying a one-time performance of Shakespeare's play by nine actors from the Royal Shakespeare Company. Michael Dobson noted that, 'in deference to Mendelssohn, the actors [...] wore early Victorian dress clothes'. There were

> no costume changes [...] no lighting effects; and the barest minimum of props. But Mendelssohn's music itself supplies all the imaginary gauze wings anyone could desire, and it here provided the frame and occasion for an astoundingly elegant, almost nonchalant performance of *A Midsummer Night's Dream*'.[24]

On the evidence provided by my foregoing survey of references to Mendelssohn in reviews of *Dream* from the last 50 years, it seems safe to say that Hortmann was wrong to claim that Mendelssohn was 'rarely heard nowadays', just as Thomas Clayton was wrong in 1986 to claim that the tradition of 'resounding Mendelssohn [...] twinkling, gauzy minifairies, [...] and pervasive fantasy' had been 'changed drastically' with Peter Hall's 1959 production, and 'even more so' with Peter Brook's of 1970.[25] What I have been trying to demonstrate with this survey is the way Mendelssohn's score perpetually rings in the ears of critical spectators, representing both the outdated theatrical conventions of a dusty, murky Victorian playhouse *and* something that stands between the modern audience and properly historicized (i.e. Elizabethan) yet fully contemporary, theatrical experience. Simultaneously distractingly old-fashioned and distractingly modern, 'Mendelssohn' is, above all else, a critical trope. The persistence of this trope expresses a familiar preoccupation or anxiety of Shakespearean performance critics – namely, the feeling that directors, actors and designers fill the space between Shakespeare's 'original' and the modern spectator with too much clutter and noise. What makes this trope so useful also makes it somewhat disconcerting and worth being wary of. As an index to or shorthand for a historically contingent (and always changing) set of staging conventions, it allows the critic to express and perpetuate three convenient but dangerously oversimplified or inaccurate ideas: first, that the meaning of Mendelssohn's music is basically stable, implying (even if only for the sake of rejection) the same magical or 'gauzy' idea for all audiences all the time; second, that Mendelssohn's music implies and/or effects a dramaturgy that determines, whether they like it or not, the kinds of meanings an acting company can convey; and third, that a clearing away of Mendelssohn and a return to original, and implicitly uncluttered, staging conventions characteristic of Shakespeare's time (or perhaps some other moment in the past) would, if properly done, inevitably facilitate the creation of transparent, original meanings. But the quest for transparent, original meanings is ultimately futile, and it is unlikely that there will ever be an adequate clearing away of intervening historical clutter. Perhaps it would be more rewarding, then, to shift critical, and indeed theatrical, focus from technological determinism – where one set of staging conventions or another is seen to govern the available or possible theatrical meanings – and toward the choices, and contexts for the choices, of particular actors, directors and critics, from whom the meaning of Shakespeare, like the meaning of Mendelssohn, is always in a state of flux.

Interlude: Introduction

A Midsummer Night's Dream is one of Shakespeare's most frequently performed plays, and its vast performance history has been well documented. The best resource for students interested in a comprehensive history of the play in performance is *Our Moonlight Revels: 'A Midsummer Night's Dream' in the Theatre* by Gary Jay Williams, which is generous in its descriptions, insightful in its analysis and replete with beautiful photographs and illustrations. A less comprehensive but equally useful, and recently updated, performance history is Jay L. Halio's *Shakespeare in Performance: 'A Midsummer Night's Dream'*. Roger Warren's *Text & Performance: 'A Midsummer Night's Dream'* is much more limited in its scope than either of the other two, but has the advantage of providing concise and very nearly contemporary descriptions of and reactions to some important productions in the 1970s and 1980s.[26] Trevor R. Griffiths's *Shakespeare in Production: 'A Midsummer Night's Dream'* presents a modern, edited text of the play; an essay on key moments in the play's performance history through 1994; a selective list of productions of the play from the end of the sixteenth century through to the end of the twentieth; and extensive footnotes, keyed to specific lines, words or stage directions, detailing specific theatrical choices that have been made by various actors, directors and playing companies over the course of the play's performance history.[27] My debt to these excellent studies and the records they provide will be everywhere apparent over the course of the chapter that follows.

Because the performance history of this play has been so well documented in books that will be readily available to students, I have decided to take a somewhat unusual approach to the task of digesting and analysing that history here. I begin with the assumption that the most important figure to consider when constructing the history of any play in performance is the spectator: the meaning of a play is to a large degree always shaped by its audience. Rather than attempt to speak, by means of historical research and inference, about *A Midsummer Night's Dream* from the perspective of various historically and culturally distant spectators – as authors such as Williams, Halio and Griffiths have done so well – I have decided to speak in this chapter from the perspective of a very specific kind of spectator, with whose viewing and interpretative habits I am very familiar: this is the late-twentieth- and early-twenty-first century academic spectator.

This kind of spectator is very likely a reader of this book, or a teacher of the reader of this book, or the kind of spectator a reader of this book is in training to become. He or she is deeply familiar with the text of the play and in some cases with the play's performance tradition, both recent and historical; he or she cannot, except by an artificial act of the imagination and the will, watch a production of *Dream* 'innocently' – free, that is, of expectations shaped by previous productions or critical interpretations of the play; and he or she is in the habit of sifting and categorizing the details of a given production so that they can be seen and analysed in terms of, alternately, previous modern productions, the history of productions in Shakespeare's time, non-theatrical literary-critical interpretations, textual history and information or interpretations that can be conveyed in the classroom. For this kind of spectator, then, the history of *A Midsummer Night's Dream* does not really have the chronological shape it is given in books such as Williams's, Halio's or Griffiths's – where theatrical interpretation and meaning begins in the past and moves linearly into the present. Rather, this kind of spectator always sees the history of *Dream* in reverse: the meanings of any given new production not only comprise within them, but also redefine and reshape, the history and various interpretations of all preceding productions, real and imaginary. To see the history of *Dream* in performance from this kind of spectator's perspective, and to interrogate the assumptions that underlie that perspective, is, I suggest, to see with new clarity how a performance tradition is developed not only out of theatrical practitioners' attitudes toward Shakespeare's text, but out of the dialectical relationship between theatrical practitioners' and literary critics' attitudes toward the text, toward the past and toward the act of creating performance history. Thus the history of *Dream* in performance in this chapter is a history that must be written backwards.

A *Dream* with no Bottom

The contemporary spectator or critic is faced with something like an embarrassment of riches when considering the modern performance history of *A Midsummer Night's Dream*. Between 1948 and 2005, in the two major academic Shakespeare journals alone, just shy of 150 discrete productions of the play were recorded and reviewed.[28] I would venture a guess that this number represents only a very small fraction of the total number of productions that were mounted in North America, the United States and Europe during that time. Surveying the vast number of productions of this play, every year, by theatre companies of every stripe, one can quickly become convinced that the text is either extraordinarily versatile or extraordinarily vacuous. The 2007–08 Cincinnati Shakespeare Theatre production presented the play as an 'adventure through a winter wonderland where ice fairies and snow-covered sprites play magical games with four young lovers' (as described in their press release). A 2003 production at Whitworth University (Spokane, Washington) featured fairies who performed 'African-style dancing, complete with a live drum ensemble' (press release). According to the press release, the 2008 theatredelicatessen (London) production, set

> deep in a gutted warehouse space hidden by the façade of smart office blocks', boasted an 'atmosphere of regret and ruin [...] No more is *A Midsummer Night's Dream* the preserve of summer parks and stately homes. This production takes the audience's pre-conceptions of the play, and turns them upside down.

More famously, on the professional stage, 2006 saw the premiere of Tim Supple's *Dream* in Delhi, India (which played subsequently in Stratford-upon-Avon at the Royal Shakespeare Company's Complete Works Festival, and has since embarked upon a world tour that continues as of this writing) – an acrobatic, multi-lingual, intercontinental collaboration in which the transition from court to forest was made when the fairies tore their way through the paper walls of the palace, uncovering a forest framework made from bamboo scaffolding, dangling ropes, and flame-red silken banners, from which the characters swung, hung, and [...] were alternately cradled, cocooned, or entrapped'.[29]

For Supple, writing on the production's website, a

> play that I have always loved and had long prepared for was revitalized through the skills of a dynamic and rich modern theatre culture with 2000-year old roots. Layers of over-familiarity and preconception were torn away.[30]

A similarly energizing, radical production was mounted by Robert LePage at the Royal National Theatre in 1992, the defining feature of which was a

> large circular pool of water [...] surrounded by a bank of mud. [...] Around the mud bank was a track of firmer material on which the lovers could run without slipping and sliding, although most of the action of the play took place in or on the water. There was, in fact, so much splashing of water and splattering of mud that plastic mackintoshes were issued to the audience sitting in the first three rows of the stalls.[31]

'By the end of his intoxicatingly inventive production,' wrote Michael Owen of the *Evening Standard* (10 July 1992), spectators 'knew they had witnessed theatre history in the making'. And Barbara Hodgdon notes that critical reception of LePage's production consistently defined it against 'two structuring absences' – the brilliant white box of Peter Brook's production on the one hand, and, on the other, the hypothetical (or imaginary) traditional *Dream*, 'complete with Athenian palace and Mendelssohn's wood'.[32]

No shortage of strikingly different variations in production style, setting and concept can be found in the annals of recent *Dream* productions. The proliferation of productions is of course a key factor driving this ingenious innovation. But, also due to the proliferation of productions, the strikingly varied performance styles and concepts have a persistent underlying similarity, namely the self-conscious insistence upon their own novelty or ingenuity. Every new production of *A Midsummer Night's Dream* announces itself as the first of its kind.[33] We might (and perhaps should) see this insistence upon novelty as a testament to the endlessly renewable and self-renewing imaginative potential of Shakespeare's play. But we might (and certainly should) also see it as a rhetorical gesture: a gesture that occurs at least in part as a reaction to a perhaps unspoken, entirely understandable anxiety about the possibility that theatre audiences might not need *another* production of *Dream*; a gesture that constructs interpretative and performative authority by means of a somewhat dubious narrative of progress; and a gesture that ensures its own replication by constructing in both performers and audience a nostalgic, commodifying attitude toward the past, where all preceding productions constitute, by their very quaintness, the identity of any given present production. This rhetorical gesture is by no means specific to the late twentieth- and early twenty-first century Shakespearean theatre, though its forms are perhaps more numerous there than they have been in previous eras, and certainly more immediately evident to contemporary critics. But the history of *Dream* in performance can be seen – and I propose to see it – as a history of reiterating this gesture, and with it, a particular attitude toward both performance and history.

Since the middle of the twentieth century, the most influential statement of the principle of innovation as the fundamental source of theatrical energy in productions of *Dream* has been Peter Brook's 1970 production for the Royal Shakespeare Company. Famously, the stage set for this production was stark, white and empty:

> Four white swings hung a few feet forward of the back wall, and two trapeze bars, their cables running up to traveling pulleys, hung at left and right. Around the top of the walls ran a metal catwalk. Ladders led to it at down right and left and at the slots in the side walls. Stage managers, lighting board operators, and drummers were visible on the catwalk, and the fairies often observed the action from it.[34]

The actors wore baggy, colourful costumes: single colours for the fairies, tie-dye for the male lovers, white for the female lovers. The mechanicals were dressed in simple street clothes: work-pants and T-shirts or tank-tops. The fairies swung into and out of the set on the swings and flying trapezes. The same actors who played Theseus and Hippolyta also played Oberon and Titania. Heavily influenced by Jan Kott's reading of the play in *Shakespeare Our Contemporary*,[35] the production's over-arching interpretative approach was psycho-sexual: it suggested that 'the events in the wood represented the dark animal fantasies beneath the public front which Theseus and Hippolyta present to the world'.[36] With its blank-slate set and its playfully but aggressively sexual thematics, Brook's production presented a challenge to the tradition of 'pretty' *Dreams* that had preceded it.

Brook was not by any means the first to challenge the tradition of pretty *Dreams* and, innovative as his *mise-en-scène* was, it might not have had the lasting effect it did had it not been presented within the context of Brook's explicit and often reiterated position that the modern theatre must of necessity be about reinvention. 'Once', he wrote in his now-classic statement of theatrical principles, *The Empty Space*, 'the theatre could begin as magic: magic at the sacred festival, or magic as the footlights came up'.[37] This is a typical late-modern idea, that modern spectators have a difficult time accessing what to earlier audiences was 'magical', and Brook expresses this idea by abstracting and conflating two highly distinct forms of earlier theatre: the theatre of ancient Greece ('sacred festival') and the theatre of the Victorian period ('footlights'). Somewhat ironically, Brook also, in almost the same rhetorical breath, announced his production as a necessary *alternative* to and advance from the specifically Victorian conventions in which productions of the play had become entrenched: quoted in the *Daily Telegraph* (14 September 1970), Brook said that his circus-inspired set allowed the actors to work 'through a language of acrobatics to find a new approach to a magic that we know cannot be reached by 19th-century conventions'. For Brook, the Victorian theatre, with its emphasis on comprehensive, overwhelming spectacle, had an enviable capacity to hold audiences spellbound – to make them feel that the theatre was 'magical'. But this capacity also seemed, looking back from the late twentieth century, to arise out of an old-fashioned interest in contrivance and gaudy artifice – out of effects that rendered an audience passive to the seductive deceptions of spectacle. It was the job of Brook's theatre to strip away contrivance and artifice, allowing an audience to experience the pleasures of theatrical magic even as it could see that the actors had, in Brook's phrase, 'nothing up their sleeves'.[38] Brook's major achievement, then, which has been and continues to be reflected and emulated (if not always successfully) in the late twentieth- and early twenty-first-century performance tradition, was his creation of a theatrical style that justified and made convincing what had been seen by twentieth-century critics of the Shakespearean theatre as the unforgivable sin: self-conscious innovation.

It is difficult at this remove, especially if one did not see the production (and there are no video recordings of it), to capture exactly what was so astonishing about it over and above its ingenious visual design. Gary Jay Williams perhaps puts it most clearly and succinctly when he ascribes the immense popularity of the production to 'its celebrative theatrical energy and overt sexuality, and its investment in the confusions and hopes of its earnest young lovers, so contemporary in spirit'.[39] Brook harnessed the particularly powerful, transient energy of live theatrical experience to make audiences in 1970 feel as though the value of the production lay in its absolute *presentness*. Irving Wardle, reviewing the play for *The Times* (28 August 1970), wrote that it forced audiences 'to encounter the play as if for the first time'. Harold Hobson, writing for *The Sunday Times* (30 August 1970), said that it was 'the sort of thing one sees only once in a lifetime, and then only from a man of genius'.

The moment in the production that perhaps most perfectly embodied the extent to which its effects derived from intensely physical, present-tense action was its final one:

> With Puck's final lines, 'Give me your hands, if we be friends/ And Robin shall restore amends' [...] the actors left the stage to an explosion of drums to come into the auditorium and shake hands with the audience. The moment, in performances in both England and the United States, was something of a lovefest [...] It seemed as if audiences were, in effect, eager to carry the young love-world of the production away with them into the world outside.[40]

But of course an audience, however energized, cannot really carry the world of a production away with it into the world outside. The poignancy and energy of the climactic moment in Brook's production depends upon the specificity of theatrical space – upon an audience's surprise and joy at the opportunity for a brief physical communion with actors who have provided them with three hours of intense emotional experience. A spectator who shook Alan Howard's/Oberon's/Theseus's hand can narrate the excitement of the experience to his or her friend, but that excitement, in both its emotional and its physical dimension, is only imperfectly communicable. To look, in 2008, at photographs of this remarkable production is very much to look backward in time: to see men and women costumed and coiffured quite recognizably in the styles of 1970, and to see them frozen in poses that we can only imagine represent exhilarating running, swinging, flirting and laughing. Those photos which seem best to capture the spirit of the production are generally those in which the actors appear with least clarity, blurred in exuberant motion. The impact of Brook's production lives on in images or memories that decrease in intensity with each passing day, and thus the terms in which that impact has been expressed in contemporary critical discourse are generally nostalgic. Indeed, a nostalgic view characterizes even the earliest responses to the play. Writing in *Shakespeare Quarterly* in 1970, Robert Speaight gave what was and has been one of the dominant opinions of the production's significance: the bare, white stage and the innovative staging made the wonder or mystery of the play

> all the deeper because it was seen so clearly – as clearly, no doubt, as it was once seen on the bare platform of the Globe. Because the words had no visual counterpart, they seized the imagination the more surely. The play was recognized as timeless, because it was neither brought up, nor brought back, to date.[41]

The intensely present-tense qualities of Brook's production ironically transported the audience into a mythical past, and put it in touch with the very spirit of Shakespeare himself – timeless and universal, but also grounded in and enabled by the particular characteristics and energies of 'the Globe'.[42]

Even as it has frequently been seen as a portal to a lost, idealized past, Brook's production has also been seen as the dawning of a new theatrical age, a revolutionary moment when what Speaight called the 'many thicknesses of muslin' laid on by the Victorian tradition were finally cleared away. Speaight, again, sounded a keynote in his *Shakespeare Quarterly* review, saying that Brook 'persuaded you to forget a century of theatrical tradition'.[43] Clive Barnes, writing in the *New York Times* (28 August 1970) promised that the production 'for good or ill, is going to exert a major influence on the contemporary stage'. Thomas Clayton, reviewing the Guthrie Theatre (Minneapolis) production of the play in 1986, referred to Brook's production as 'epoch-making' and 'a modern benchmark'.[44] Writing in 1995, Jay L. Halio quoted Barnes's review and said that in the present moment his words 'resound with prophetic truth'.[45] For Halio, Brook's production 'made many rethink the play from first to last and, what is just as important, feel it again, perhaps for the first time fully'.[46] Words such as *landmark*, *benchmark*, *watershed*, *seminal*, and *revolutionary* are regularly used to characterize Brook's production, often even by those who were not wholly charmed by it.

But the evidence of the subsequent performance tradition suggests that seeing Brook's production as the beginning of a new theatrical era is as problematic as seeing it as providing a transcendent connection with the sixteenth century. The steadily increasing number of Shakespeare festivals and theatres from the mid-1960s onward made dramaturgical and sceneographic innovation and experimentation almost inevitable – especially in the case of such a popular play as *Dream*. And while the spirit and substance of such innovation could often be traced back to the daring of Peter Brook, just as often it took the form of ostentatious, fantastic visual display characteristic of the late nineteenth-century staging tradition. Thus, in a review of a 1976 southern California production, Stephen Booth could complain of an overbearing and distracting 'Walt Disney-enchanted forest backdrop'.[47] R. C. Fulton described a production staged in Alabama in 1981 this way:

[t]hroughout the woodland scenes and again at the very end [...] a huge white disc appeared on a black curtain. At its first appearance it was the fullest of moons; then it became a screen for changing woodland icons, images of trees, single flowers, wild patches of nature.[48]

In a 1985 production at the Old Globe Theatre in San Diego, the playing space was

reminiscent of a vast, attenuated green marble ballroom floor surrounded by a darkened forest. Located at stage right was a black, vine-encrusted spiral staircase, while up left were two huge open doorways that dwarfed the actors and gave a slightly surrealistic tone to the sparsely furnished stage. Oversized, weed-like lanterns, six-foot-tall squirrels, and a gigantic wagon served as mythic props in the fairy world.[49]

Even the forest-set for the 1986 Royal Shakespeare Company production (directed by Bill Alexander) could be described as

a world of sheer fantasy. One of the children playing a fairy wore a bellhop's uniform, another a 'twenties sailor suit. A gigantic spider's web dominated the stage; Titania slept on a huge toadstool; there were Chinese lanterns instead of musk roses, and a gypsy caravan out of *The Wind in the Willows*.[50]

Most productions that have been reviewed by academics since the late 1980s eschew this kind of scenography, but even casual theatregoers will be familiar with the ubiquitous annual productions of *Dream* in idyllic outdoor settings, often presented with free admission and the aim of reaching the widest audience possible – children in particular. As recently as 2007 the Public Theatre's production in New York's Central Park was touted in a press release with language that might as easily have been applied to Herbert Beerbohm Tree's 1900 production: 'The soft singing voices of child fairies sweetened the air [...] [S]moke, thunder, lightning, and fairy dust captivated the audience'. A production the same year in Regent's Park, London, was announced as being performed in 'the most magical place – The Open Air Theatre', a theatre 'surrounded by the heady scent of roses', where, '[a]s dusk deepens and the fairy lights twinkle, the theatre is transformed' (press release). Meanwhile, the more 'serious' professional Shakespearean stages have developed a tradition of staging that does not emulate what Brook presented as a stripping-away of superfluous spectacle. Rather, the emphasis is very much on a visual spectacle that is (often ingeniously) presented as a variation on, contrast to, or even a challenge to 'Victorian' staging conventions. According to Robert Smallwood, the 1989 Royal Shakespeare Company production, directed by John Caird, featured a

> cluttered, black-and-grey-dreamland-rubbish-dump of [a] set [...] a sort of ruined adventure playground to which the fairies, snappers-up of unconsidered trifles, have brought back an accumulation of household junk – old bicycles, sewing machines, a broken piano, iron railings, a cello, chandeliers, and assorted items of domestic plumbing.

The fairies were presented with 'detachable white wings and elongated ears, wearing misshapen tutus and heavy leather boots, escapees from some ghastly delinquents' ballet class'.[51] This visual design is, of course, anti-Victorian, but, paradoxically, the fact that it is so *explicitly* and specifically anti-Victorian indicates how immediate in even a late twentieth-century spectator's consciousness Victorian staging conventions are assumed to be. A quasi-junkyard setting, and/or a setting filled with dreamlike versions of household objects, and/or quasi-punk fairies clad in heavy boots and unconventional tutus are, like the anti-Victorian ethos they embody, completely conventional in late twentieth- and early twenty-first century productions, as is evident in reviews and descriptions of the 1993 production at Stratford, Ontario (directed by Joe Dowling), the

1995 production at the Royal Shakespeare Company (directed by Adrian Noble), the 2005 production at the Royal Shakespeare Company (directed by Gregory Doran) and the 2008 production at the Oregon Shakespeare Festival in Ashland, Oregon (directed by Mark Rucker). In the light of this ongoing competition between quasi-Victorian and anti-Victorian staging traditions, where the 'magic' of an idealized or hyperbolical forest is in each case conflated with the magic of the theatre, the real impact of Brook's production must be understood as the product of – and in some important ways entirely limited to – a very specific cultural and historical moment.

For the purposes of the kind of history I am writing, what is particularly important about the cultural and historical moment in which Brook's *Dream* was produced is that it was a time of energetic expansion in both the professional Shakespearean theatre and the profession of literary studies, and also a time of remarkable cross-pollination between the two professions. The first two decades of the Royal Shakespeare Company's existence, 1960–78, comprising the artistic directorships of Peter Hall and Trevor Nunn, coincided with the English-language publication of Jan Kott's *Shakespeare Our Contemporary* in 1964 and the publication of J. L. Styan's *The Shakespeare Revolution* in 1977. Kott's book, a huge influence on Peter Brook (he wrote the Preface), argued for the vigorous, polemical application of critical interpretations of Shakespeare to the social and political problems of modern life, and vice-versa. Styan signalled a sea-change in literary criticism of Shakespeare by drawing upon, and challenging other scholars to draw upon, the work of contemporary theatrical practitioners (productions by Peter Brook and Tyrone Guthrie, among others, provided keynote examples) in order to broaden and enrich the interpretative work that might be undertaken with the Shakespearean text. As much as these books and these directors electrified the theatrical world and stimulated critical imaginations, they also provoked a great deal of resistance – perhaps most notably and in most sustained form from John Russell Brown, a prolific Shakespeare scholar and, from 1973 to 1988, an associate director at the National Theatre in London.[52] This vigorous dialogue between theatre and academy (of which these critics and directors are only a very partial representation) was most crucially concerned with the role of theatrical innovation – 'design theatre' – in making meaning out of, or imposing meaning upon, the Shakespearean text. The increasingly high public and academic profile of Royal Shakespeare Company directors emerged contemporaneously with a rapid flowering of local and regional Shakespeare festivals and theatres in the United States: the Utah Shakespeare Festival in 1961, the Champlain (Vermont) and Great Lakes Shakespeare Festivals in 1962, the Guthrie Theatre (Minneapolis) and the Shakespeare Theatre of New Jersey in 1963, the Theatre at Monmouth (Maine) in 1970, the Alabama Shakespeare Festival in 1972, the California Shakespeare Theatre in 1974 and Shakespeare & Co. in Lennox, Massachusetts in 1978 – to name only a few. And this flowering was accompanied by a corresponding surge in academic interest in reviewing Shakespeare of all kinds – an enterprise that was crucially concerned with defining the role and limits of theatrical innovation with respect to the meanings inherent to or imposed upon Shakespeare's texts.

The performance history of *Dream* in the twentieth century can be seen as an ongoing struggle between the rhetoric of authenticity, where visual spectacle is seen as a detriment to the glories of Shakespeare's language, and the rhetoric of nostalgia, where the magical world Shakespeare evokes is seen as co-extensive with the theatrical magic sought by an earlier (usually Victorian) era. Sometimes, as we have seen in the case of Robert Speaight or Peter Brook, these two rhetorics amount to the same thing, or struggle for precedence within and around the same production. Perhaps the most important productions of *Dream* before Brook's were those of Peter Hall at Stratford-upon-Avon in 1959 and 1962 (the latter a revival of the former with a different cast), and on film (using many actors from the 1962 cast) in 1967. Like Brook after him, Hall's goal was to 'take *The Dream* back to its beginnings',[53] and as they would with Brook's production, a number of critics felt that Hall's production had effected 'a complete break with modern tradition and an attempt to get back to something like the Elizabethan original'.[54] The visual means by which Hall signalled a return to Elizabethan principles was by setting the production in what resembled a cross between a nobleman's hall and an Elizabethan theatre. When 'the wood near Athens is required, walls melt away, and in and through transparencies shadowy trees glow and glimmer, and bushes in pots and branches are brought on by the actors themselves'.[55] In a move that anticipated Peter Brook, Hall directed the actors in the 1959 production to present themselves *as* performers – in this case, as performers who might be presenting the play as an entertainment accompanying a noble Elizabethan wedding. The problem with this approach, of course, is that Hall's audiences were not and could never pretend to be guests at a noble Elizabethan wedding, and the ' "well meaning amateurs," as the actors pretended to be, stumbled about far too often so that the theatre audience found themselves much in the same position of

Theseus and Hippolyta watching the rude mechanicals stage their play'.[56] Hall's initial attempt to recapture the authentic *Dream* conceived authenticity too narrowly, presenting the audience with historical demands it could not possibly meet.

Hall's subsequent and more successful productions reconceived the locus of authenticity: now the meaning of the production and the play derived from the language's independence of the production's scenic or visual elements. Thus, while the nobleman's hall set of the 1959 production was retained in the 1962 revival, the artificially clumsy acting and the 'unmusical verse speaking' were eliminated, and many of the 1959 textual cuts were restored.[57] The 1967 film (based on Hall's stage production) takes full advantage of film's visual privileges, setting the action outdoors in a wet, muddy, foggy, fecund countryside: famously, the lovers become more begrimed and less clothed as their sexual mishaps in the forest intensify. But, importantly, the 1967 film also used film's technological sophistication to separate language from image: 'while most of the scenes were actually shot in the open air, the great clarity of speaking was accomplished partly by "post-synch," that is, dubbing the sound track in a studio, a technique affording lightness and precision' in the verse-speaking.[58] As with Brook's production three years later, Hall's film cultivates a gap between breathtaking spectacle and headlong physical action on the one hand, and dazzling verbal precision on the other; the effect of this gap is to suggest that the play's true meaning lies in the language – artificial, highly controlled, original and complete – and that the visual spectacle is a necessary vehicle (but *only* a vehicle) by means of which to transmit that language to modern audiences.

Halio argues that Hall's film 'was a conscious attempt to get away from conventional representations' of the play – in particular those associated with 'Mendelssohn's music and pre-Raphaelite art'.[59] This argument, like Hall's own sweeping claim that he was returning the play to its beginnings, suggests that the production was the first to respond really energetically and in modern terms to an essentially static and long outdated tradition of staging. But, in fact, Hall was responding most specifically to a fairly recent and thoroughly modern tradition of staging that extended only as far back as perhaps 1934. In that year, the German director Maximillian Reinhardt had staged his enormously popular, enormously spectacular *Dream* at the Hollywood Bowl in California; this production was transformed the following year into a big-budget Warner Brothers film starring Olivia de Havilland, James Cagney, Victor Jory and Mickey Rooney. Full of Mendelssohn's music, dancing fairies and lavish indoor and outdoor sets, Reinhardt's production both hearkened back to an earlier, ostensibly more spectacular era of staging (his theatrical production of *Dream* was a fixture on the German stage between 1905 and 1927) and demonstrated how fully the play's language could be made visual by means of the most modern technology. Reinhardt's production certainly influenced Tyrone Guthrie's spectacular staging at the Old Vic in 1937 – Robert Speaight called it a 'flagrantly Victorian fantasy'[60] – starring Robert Helpmann and Vivien Leigh, which in turn provided a kind of source for Michael Benthall's 1954 Old Vic production, in which the Old Vic and 'members of the Sadler's Wells Ballet combined forces to present a scenically lavish production that exploited to the utmost Mendelssohn's music [...] and the acting (and dancing) talents of such notables as Robert Helpmann [...] Moira Shearer [...] and Stanley Holloway'.[61] These star-studded, spectacularly musical productions provide the necessary context within which to understand the impact of Hall's production, which, in its 1959 incarnation, featured a cast of as-yet-unknowns and an under-emphasis even on what Muriel St Clare Byrne called the 'verbal music' of the play.[62]

A narrative of progress moving from Reinhardt's film to Hall's might construct the forward-moving history of *Dream* in performance as the triumphant liberation of modern productions, on the screen as well as the stage, from the visual and musical vocabulary of the Victorian era – a sloughing off of accrued 'traditional' layers that stood between spectators and an authentically enjoyable experience of the play. But such a narrative is easily complicated when we understand that the quasi-Victorianism of productions such as Reinhardt's, Guthrie's and Benthall's (as well as those of William Bridges-Adams at Stratford-upon-Avon in the 1930s) was itself a reaction to a prior, almost opposite mode of staging, and moreover a reaction that could as readily be understood as a reclaiming of authentic Shakespearean theatrical experience. In 1914, at the Savoy Theatre in London, Harley Granville-Barker staged what has been called, with predictable overstatement, an 'epoch-making' production of *Dream*.[63] Influenced by contemporary practitioners such as William Poel, Nugent Monck and Ben Greet, who believed that the recovery and application of Elizabethan staging practices would reform the modern performance tradition, Barker produced his plays on a stage meant to mimic – with its bright frontal lighting and its large apron – the Elizabethan thrust stage and the intimate relationship it might have allowed between audiences and actors.

Barker's *Dream* was visually striking, but not strictly spectacular and certainly a departure from earlier 'realistic' or highly representational stagings, where forests and palaces were constructed in as much detail as possible. The play's different settings were generally created with impressionistic painted curtains; the interior of Theseus's palace in the final scene was evoked by quasi-classical modern pillars and a dais set against a black curtain painted with stars; the fairies were costumed entirely in gold and moved with jerky, mechanical gestures. As he simplified the visual approach to location in *Dream*, Barker also simplified the directorial approach to the play's text, cutting fewer lines (a total of about three from the entire play) than any director before him. This insistence upon the importance of the Shakespearean text constituted the general principle underlying all of Barker's work with Shakespeare: 'We have the text to guide us [...] and that is all' he wrote in a letter to the *Daily Mail* in 1912. 'I abide by the text and the demands of the text, and beyond that I claim freedom'.[64]

Like Peter Hall many years later, Granville Barker sought to present the play in some approximation of what an Elizabethan audience would have seen, and this partly involved insisting upon an authentic 'Englishness' within the play – replacing Mendelssohn's music with English folk music and conceiving of Puck as, in the words of a reviewer, 'a genuine rustic hobgoblin, an authentic fragment of Warwickshire folk-lore'.[65] And also like Hall many years later, Barker's gestures toward authenticity were seen by some critics as distracting modernizations that interfered with or worked at cross purposes to the kind of theatrical realizations Shakespeare's text demands. While acknowledging the efficacy of Hall's simple set, as well as the way it evoked both an Elizabethan hall and an Elizabethan theatre, Muriel St Clare Byrne nevertheless regretted that Hall did not take advantage of 'the useful depth and space which the Stratford stage can provide, which in this play can be so helpful for the suggestion of woodland paths and vistas and groves in which fairies can lurk'.[66] Similarly, when William Bridges-Adams staged *Dream* in 1920 – the first production in England, due to World War I, since Barker's – the reviewer for the *Observer* (25 April 1970) found its use of Mendelssohn's music and realistic forest set salutary. In an implicit reference to Barker's golden fairies and abstract sets, this reviewer expressed relief that 'Mr Bridges-Adams is not freakish, or futurist, or rebellious in any direction [...] [H]e gives you, when needed, a landscape, a garden, or what not, which the scene painter shows as definitely a landscape or a garden'. And this relatively understated scenic verisimilitude was seen, in contrast both to the 'sham-realistic style' of the Victorians and the 'futurism' of Barker, as an example of the way Bridges-Adams's production gave the sense of 'a drama which is feeling its way back to its origins'. It was possible for the grandiose style of Reinhardt to take hold between the late 1930s and mid-1950s precisely because of critical reactions such as this – still current even today – which express a longing for a middle ground between the self-consciously abstract spareness of Harley Granville Barker and the extravagantly detailed pictorialism of the Victorians.

The epitome, from the modern critical point of view, of extravagant Victorian pictorialism was Herbert Beerbohm Tree's 1900 production of *Dream* at Tree's own Her Majesty's Theatre in London: it featured a three-dimensional re-creation of an Athenian palace (including nine huge pillars), an army of fairies wielding battery-operated lamps and forest scenes decorated with real trees filled with mechanical, chirping birds. Infamously, in a 1911 revival of the production, Tree added real rabbits to his forest scene, coaxed onto and around the stage with trails of bran. In spite of the fact that Tree cut fewer lines than many earlier productions (and, no doubt, a great many later ones as well), his explicit belief that producers should stage Shakespeare 'as beautifully as they can afford',[67] and the extravagant means with which he undertook to do this, has made him a perennial case in point for the problem of a director standing in the way of Shakespeare's text. In 1895, George Bernard Shaw attacked the dramaturgy of Tree and his contemporaries, arguing that every scenic accessory presented 'the deadliest risk of destroying the magic spell of the poet'.[68] Writing in 2005, Gerald Pinciss found that Shaw's judgement could still 'stand for all [the] elaborate spectacles' of that age.[69] This sentiment has also been echoed by Halio: 'Splendid as Tree's production doubtless was, it was a far cry from Shakespeare's bare boards festooned chiefly with eloquent poetry'.[70] Of course, bare boards festooned chiefly with eloquent poetry is hardly the norm even for twenty-first-century productions of *Dream*; moreover, to a theatregoing culture such as ours, where it is quite common to see *Dream* performed in an outdoor setting whose physical beauties are meant to give resonance and meaning to the events of the play, Tree's production might not seem so strange or excessive if we were somehow able to view it. Tree's stage forest might easily be seen as a forerunner, only in the wrong medium, of Peter Hall's green and foggy England in his 1967 film – a literal and thematic outgrowth of the imagery of the play.

Tree's production was deeply influenced by an earlier one, and one whose pictorialism I think would probably have seemed, could we travel back in time, even more strange and excessive: this was Charles Kean's 1856 production at the Princess's Theatre. Where Tree's pictorialism might be understood as attempting to realize in physical form the authentic spirit of the play's language and imagery, Kean sought to create an authentic historical world on the stage, irrespective of the importance of that historical world to the plot and language of the play. Thus, his *Dream* was set against gorgeous backdrops depicting the Athens of Pericles (fifth century BC) – Athens 'at a time when it had attained its greatest splendour in literature and art – when it stood in its pride and glory, ennobled by a race of illustrious men'.[71] Peter Quince was discovered in a carpenter's workshop fitted out with 'tools copied from discoveries at Herculaneum'.[72] In this way, Kean's *Dream* was as similar as this play could have been to his extremely influential, historically super-accurate productions of *Richard III* and *King John*. And his staging of the forest scenes was at least as spectacular as, if not more so than, those of Tree and other Victorian producers: like the forests of other nineteenth-century productions, Kean's was filled with flying and dancing fairies, artificial moonlight and realistic foliage; in addition, he cut about 800 lines of the play in order to keep running time under three hours – even as he added in a great many dances, musical numbers and spectacular processional entrances. The legacy of Kean's forest lives on – via Tree and his twentieth-century successors – in modern outdoor and indoor stagings of *Dream*; the legacy of his historically and geographically detailed dramaturgy lives on in modern stagings of many other Shakespeare plays – a *Measure for Measure*, for example, set in 1940s Vienna, or a *Comedy of Errors* set in Las Vegas – but not, generally, in the staging of *Dream*, where the 'magic' of the forest tends to suggest that the specific identity of other locales might remain abstract. Indeed, the interest Kean showed in creating an authentic historical setting for *Dream* is perhaps the single staging tradition for this play which has truly died out[73] – though, of course, the concern to achieve authenticity has not.

Ironically, Tree and Kean were direct theatrical descendants of what might be called the first deliberately 'authentic' production of *Dream* in the modern era: that staged by Lucia Elizabeth Vestris, an English actress and singer, at Covent Garden in 1840. As with Kean and Tree, the scenery for Theseus's court was a detailed evocation of ancient Athens. The mechanicals' scenes occurred in front of a painted backdrop illustrating a carpenter's workshop. In the forest scenes 'Vestris attempted to differentiate pictorially each forest locale. The lovers met [...] with a stream and a raised bank in the background, under a mist-veiled moon that slowly sank, its reflection disappearing in the stream'.[74] At the same time, Vestris made relatively light cuts in the text (390 lines), set the production's

13 songs only from Shakespearean text and retained all the scenes as well as the structure of Shakespeare's plot. The Vestris production marked a turning point in the performance history of *Dream* – or, perhaps, what scholars might call, were the Vestris production staged today, a *returning* point: for, between 1630 and 1840 we have almost no record of any productions of what students and scholars today would call 'Shakespeare's' *Dream*.

In 1692 Elkanah Settle's spectacular operatic adaptation, *The Faerie Queen*, with music by Henry Purcell, premiered at the Dorset Gardens Theatre. The distinguishing characteristics of this production – extensive textual cuts in order to make room for newly written dialogue and songs, the near-elimination of the mechanicals and the addition of dance numbers featuring fantastic and pastoral creatures, and an indifference to the structure of Shakespeare's plot except in so far as it could serve as a scaffold on which to hang huge musical numbers – would be typical of all subsequent adaptations over the next 150 years. The major adaptations in this period, besides *The Faerie Queen* (which was so expensive to produce that it all but disappeared after 1693) were those of David Garrick and Frederick Reynolds. Garrick's production, which premiered at Drury Lane in 1754, was an opera called *The Fairies*; featuring 28 songs and only 560 lines (just over a quarter) of Shakespeare's text, this production was very popular in the 1754–55 season. In 1763 Garrick attempted, unsuccessfully, to revive *The Fairies* – augmented with new songs (it now had 33) and more of Shakespeare's text, presented under the title *A Midsummer Night's Dream*. This production was a flop and did not run past opening night. It did, however, provide some of the textual basis for Frederick Reynolds's 1816 operatic adaptation at Covent Garden. Reynolds's production featured 24 songs and reorganized Shakespeare's plot in order to conclude with what an 1817 playbill advertised as

A GRAND PAGEANT commemorative of *THE TRIUMPHS OF THESEUS* in which is introduced the Cretans, the Thebans, the Amazons, the Centaurs, Ariadne in the Labyrinth – Mysterious Peplum, or Veil of Minerva – the Ship Argo – & the Golden Fleece.[75]

As the apotheosis of the eighteenth and early nineteenth centuries' drive to use 'stage technology [...] to provide material representations of a fairy forest world' and to create 'a virtual, alternative reality',[76] Frederick Reynolds' opera was extremely influential – indeed, its influence might be seen to this day in most large-scale professional productions of *Dream*. It is just possible to lock Reynolds up in the early nineteenth century, together with his eighteenth-century forbears – to sequester him on the other side of a door at the threshold of which stands Lucia Elizabeth Vestris and her innovative, inspired commitment to the text, a commitment that would struggle valiantly (and eventually victoriously) to escape the grip of stage technology and its overbearing ability to provide material representations of the fairy world. In the locked room we have 'Adaptation', and in the sun-dappled world that unfolds from that room's doorstep, we see running freely 'Shakespeare's Text', or its closer and more distant cousins, each in possession of an oddly shaped key that may or may not open the door – there, off in the middle distance, always receding – labelled 'Original Performance'. That is one way to look at the narrative of *Dream* in performance: as an endless but hopeful journey, the existence of whose ultimate goal is actually proved by how elusive that goal is.

It is also, of course, possible to see the narrative of *Dream* in performance as an endless and ultimately deluded journey, enabled by the manufacture of beautiful, oddly shaped keys that we know will never unlock the forever receding door. And in fact, we might really prefer that the door remain closed.

The earliest 'modern' (as opposed to early modern) first-person response to a production of *Dream* – a production about whose text and dramaturgy we admittedly know nothing, but which I like to imagine was simply an attempted revival staging of a now-outdated play – was provided by the diarist Samuel Pepys in 1662:

> Then to the King's Theatre, where we saw 'Midsummer Night's Dream,' which I have never seen before nor shall ever again, for it is the most insipid ridiculous play that I ever saw in my life. I saw, I confess, some good dancing and some handsome women, which was all my pleasure.[77]

To Pepys, as to us, *Dream* was a relic from another age, and even the gestures made by the King's Theatre to bring it into the contemporary moment did not suffice to disguise its antiquity and its opacity. It is not easy, but is perhaps interesting, to imagine – as I shall in the chapter's next short section – that an unaccommodated *Dream*, stripped of the music, dancing, acrobatics, innovation and above all the energetic public and academic discourse that have accompanied it through the last three and a half centuries, is but a bare, poor thing.

Unaccommodated *Dream*

The original performance of *A Midsummer Night's Dream* was probably in 1595 or 1596. If this date range is correct, the play would have been performed by the Lord Chamberlain's Men, the theatre company for which Shakespeare worked throughout his career (it became known as the King's Men after the death of Queen Elizabeth I in 1603). Like all theatre companies in England during the sixteenth century, the Lord Chamberlain's Men would have consisted of 12 to 15 professional adult male actors and three or four professional boy actors. The play was probably first performed in a playhouse called the Theatre, in Shoreditch, just north of the city of London. (Some critics have speculated that the play may have been written specifically to celebrate the occasion of an Elizabethan court wedding; as Gary Jay Williams convincingly demonstrates, there is no evidence to support this speculation and it is in fact much more likely that the play was, like all of Shakespeare's plays, written for the commercial theatre.[78]) Built in 1576, the Theatre was the oldest permanent, purpose-built playhouse in London. It was a round, open-air playhouse with a capacity of perhaps 3,000 spectators seated in galleries and standing in the pit surrounding the large, bare thrust stage. The titlepage of the first printed edition of the play says that it 'hath beene sundry times publickely acted', which suggests, albeit vaguely, that it was popular between its first performance and the turn of the seventeenth century. A book called *Palladis Tamia*, published in 1598, refers to Shakespeare as one of 'the most excellent' English dramatists, and includes *Dream* in a list of his achievements in comedy. Court records from the early modern period indicate that *Dream* was probably performed before King James I on New Year's Day, 1604, and definitely performed before King Charles I on 17 October 1630.[79] The play was printed in quarto for the first time in 1600 and again in 1619. It also appeared in the *Folio* edition of Shakespeare's works, 1623. These are things we know.

Though we know the names of some of the actors in the company that performed *Dream* at the end of the sixteenth century, we do not know which roles they played. We do not know if the smaller fairy roles were played by boys or men. Though we know approximately where the Theatre was, we do not know what it looked like.[80] We do not know what kinds of costumes the actors wore to represent Athenians, mechanicals or fairies. A critic can make educated and imaginative guesses at these things, but the kinds of guesses he or she makes, and the meaning attributed to them, are determined by his or her particular historical moment, and so change readily and rapidly. And even if we had detailed information about these things, a vivid and accurate physical picture of the sixteenth-century theatre and playing company would still be only a picture. It would not give us access to what we really want to know: what was it *like* to be a part of that picture, not as a historically distant observer but as a contemporary person? How was the weather at the opening performance? Which jokes did even the contemporary audience find too corny or clever to laugh at? Was the actor playing Bottom known for being a ham 'in real life'? Did anyone notice or care that the female characters were silent throughout much of the final scene? Did Shakespeare's verse cast a spell upon the audience? To attempt to imagine the 'original' performances of *Dream* is to stare into a void: we do not know what it would mean for the play to be real in its own time. As I have attempted to demonstrate in the preceding pages, the substance and meanings of *Dream* in any given present moment originate in that moment, out of performance, out of criticism, out of the interaction between the two, and in dialectical relation to an idea about the past. The difficult task facing both performance and criticism is to develop an idea about the past – past performances, past criticism, past spectators – that is neither nostalgic nor teleological, that does not evaluate meaning deterministically and in relation to a no longer extant original, but which understands that performers, spectators and critics are agents in the creation of theatrical effects and Shakespearean meanings.

Acknowledgement

I am very grateful to Regina Buccola, Genevieve Love and Paul Menzer for their careful reading of earlier drafts of this chapter.

Notes

1   Gary Jay Williams, *Our Moonlight Revels: 'A Midsummer Night's Dream' in the Theatre* (Iowa City, IA: University of Iowa Press, 1997), p. 109.
2   The 1861 production was a revival of a production that debuted in 1853. Williams suggests that Mendelssohn's music may have been a part of the original production, but notes that no composer is given on the playbills until 1861 (Williams, *Our Moonlight Revels*, p. 112, n. 10).
3   Robert Speaight, 'Shakespeare in Britain', *Shakespeare Quarterly* 21 (1970), pp. 439–49, p. 448.
4   Williams, *Our Moonlight Revels*, pp. 104–9.
5   Williams, *Our Moonlight Revels*, p. 107.
6   Williams, *Our Moonlight Revels*, p. 121.
7   Williams, *Our Moonlight Revels*, p. 135.
8   Williams, *Our Moonlight Revels*, p. 107.

9   Williams, *Our Moonlight Revels*, p. 146.
10 Jay L. Halio, *Shakespeare in Performance*: 'A *Midsummer Night's Dream*' (Manchester: Manchester University Press, 1995), p. 34.
11 Halio, *Shakespeare in Performance*, p. 35.
12 James Sandoe , 'The Oregon Shakespeare Festival', *Shakespeare Quarterly* 1 (1950), pp. 4–11, p. 8.
13 A. C. Sprague, 'Shakespeare on the New York Stage, 1954–1955', *Shakespeare Quarterly* 6 (1955), pp. 423–27, p. 423.
14 Williams, *Our Moonlight Revels*, p. 195.
15 Robert Speaight, 'The Old Vic and Stratford-upon-Avon, 1960–61', *Shakespeare Quarterly* 12 (1961), pp. 425–41, p. 427.
16 Mildred Kuner, 'The New York Shakespeare Festival, 1967', *Shakespeare Quarterly* 18 (1967), pp. 411–15, p. 412.
17 Lynn K. Horobetz, 'Shakespeare at the Old Globe, 1971', *Shakespeare Quarterly* 22 (1971), pp. 385–87, p. 385.
18 Arthur Ganz, 'Shakespeare in New York City', *Shakespeare Quarterly* 34 (1983), pp. 103–7, p. 106.
19 Alfred Weiss, 'The Edinburgh International Festival, 1990', *Shakespeare Quarterly* 42 (1991), pp. 462–71, p. 468.
20 Stanley Wells, 'Shakespeare Production in England in 1989', *Shakespeare Survey* 43 (1990), pp. 183–204, p. 200.
21 Claire McGlinchee, 'Stratford, Connecticut Shakespeare Festival, 1958', *Shakespeare Quarterly* 9 (1958), pp. 539–42, p. 541.
22 Judy Salsbury, 'Shakespeare at 'The Mount'', *Shakespeare Quarterly* 30 (1979), pp. 177–78, p. 177.
23 Wilhelm Hortmann, 'Shakespeare in West Germany', *Shakespeare Quarterly* 32 (1981), pp. 382–85, p. 384.
24 Michael Dobson, 'Shakespeare Performances in England, 2001', *Shakespeare Survey* 55 (2002), pp. 285–321, p. 313.
25 Thomas Clayton, 'Shakespeare at the Guthrie: *A Midsummer Night's Dream*', *Shakespeare Quarterly* 37 (1986), pp. 229–36, p. 232.
26 Roger Warren, *Text & Performance: 'A Midsummer Night's Dream'* (New York: Macmillan, 1983).
27 Trevor R. Griffiths, *Shakespeare in Production: 'A Midsummer Night's Dream'*, (Cambridge: Cambridge University Press, 1996).
28 The two journals to which I am referring are *Shakespeare Survey* (founded in 1948) and *Shakespeare Quarterly* (founded in 1950). The archive of reviews from these two journals is the source of much of the critical commentary that gives shape to this chapter. My 'Census of renaissance drama performance reviews in *Shakespeare Quarterly* and *Shakespeare Survey*, 1948–2005' (*Research Opportunities in Renaissance Drama* XLV [2006], pp. 41–104), provides the complete list of recorded, reviewed productions of this play as well as the rest of the plays in the Shakespeare canon.
29 Susanne Greenhalgh, '*A Midsummer Night's Dream*', *Shakespeare Bulletin* 24.4 (2006), pp. 65–69, p. 68.
30 Tim Supple, 'Making the Dream', online: www.dreamonstage.co.uk.
31 Halio, *Shakespeare in Performance*, p. 123.
32 Barbara Hodgdon, 'Looking for Mr. Shakespeare after "The Revolution": Robert LePage's Intercultural Dream Machine', in *Shakespeare, Theory, and Performance*, ed. James Bulman (London: Routledge, 1996), pp. 68–91, p. 71.
33 Contemporary performance criticism of this play has been to some degree preoccupied with discovering and labelling 'the next Peter Brook' – the new production, and production style, that will seem to overturn all previous. LePage's 1992 production is frequently proffered as a candidate. Halio devotes a chapter to this production, and his chapter title wonders if it might be the 'new watershed' in *Dream*'s production history (Halio, *Shakespeare in Performance*, p. 122). Peter Holland voiced a similar idea at the end of his review: 'I have seen

the future, and it is muddy' ('Shakespeare Performances in England, 1992', *Shakespeare Survey* 46 [1993], pp. 159–89, p. 189).

34   Williams, *Our Moonlight Revels*, p. 224.

35   Kott's book was first published in Polish in 1961.

36   Warren, *Text & Performance*, p. 56. For further, and more detailed, discussion of Kott's influence on productions of *Dream*, see Adrienne Eastwood's and Dorothea Kehler's chapters in this volume.

37   Peter Brook, *The Empty Space* (New York: Touchstone, 1968), p. 88.

38   Brook, *The Empty Space*, p. 88.

39   Williams, *Our Moonlight Revels*, p. 233.

40   Williams, *Our Moonlight Revels*, p. 231.

41   Robert Speaight, 'Shakespeare in Britain', p. 448.

42   While it is certainly possible, even likely, that *Dream* was revived at the Globe during the seventeenth century, there is no actual record of a performance there. Moreover, the play was written before the Globe was built. Speaight's idea about the play's ability to communicate in an unmediated, Shakespearean way is thus enabled by a nostalgic abstraction of 'the Globe' to represent or symbolize, anachronistically, Elizabethan theatrical experience in general.

43   Speaight, 'Shakespeare in Britain', p. 448.

44   Thomas Clayton, 'Shakespeare at the Guthrie', p. 232.

45   Halio, *Shakespeare in Performance*, p. 49.

46   Halio, *Shakespeare in Performance*, p. 71.

47   Stephen Booth, 'Shakespeare in California and Utah', *Shakespeare Quarterly* 28 (1977), pp. 229–44, p. 232.

48   R. C. Fulton, 'Alabama Shakespeare Festival, 1981', *Shakespeare Quarterly* 33 (1982), pp. 345–52, p. 350.

49   Michael Flachmann, 'Shakespeare in San Diego, 1985', *Shakespeare Quarterly* 37 (1986), pp. 503–6, p. 503.

50   Roger Warren, 'Shakespeare at Stratford-upon-Avon, 1986', *Shakespeare Quarterly* 38 (1987), pp. 82–89, p. 88.

51   Robert Smallwood, 'Shakespeare at Stratford-upon-Avon, 1989 (Part 1)', *Shakespeare Quarterly* 41 (1990), pp. 101–14, p. 109.

52   See, in particular, Brown's *Free Shakespeare* (London: A & C Black, 1974).

53   See Warren, *Text & Performance*, p. 47.

54   Muriel St Clare Byrne, 'The Shakespeare Season at the Old Vic, 1958–59 and Stratford-upon-Avon, 1959', *Shakespeare Quarterly* 10 (1959), pp. 545–67, p. 545.

55   Byrne, 'The Shakespeare Season at the Old Vic', p. 555.

56   Halio, *Shakespeare in Performance*, p. 47.

57   Halio, *Shakespeare in Performance*, p. 48.

58   Halio, *Shakespeare in Performance*, p. 105.

59   Halio, *Shakespeare in Performance*, p. 105.

60   Robert Speaight, *Shakespeare on Stage* (New York: Little Brown, 1973), p. 157.

61   Halio, *Shakespeare in Performance*, p. 44.

62   Byrne, 'The Shakespeare Season at the Old Vic', p. 554.

63   Halio, *Shakespeare in Performance*, p. 41.

64   Eric Salmon, *Granville Barker and his Correspondents* (Detroit, MI: Wayne State University Press, 1986), p. 528.

65   This is a quotation from *The Nation*'s review of the 1914 production, given in J. L. Styan, *The Shakespeare Revolution* (Cambridge: Cambridge University Press, 1977), p. 101.

66   Byrne, 'The Shakespeare Season at the Old Vic', p. 555.

67   Williams, *Our Moonlight Revels*, p. 131.

68   George Bernard Shaw, *Our Theatres in the Nineties* (London: Constable, 1932), p. 179.

69   Gerald Pinciss, *Why Shakespeare: An Introduction to the Playwright's Art* (London: Continuum, 2005), p. 177.

70   Halio, *Shakespeare in Performance*, p. 32.

71   This quotation is from Kean himself, in his acting edition of the play (cited in Williams, *Our Moonlight Revels*, p. 120).

72   From Kean's acting edition of the play (cited in Williams, *Our Moonlight Revels*, p. 121). For a description of the realistic details of Kean's Athens backdrops, see Halio, *Shakespeare in Performance*, p. 29.

73   Readers will undoubtedly supply numerous examples to contradict this claim. As to the issue of the persistence of staging traditions, see my 'Prologue', above, on Mendelssohn's music. Other staging conventions that have continually given shape to productions of this play and have almost always been discussed by performance critics and directors as either no-longer-occurring (finally) or once-again-occurring (surprisingly) include: Puck being played by an actress; the doubling of Oberon with Theseus and Titania with Hippolyta; the over-zealous suppression or expression of the play's psycho-sexual 'dark side'; and the actual appearance of the textually absent Indian boy.

74   Williams, *Our Moonlight Revels*, p. 100.

75   Williams, *Our Moonlight Revels*, p. 81. The actual playbill can be seen at the Folger Shakespeare Library in Washington, DC.

76   Williams, *Our Moonlight Revels*, p. 89.

77   Samuel Pepys, '29 September 1662', in *The Diary of Samuel Pepys*, ed. Robert Latham and William Matthews, vol. 3 (Berkeley, CA: University of California Press, 1970), p. 208.

78   Williams, *Our Moonlight Revels*, chapter 1.

79   Halio, *Shakespeare in Performance*, p. 14, and James G. McManaway, 'A New Shakespeare Document', *Shakespeare Quarterly* 2 (1951), pp. 119–22.

80   In August 2008, archaeologists from the Museum of London were called to a building site in Shoreditch in order to examine what they now believe to be the foundations of the Theatre.

CHAPTER THREE

Soundings in *A Midsummer Night's Dream*

Tom Clayton

Fore-play – and Aft-play

Concerned with the language, the dialogue, the sense and the sound of *Dream*, this chapter shares something of the nature of a preface as 'rambling, never wholly out of the way nor in it', as John Dryden described it – in a preface, naturally (to his *Fables Ancient and Modern* in 1700). Given my focus here, it seems right to cite a bit at once to chew on, the first and last six lines of the play:

THESEUS
    Now, fair Hippolyta, our nuptial hour
    Draws on apace. Four happy days bring in
    Another moon – but O, methinks how slow
    This old moon wanes! She lingers my desires
    Like to a stepdame or a dowager
    Long withering out a young man's revenue.
PUCK
    ... Now to 'scape the serpent's tongue,
    We will make amends ere long,
    Else the Puck a liar call.
    So, good night unto you all.
    Give me your hands, if we be friends,
    And Robin shall restore amends.

                        (I.i.1–6; V.i.424–29)

Theseus, Duke of Athens, the mortal with the highest rank, speaks first, and the King of fairies' jester speaks last. In these part-speeches alone we have verbal evidence of a richly complex and entertaining play of differences harmonized. As a hybrid figure of Greek mythology (in which there were no 'dukes') Theseus is eminently human, while Puck the jester is a fairy, a denizen of Elizabethan folklore. Theseus is Shakespeare's enhanced courtly contemporary, and the two speak in very different kinds of verse, Theseus's blank, Puck's predominantly heptasyllabic, here and often.[1] The duke, with a vital and vivid line in imagery and figure, speaks affectionately to his prospective bride. The jester addresses the audience with a blend of geniality and mock threat that together end the play with charm and wit. With the former lines the play is just beginning, with the latter it is ending – with transition from the stage world of make-believe to its real-world extension, the better for the experience.

Merriage (*sic*): Getting into *A Midsummer Night's Dream*

Readers not told or shown in advance how and what to think about the play are likely to get it pretty much right: they read to understand, respond and appreciate – for the unique pleasures that reading affords. If they are lucky and have the fortitude, they will retain this attitude as critics, scholars, teachers, adults of every calling, when experience contextualizes and deepens learning, and vice versa. Agreement will probably centre especially on the plot and characters: the vicissitudes of love and its winning through in a world fraught with obstacles on the way to marriage and mutuality after – if we think of Oberon and Titania as 'married' king and queen, and tacitly most do: 'traditional' fairies marry. We shall likely agree, too, that a second major theme along with love is imagination – as anatomized (partly in error but brilliantly) by Theseus at the beginning of Act V: 'The lunatic, the lover, and the poet | Are of imagination all compact' (V.i.7–8). A third is sympathy and kindness, as advocated and manifested by Theseus in choosing *Pyramus and Thisbe*, a play of lovers after all – however clumsy in script and execution – as a wedding entertainment: 'the kinder we to give them thanks for nothing' (V.i.89 ff.).[2]

With the range of characters and actions we expect some kind of micro-survey of human nature and society, an introduction to persons better and worse but like us, albeit translated into extraordinary fiction. And we shall see the play as a comedy in the modern sense perhaps more quickly than in any other: comedy is to laugh at, and the play abounds in actions, persons and utterances to laugh at intermittently from beginning to end. There is scarcely a person – or mythical figure or fairy – in the play who is not a cause or a source of laughter at some point, not even Hippolyta. No po-faced Amazon misandrist she, but a – benevolent – member of the horsy set who is sensitive, compassionate, kind, understanding, enthusiastic and also witty, as a commentator on *Pyramus and Thisbe*. She shows her country colours most clearly in a picturesque mythico-Elizabethan vignette:

> I was with Hercules and Cadmus once
> When in a wood of Crete they bayed the bear
> With hounds of Sparta. Never did I hear
> Such gallant chiding; for besides the groves,
> The skies, the fountains, every region near
> Seemed all one mutual cry. I never heard
> So musical a discord, such sweet thunder.
>
> (IV.i.111–17)

This is the middle speech (7 ll.) between two speeches by Theseus (of 9 ll. each). The speeches' complementarity demonstrates the couple's mutuality even if there *is* a touch of – jovial – competition over which dogs are the superior choristers and Hippolyta drops the names of mythical superstars she has known. The music made by hunting hounds was a genuine concern to Elizabethans, which Theseus and Hippolyta are far more than they are figures from Greek mythology medievalized as in Chaucer's *Knight's Tale*, one of Shakespeare's sources.

Induction

Of Shakespeare's plays, only *The Taming of the Shrew* has a formal 'Induction', but every one of them has in effect if not in fact an induction, prologue, proem or prelude of some kind. *Dream* opens with exposition interspersed with precipitate action preceded by sponta-neous and perfunctory planning – but that is the business of sub-scenes 2–5 of scene i.[3] The opening sub-scene (1–19) is the prologue-in-effect, the stage set in a dialogue between the mature mythic lovers opposed in war but united in peace. It is punctuated by directions to Theseus's silent master of the revels, Philostrate, that are given as much to proclaim the theme, tone and attitude of the play as because anything dramatic follows from them beyond Philostrate's exit:

> Go, Philostrate,
> Stir up the Athenian youth to merriments.
> Awake the pert and nimble spirit of mirth.

Turn melancholy forth to funerals –
The pale companion is not for our pomp.

(I.i.11–15)

More than anything else in the opening dialogue, perhaps, this speech vouches for the bond of affection between Theseus and Hippolyta as already firmly established. Some have found cruelty and violence in Theseus's next words, by taking the first two lines literally and tuning out the second two:

Hippolyta, I woo'd thee with my sword,
And won thy love doing thee injuries.
But I will wed thee in another key –
With pomp, with triumph, and with revelling.

(I.i.16–19)[4]

But they have the same festive and proclamatory tenor as the direction to Philostrate, and seem to establish the prevailing tone, which is in fact advanced by Hippolyta herself in her speech in answer to Theseus's first, quoted at the beginning above. Hippolyta's response is entirely complementary, eloquent in its own right, temperately affectionate and downright spirited in her way of characterizing the appearance – but not the attitude – of one of the weapons that brought them together:

Four days will quickly steep themselves in night,
Four nights will quickly dream away the time;
And then the moon, like to a silver bow
New bent in heaven, shall behold the night
Of our solemnities.

(I.i.7–11)

Whether or not Shakespeare was aware of a tacit bond between the speeches or expected his auditors to recognize it if he was, 'the silver-bow | New *bent*' is related to '*draws*' in Theseus's second line, as though a secondary sense had captured her imagination and prompted the image from archery – which is explicitly present in *King Lear* when the king threatens Kent, 'The bow is *bent and drawn*; make from the shaft' (I.i.149, emph. added).

Dream is a sublimely writerly, poetical play, and the qualities that make it so can be defeated as such in performance only with difficulty and determination, as by Hippolyta's delivering her speech ruefully if not with a snarl; those who see strife in the opening scene are nearer the company of the players, and those who do not are nearer the poets. As Andrew Gurr describes the theatrical tension of Shakespeare's day, 'The contrast between the attractions of witplay and swordplay is part of the larger story of the conflict between stage verse and stage spectacle, and the priority that the poets fought the players for, of hearing or beholding'.[5] For all it can say on stage and screen even when uncut, *Dream* is an exquisitely lyrical, melodious and colourful, at once profound and witty, play that really must be *read* to be fully appreciated – not that it can be *fully* appreciated ever. And it should be read not only in silence but aloud, even if 'heard' only by reading word-for-word and line-by-line in silence. But it *must* be heard: so it was written to be, and so most writing is, whether consciously intended to be heard or not.

Much of Jacobethan drama is pre-eminently verbal drama, Shakespeare's above all, and it was the language that made, it is the language that *makes*, the play. Take the dialogue away from the action, and what is left? Take the action away from the dialogue, and what is lost? Not much that matters to an imaginative reader, who if he or she will have a stage can re-enact the play in what the late Maynard Mack aptly called 'the theatre of the mind', the resources of which are nearer unlimited than any we see in performance, whoever the director and whatever the staging.[6]

One can find a suggestive measure of any play – or speaker – by looking at the first (and last) lines, those of *Dream* quoted at the beginning above. Theseus's 'Now, fair Hippolyta, our nuptial hour | Draws on apace' is *Dream*'s opening line and two-fifths, and it strikes the keynotes of the play in the first line alone with its stress on '*fair* Hippolyta' and '*our* núptial hoúr'. What is packed into the first line's special effects would not be much noticed in performance no matter how circumspectly delivered, perhaps, nor is it certain that these were consciously in the poet's mind when writing. But language is the poet's instrument, and his study makes him play and write it instinctively like the composer he is. If with much the same words he had wanted 'Now' as well as 'fair' stressed, he might have written 'Now, my fair Hippolyta', but there is felicity in the unstressed '(h)our''s giving stress to '*nup*tial' and taking suggestive stress of its own in the stressed homophonic 'hour' that ends the line, enjambing onto the clause's verb 'draws' and its modifier, 'apace'. All slowly indeed to his perception, and the rest of his speech complains of ageing stepdame and dowager-like moon's 'linger[ing] his desires'. Her comforting reply says, in effect but ever so graciously and brightly, 'down, boy'. The sound effects enhancing meaning, combining in intricate patterns, are obvious to the eye in the script and the ear in the sounding; especially noticeable are the long vowels and diphthongs emphasizing Theseus's impatience.

Close Reading and the Poetic

Here by the *poetic* I mean rich and vivid verbal expression and all it conveys by design in sense, reference, sound and resonance – much of which is lost in paraphrase or modern 'translation' – that affects auditors and readers.[7] The most important element is sense, meaning, which is expressed particularly by the words, in both literal and figurative use, and their arrangement, both 'natural' and artificial (e.g. Milton's famous 'Him the Almighty Power | Hurled headlong flaming from th'ethereal sky', *Paradise Lost* I.44–45). Samuel Johnson's succinctly expressed Enlightenment view of 'poetry' still has relevance, too: 'The end of writing is to instruct; the end of poetry is to instruct by pleasing'.[8]

In poetry 'pleasing' is often very complex, owing to orders of expression not typical of most prose works. Common integral devices are imagery, tropes (or figures of thought) and, in Shakespeare's day and writings, figures of speech; that is, of arrangement. It is the imaginative quality and concrete and often far-reaching detail of the language that have effects both immediate and often profound. Any number of speeches or passages or phrases have the intoxicating power of incantation even when that is not the mode of expression, as it is on five occasions – with each anointing – in *Dream*. The kind of critical activity poetry demands, if it is to be understood and felt beyond its general sense and surface qualities, is 'close reading', ever and always an invaluable practice for writings of all kinds from the fine print in sub-prime mortgage contracts meant to deceive, to the fine lines of literature designed to enthral (see any translation of Longinus *On the Sublime*).

A major reason for 'close reading' is to determine, recognize, understand and enjoy as much as possible of all that is there. Since every passage, indeed every use of the same word, differs by context and in some degree content from every other, however close it may seem, it would be self-defeating to offer a checklist approach to that reading. But what it takes in particular is the skill and willingness to read the words, not only individually but in combination and order, to use the *Oxford English Dictionary* (OED) liberally, even or especially including words one thinks one knows already,[9] and to take full account of sound, including the rhythm and metre above all but also the arrangement of consonant and vowel sounds and their inferential relation to the sense and feeling.[10] For the purpose of enlarging understanding (and 'delight'), one may begin anywhere. The examples discussed above and in the rest of this chapter came up by several means, including selection, both random and deliberate in the case of heptasyllabics, which abound in this play, as well they might since they are the distinctive verse form of fairies and a rhythmic source of mesmerism and magic. The four-beat measure is distinctively lilting and rocking, and lends itself readily to dance as well as to song.

As a word, a passage, a speech means in relation to context as well as in content and expression, so do larger units. For example, the Hempen Homespuns' first scene (I.ii) is in tradesmen's prose artfully endowed by Shakespeare with idiosyncrasy, spirited pretension and corresponding malapropism. It comes with unpredictable, vivid and striking contrast after the first long scene (I.i) of lovers' troubles in court discourse ending with the passionate soliloquy in heroic couplets by Helena pining for her fickle Demetrius. As soon as the Homespuns' scene is concluded by – who else? – Bottom, with 'Enough. Hold, or cut bowstrings' (I.ii.100),[11] the still less predictable fairies are ushered in in the next scene (II.i) by Puck's enneasyllabic (nine-syllable) challenge and cue to an itinerant fairy, 'Hów now, spírit, whíther wánder yoú?' (II.i.1). The fairy responds with a pyrotechnic burst of verse in 16 lines of metrical variety and kaleidoscopic fairy-court and country imagery, modulating at the end into courtly pentameters and a closing heroic couplet, blowing off Puck as a '*lob* of spirits', which hardly needs glossing.[12] Although King and Queen mostly speak and Puck sometimes speaks in blank verse or heroic couplets, the characteristic fairies' measure is heptasyllabics. These incorporate variations in other odd-numbered lines also beginning and ending with a stress (like Puck's first in II.i just quoted), or in tetrameters or even-numbered short lines stressed at beginning and end, like the fairy's first four – hexasyllabic (six-syllable) – lines here. The individual lines' measure and rhyming are:

Over hill, over dale,	a 6 syllables	amphimaceric dimeter[13]
Thorough bush, thorough brier,	b 6	'
Over park, over pale,	a 6	'
Thorough flood, thorough fire,	b 6	'
I do wander everywhere	c 7	heptasyllable
Swifter than the moonës sphere,	c 7	'
And I serve the Fairy Queen	d 7	'
To dew her orbs upon the green.	d 8	iambic tetrameter
The cowslips tall her pensioners be.	e 8	'
In their gold coats spots you see;	e 7	heptasyllable

Those be rubies, fairy favours;	f 8	trochaic tetrameter
In those freckles live their savours.	f 8	trochaic tetrameter
I must go seek some dewdrops here,	g 8	iambic tetrameter
And hang a pearl in every		
cowslip's ear.	g 10	iambic pentameter
Farewell, thou lob of spirits;		
I'll be gone.	h 10	iambic pentameter
Our Queen and all our elves come		
here anon.	h 10	iambic pentameter
		(II.i.2–17)

Altogether a merry round of the fairy's rollicking bollocking of Puck that must be read aloud or at the very least heard with the inner ear to do justice to both the ear and the speech. The insistent beat of the pulse of the first seven lines propels the sense along through space, detailing the fairy's movements 'everywhere, | Swifter than the moonës sphere'. The fairy's first line may occasion mnemonic irrelevance in those who learned the Caisson Song before they first encountered *Dream*, but only momentarily.[14] The incantatory effect of heptasyllabics is achieved by the unvarying regularity of their distribution of stresses and unstresses within the line. Word, verse and arrangement sweep right on with twice-repeated prepositions 'Over' and 'Thorough' in alternating lines that pan movement with the verb understood from Puck's question but reiterated in a strong assertion of service and status both at once: '*I* do *wan*der *eve*ry*where*, | And I *serve*', etc.

Sounding Sense

As noted, a critical element of the script is lost in the reading unless it is actively elicited and realized aloud: without the sound, much of the meaning and feeling of any line or speech is flattened or lost altogether. In Shakespeare's verse dialogue, metre makes meaning. It *must* be heard somehow for the meaning to be inferred, understood, experienced. Meaning is the primary matter of verbal expression, and stress is an important means of conveying it, as one of the so-called 'suprasegmental phonemes' of pitch, stress and juncture. A reading from which sounding is absent misses more than a little of the designed emphasis and sense, important dimensions of meaning as well as crucial ones of drama.

It might seem eccentric to adopt aspects of the different pronunciation of Shakespeare's day, but it can often be done unobtrusively and with advantage to sense as well as sound; this applies mainly to stress. Using the pronunciation of the period requires special effort – which was made in June 2004 for several 'original-pronunciation' performances of *Romeo and Juliet* directed by Tim Carroll at Shakespeare's Globe Theatre in London, with David Crystal as the advising historical linguist (see his *Pronouncing Shakespeare*).[15] Both the actors and the audience liked it, and its dialectal sound was not difficult for a British audience to understand. But metre, rhythm and stress are a different matter altogether, and these were largely neglected, with secondary stresses lost accordingly. It is quite possible to observe the secondary stress without making the language sound alien, so long as the sense is observed and the other resources of expressing meaning aloud are in play – not only degree of stress but also pitch and sometimes length. Note, for example, the opening speech of the play, where Theseus's impatience to be wed is conveyed partly by the long vowels and diphthongs in 'F*our* h*a*ppy d*a*ys bring in | Another m*oo*n; but O, *me*thinks, *how slow* | This old m*oo*n wanes' I.i.2–4). In English, stress is phonemic, length is not; but length can be used to telling effect when it compounds the expression of the words, as here.[16]

A fluent, imaginative and practised poet from the Midlands translated to London as Shakespeare was could write differential dramatic dialogue with ease for a wide range of persons, and *Dream* is one of the finest examples: consider the social and creational range of characters, (super-)human from top to Bottom, fairies from royalty to Robin the jester Puck. And consider the idioms required or at least expedient to express the individualities and differences by diction, syntax, range of reference, verse form, phonic palette from court to country, the easy art of the *Dream* and the laboured miscarriage and comic success of art in *The Most Lamentable Comedy and Most Cruel Death of Pyramus and Thisbe*. 'This palpable, gross play' metadramatically demonstrates the art of *Dream* by the excellence of *Pyramus*'s own systematic and uproarious failure, assisted by the *Mystery Science Theatre 3000*-style kibitzing of the internal audience of Athenian courtiers. Its failings are its excellencies, in the sure hands of a master playwright with corresponding players and audience.

All the dialogue works toward performance, but all of it works without it, too, and without it is how it must begin with every kind of reader, for pleasure, for learning, for performing. First with the eye, but also with the inner ears and then the outer aided by the lips.

Here are the last lines of Helena's soliloquy on love at the end of I.i (226–51):

As waggish boys in game themselves forswear,
So the boy Love is perjured everywhere.
For ere Demetrius looked on Hermia's eyne
He hailed down oaths that he was only mine,
And when this hail some heat from Hermia felt,
So he dissolved, and showers of oaths did melt.
I will go tell him of fair Hermia's flight.
Then to the wood will he tomorrow night
Pursue her, and for this intelligence
If I have thanks it is a dear expense.
But herein mean I to enrich my pain,
To have his sight thither and back again.

Helena seems to impugn all young men in the game of love personified by Cupid, whose ubiquitous perjury seems proved by Demetrius's leaving her for Hermia. But so betrayed, she will now betray the eloping Hermia to Demetrius for a welcome but costly thanks, if any; and she will intensify her own jealousy by pursuing him as he pursues Hermia. '*Dear* expense' and '*enrich[ed]* pain' keenly express the ambivalent experience of loving where one is not loved: misery loves company – that of the one causing it. The condensed paraphrase (word count 87) reductively gives the plot with the general sense and feeling of the passage. The 97 words of the original afford far more than amplification by 10 words, and it would take many times as many to convey all that *is* going on in the passage, which is perhaps most striking in its use of figures and a conceit – the kind of thing that especially cannot be conveyed in paraphrase – in the sentences occupying the first three heroic couplets. These express the cause of the action Helena tells herself (and us) she is about to take as a result. The two sentences are followed by the three sentences occupying the next three heroic couplets and concluding lines of the scene.[17]

I am concerned here primarily with the verbal expression and orders of meaning, not with comprehensive criticism. At this level, and with a view especially to the hearing and reading aloud, and understanding accordingly, the verse form of these 12 lines is heroic couplets, and the pentameters are metrically and rhythmically regular – which is not to say monotonous or even invariant – except for the last line, 251, which is necessarily variant ('To have his sight thíthĕr ănd báck ăgaín') as two or three other lines could be. The stronger secondary accents of Shakespeare's day can be incorporated to advantage and without loss, if integrated without self-consciousness, in such words as 'every*where*' (241) and 'intelli*gence*' (248); in fact rhythm and metre require the stresses. As to the possible metrical variants, 'Sŏ thĕ bóy Lóve' *could* be so stressed (as a pyrrhic and a spondee) or conventionally as two iambs, which perhaps better serve the sense, logic and flavour: that is, by contrast with the merely 'waggish boys' of the preceding line, Love is *the* boy, the archetypal mischievous boy.[18] In 246, stressing 'I' seems unlikely;[19] 'I *will* go *tell* him' has the metrical stresses and gives special and pertinent prominence to Helena's 'will'fullness. In 247, few would object to reversing the stresses in the first foot to '*Then* to'. Monosyllabic adverbs are usually stressed and prepositions are not. Here, however, 'to' stressed gains and gives force to the immediate *movement* consequent upon Demetrius's learning 'of fair Hermia's flight', and to the direction and destination. In 248 not stressing the 'and' in a stress position prosifies with three unstressed syllables in a row. More importantly, it de-emphasizes the force of the concluding 'and' clause as both conclusive and ironical – but not ruefully so. The sentimental thought Helena is expressing – as indicated partly by 'But' in 250 – is that, if she receives even so little as thanks for her effort, it will be a cherished as well as costly (in two ways 'dear') expense worth incurring. At the same time, at odds with Helena's reflection is a glancing irony in the language to the effect that so little return as 'thanks' is dearly bought, and the paradox is made painfully explicit in her next and last two lines: not that she deliberately seeks – 'means' – 'to enrich my pain', but that that is the inevitable effect of pursuing the Demetrius otherwise engaged.

Many words had – and have – varying numbers of syllables according to the needs of the verse, especially verbs in the past tense ending in '-ed', of which there are no variants in these lines: 'hailed' (243) is one syllable and 'dissolved' (245) two syllables, though in other contexts either could have an extra (unstressed) syllable by the sounding of the *e*. Both 'Hermia' and 'Demetrius' vary in number of syllables according to metrical requirements. 'Hermia' usually has two but has three (with consequent secondary stress on 'Herm*ia*') several times in the play, especially at the end of lines. 'Demetrius' has four syllables with secondary stress on 'Demetri*us*', but sometimes only three as in 242, probably pronounced 'De*met*r's' with a schwa in place of the two separately-sounded vowels, *iu*.

Perhaps the most striking part of the passage is also the most metaphorical:

For ere Demetrius looked on Hermia's eyne
He *hailed* down oaths that he was only mine,

And when this *hail* some heat from Hermia felt,
So he dissolved, and showers of oaths did melt.

(I.i.242–45)

The sense of 'hailed' as a verb seems at first to be 'called, shouted' (*OED hail*, v. 2) in line 243, with the suggestion of swearing by heaven. But this sense congeals to ice-pellets in the next line, 'when this *hail* some heat from Hermia felt'.[20] Then those hail 'showers of oaths' melted, proved meaningless; and Demetrius himself 'dissolved' – melted away, ceased to be, as hers. The effect is enhanced by the insistently alliterating *h*'s, eight instances in four lines, seven in stress positions. The source of heat was Hermia herself but perhaps tacitly her 'eyne' because sunlike, as the eyes of Petrarchan beauties were (hence the contrarian denial in Sonnet 130.1, 'My mistress' eyes are nothing like the sun').

The passage accelerates in the second set of six lines (246–51) with the aid of enjambment in lines 247–48, which some editors recognize by sparing end-line punctuation there and some do not. Thus ends a soliloquy that began (226 ff.) with emotional and rueful reflections on the paradoxes of amorous attraction, all but concealing the hint of an ultimately happy outcome in 'as he *errs, doting* on Hermia's eyes' in a state of irrational infatuation, curable by anti-dote. And it ends the scene with the audience in on some of the complexities of the plot to come – but with little inkling of just how intricate and surprising they are to be. Next, the utterly unforeseeable Hempen Homespuns come comically into view and hearing in the play's second scene. Bathos follows pathos.

Heptasyllabics and *Dream*'s Epilogue

Dream abounds in a metre perfect for its purposes but not accorded much attention by literary metrists. For example, the *New Princeton Encyclopaedia of Poetry and Poetics* says this:

> HEPTASYLLABLE. In most metrical systems, lines of 7 syllab[l]es are almost always variants of octosyllables (q.v.), not an autonomous meter. In Eng. such lines appear most prominently in the verse form known as '8s and 7s', as in Milton's *L'Allegro* and *Il Penseroso*...[21]

Heptasyllables are by definition not full tetrameters. Being a measure made up mostly of metrically identical lines of seven syllables, they deserve their own term, *heptasyllabics*,[22] which *hendecasyllabics* (lines of 11 syllables) have long had. This term is also considerably more economical than are the cumbersome *acephalous iambic* and *catalectic trochaic tetrameter,* and it begs no questions about which of the 'exceptions' it is (namely, neither). Heptasyllabics are an autonomous metre in Shakespeare, where octasyllabic lines are the variants.[23] They are associated especially with the supernatural and used by fairies (*Dream*), witches (*Macbeth*), and spirits (*The Tempest*), and in incantations (*Dream*), 'scrolls' (*The Merchant of Venice*), a dirge (*Cymbeline*) and so on.[24] Heptasyllabics are the verse form of the epilogue in both *Dream* and *The Tempest*, where the *variations* seem particularly significant in a speech that possibly doubles as Shakespeare's farewell to the stage.[25]

An epilogue may be a vital part of the play, not just a redundant afterword, but its relatively low formal status may be inferred from the article in Wikipedia ('This article may require cleanup to meet Wikipedia's quality standards. Please improve this article if you can [April 2007]'),[26] and from its brief treatment in three of the four best glossaries of literary terms (Oxford, Penguin, Prentice Hall) and its (surprising) absence from the fourth (Abrams).[27] OED gives a range of meanings:

1. *Rhet.* The concluding part or peroration of a speech. *Obs.*
   b. A summary. *Obs.*
2. The concluding part of a literary work; an appendix.
3. A speech or short poem addressed to the spectators by one of the actors after the conclusion of the play.

At the end of *Pyramus and Thisbe*, Pyramus is suddenly resurrected as Bottom with characteristic dysphasia (hypallage in classical rhetoric) to invite the duke to 'see the epilogue, or to hear a Bergomask dance between two of our company' (V.i.345–46).[28] The duke responds, 'No epilogue, I pray you. [...] But come, your Bergomask; let your epilogue alone' (347, 352–53), possibly with a soupçon of double entendre. Sometimes said to try to prevent or delay a barrage of fruit and other missiles while the other actors make their retreat, an epilogue typically apologizes for any defects perceived by the audience and seeks their indulgence and applause for the better parts. Whatever its purposes, it has the power of its position to speak with authority, to have as well as be the last word; and a well-tuned epilogue ends a play on a tonic note, as *Dream*'s does.

If we shadows have offended,
Think but this, and all is mended:
That you have but slumbered here,
While these visions did appear;
And this weak and idle theme,
No more yielding but a dream,
Gentles, do not reprehend.
If you pardon, we will mend.
And as I am an honest Puck,
If we have unearnèd luck
Now to 'scape the serpent's tongue,
We will make amends ere long,
Else the Puck a liar call.
So, good night unto you all.
Give me your hands, if we be friends,
And Robin shall restore amends. [*Exit.*]

(Epilogue 1–16)[29]

The speaker is 'Puck' in the first quarto and most modern editions, 'Robin' in the *Folio* and others. Since the speech prefix in the script is nothing the audience hears, it matters not which name is there: the character-speaker-actor is the same in either case. But the importance of the difference is expressed in the speech itself, where 'an honest Puck' (9) and 'the Puck' (13) refer to a species of 'evil, malicious, or mischievous spirit or demon of popular belief' (*OED* 1.a).[30] By contrast, 'Robin [Goodfellow]' is the individual, who, treated kindly and propitiated, will 'restore amends' (16). The Epilogue may not rival Theseus's two monologues in V.i, but it is striking and affecting in its own write.[31] Though not in the eloquent blank verse of Theseus's soaring imagination (V.i.2–22) and sympathetic perception (V.i.89–105), it is aptly in the fairies' own measure, heptasyllabic couplets, variant only – and very deliberately – in lines 1–2 (trochaic, falling rhythm), transitional 9 (iambic, rising rhythm), and 15–16 (iambic, out on the upbeat). The rest of the lines (3–8, 10–14) are uniform heptasyllabics, each with four stresses including the first and last words in each line.

The Epilogue asks the audience to think, to use its imagination ('there is nothing either good or bad but thinking makes it so', *Hamlet* II.ii.253–54), and to act charitably. It is developed as two complementary octaves. Each octave makes its case in the first three couplets, and its appeal in the fourth. Both concluding couplets are addressed to the audience, explicitly as 'Gentles' in line 7, implicitly by the imperative 'Give me your hands' in line 15. *Gentles* are 'persons of gentle birth or rank' – flattering the many in the theatre who were not of high station – and also persons 'mild in disposition or behaviour; kind, tender' (*OED gentle* a. & n. A.8, B.1). But could this expression also be an English cousin of Irish folklore, where fairies were referred to as 'gentle people' (A.1.e) and 'gentry' (3.b)? Probably not, since the record has those applications no earlier than the nineteenth century. Tempting, nevertheless, as the speaker's way of calling upon his kin to show their special kindness. The last line of each octave promises conditional but assured reciprocation: 'If you pardon, we will mend' (8) – forgiveness leads to healing – 'And Robin shall restore amends' (16). The argument of the first octave is that, if we 'shadows' – fairies, actors, fictitious dramatis personae, insubstantial figures – 'have offended', the audience should view themselves as sleeping and the stage action as visions in their dream. The figments of their imagination should be not reproved but reprieved, with the players to 'mend' (perform better) in response. Bottom had imaginatively translated his lived experience into just such a vision – fit for a ballad – in coming to terms with the incredible (see his soliloquy in IV.i.198–215) but, as we know from our privileged position, ever so real.

Octave 2 repeats and in personal terms applies the appeal of octave 1, here with the speaker identifying himself first as an '*honest* Puck', a bit of an oxymoron, but the stress on 'am' gives assurance of its truth: if there is no audience hissing, '*We* will make amends ere long'. If we don't, or if you don't believe we will, then '*the Puck* a liar call' – at once a reassurance and a threat, since the Pucks were not to be trifled with or crossed. Line 14's 'good night' might seem ambiguous if not menacing, if it were the closing note. But the following and play-concluding couplet dispels any such threat of mischief or disharmony, merging fairy, stage, player and audience: 'Give *me* your *hands*, if *we* be friends, | And *Robin* shall restore amends' (15–16). Such regular iambics in the last two lines place the appropriate rhythmic, metrical and semantic stress on 'me' and 'we', a bonding across the divide between species. But stressing the imperative 'Give' sacrifices nothing and complements the 'restore[d] amends'. 'The Puck' generic may not be a friend to man, but 'Robin' is another story – of friendship shown by the given name, even a *Christian* name, as it is called where that religion is the norm. 'Give me your hands' is obviously an appeal for applause, but it just as obviously prompts an actual as well as symbolic shaking of hands, by Robin with the groundlings near the stage or with even more by going into the audience as he did in Peter Brook's famous and epochal production (1970), where he was followed by the entire cast, in the spirit and in keeping with the letter of *A Midsummer Night's Dream*.[32]

Epilogue

The ultimate root of *audience* is the Latin word for 'to hear', *audire*, and in Shakespeare's day and for long after, as already noted, it was as common to *hear* a play as *see* it.[33] Dramatic dialogue unheard is dialogue deprived of one of its most significant and expressive dimensions, sound and all that that entails, especially in verse, with its rhythm and metre, and the sense they make by indicating stress, modulated, of course, by pitch and all the other variations as necessary. All readers should hear as they read, whether aloud or not, because much of the meaning as well as the very life of the script depends upon just such a sensitive and sympathetic hearing, the one the players endeavour to accommodate by mediating the script for the audience in performance. In the course of performance, the experience in the theatre for players and audience alike is more real than the historical reality of all under other circumstances: it *is* the reality for that time and place, not seldom richer and deeper than the other but also transforming it by the connection.

Glossaries of Literary and Theatrical Terms

Abrams, M. H., *A Glossary of Literary Terms*, 8th edn, with contributions by Geoffrey Harpham (Boston, MA: Wadsworth/ Thomson, 2005).

Baldick, C., *Concise Oxford Dictionary of Literary Terms*, 2nd edn (Oxford: Oxford University Press, 2001).

Cuddon, J. A., *The Penguin Dictionary of Literary Terms and Literary Theory*, 4th edn, rev. by C. E. Preston (London: Penguin, 1998).

Harmon, W., and Hugh Holman, C., *A Handbook to Literature* (Upper Saddle River, NJ: Prentice Hall, 1996).

Hodgson, T., ed., *The Batsford Dictionary of Drama* (London: Batsford, 1988).

Pickering, D. and Law, J. *The Penguin Dictionary of the Theatre* (2001), rev. edn (London: Penguin, 2004).

Preminger, A., and Brogan, T. V. F. eds, *The New Princeton Encyclopedia of Poetry and Poetics* (Princeton, NJ: Princeton University Press, 1993).

Notes

1   Metrical terms can seem daunting, but they are easy to find in glossaries (e.g., those listed at the end of this chapter) and they greatly facilitate discussion in which metrics are important.

2   Theseus's monologue on kindness often goes unnoticed (not very sexy), but it is as important to the play and Shakespeare's lifelong concerns as the earlier one on the imagination.

3   *Sub-scene* is not a standard term. I use it by analogy for a unit of a *scene*, which ends when all characters leave. A sub-scene begins and ends with a significant arrival or departure, either of these altering dialogue and action according to who is present.

4   These lines are a masterstroke of elevated mood, theme and expression threaded together by alliterating keywords in every line: 'woo'd', 'won', 'will wed', and 'with', 'with', and 'with revelling'.

5   Andrew Gurr, *The Shakespearean Stage 1574–1642*, 3rd edn (Cambridge: Cambridge University Press, 1992), p. 173.

6   For a sympathetic and insightful study of some of the theatrical (and filmed) vicissitudes of the play, see Jay L. Halio, *Shakespeare in Performance: 'A Midsummer Night's Dream'* (Manchester: Manchester University Press, 2003) and also Jeremy Lopez's chapter in this volume. The most visually original and complex renderings may be hugely entertaining and provocative, but those that most fully realize the expressiveness and values of the dialogue arguably best serve the play, the playwright and even the audience. The fullness and variety of the imagery is due in part to the spare resources of the staging in Shakespeare's day, and it is all too easy for the richness and special effects of our contemporary dramatic media to flex their muscles, wringing the dialogue dry.

7   What is seen on stage (or screen) and expressed or heard in non-verbal sound effects communicates by sign systems that are not essentially verbal though they can be interpreted as though they were, and in verbal drama they always correlate, if sometimes negatively, with what is said and how it is said.

8   Samuel Johnson , 'Preface' to *Shakespeare's Works*, in *Samuel Johnson on Shakespeare* (1765), ed. W. K. Wimsatt, Jr (New York: Hill & Wang, 1960), pp. 23–69, p. 29.

9   The continuously-updating *OED* is accessible online at no charge through many libraries and other institutions, and for a fee through the *OED* direct. Online: http://dictionary.oed.com.

10   Another area of the relative, since Shakespeare's pronunciation in his own day was not entirely the same as any variety of contemporary English, between varieties of which differences abound. For an excellent study of the subject, see Charles Barber's *Early Modern English*, and in this connection his phonetic transcriptions of poems or songs by Sir Thomas Wyatt (1503–42), Thomas Ford (c. 1580–1648, e.g. 1607) and Andrew Marvell (1621–78) (Charles Barber, *Early Modern English* [Edinburgh: Edinburgh University Press, 1997], pp. 137–40).

11   A line often glossed but seldom explained in detail because, though the tenor is clear enough, the vehicle is not. Peter Holland has the fullest recent editor's note (p. 152b): 'the most likely source is that the English longbowmen if defeated would cut their bowstrings to prevent their use by the enemy' (Charles Hertel in *The Explicator*, 33 [1975], item 39).

12   But here it is. *OED lob*, n. 2: 'A country bumpkin: a clown, lout. Now *dial.*'

13   Alternative term, acatalectic cretic dimeter. Lewis Turco says that 'the *short rocking foot* ('˘') [...] is called *amphimacer* (*cretic*) in accentual-syllabic verse, where it is never found in English language poetry written in that prosody', with the apparent exception of ll. 2–5 here, but they are not a whole poem and may be too few lines to count (Lewis Turco, *The Book of Forms: A Handbook of Poetics,* 3rd edn [London: University Press of New England, 2000], p. 30).

14 'Over hill over dale we have hit the dusty trail | As our caissons go rolling along', etc.

15 David Crystal, *Pronouncing Shakespeare: The Globe Experiment* (Cambridge: Cambridge University Press, 2005).

16 Onomatopoeia is phonemic, in a sense, but there are not many such sounds in the language; e.g., 'buzz, buzz' (*Hamlet* II.ii.389).

17 The first quarto and the *Folio* have three sentences to Oxford's five. The punctuation in Oxford is editorial, and it probably always was, except in Quince's prologue (V.i.108–17) and Shakespeare's manuscripts, of which there is a single surviving example. This example is a scene of three pages (147 ll., the 'ill-Mayday scene') of the manuscript play, *Sir Thomas More*, that many if not all scholars believe is in Shakespeare's hand. In it the punctuation is very sparing: mostly commas, a few periods, a colon (*with* a comma!) and four semi-colons. In any case, the deliberate mispunctuation of Quince's prologue is proof in itself that punctuation in Shakespeare's day and practice was systematic enough for *mis*punctuation to be recognizable and understood as such (because of what it does to the syntax and sense).

18 Shakespeare's verse seems to be far more regular metrically than is always recognized, much less practised, partly because 'variation' as such tends to be preferred to regularity on principle, and partly because the unconscious tendency toward prosification – the inevitable effect of numerous 'variants' – is widespread. I discuss these issues in 'Metre and Meaning in Shakespeare', forthcoming in a festschrift to be published as a special issue of the *Ben JonsonJournal* in 2009. In lines like 241, I suspect that 'the' in this position (iambic metrical-stress) should be stressed more often than not. The word in the position seems a bit less likely to be stressed if a monosyllabic article (as here) or preposition is followed by two words that could be stressed (as monosyllabic nouns or verbs, here 'boy Love'). Stressing 'Sŏ thĕ bóy Lóve' is the closest four-syllable metrical equivalent of two iambs, called a 'double iamb' by Turco, and corresponds with the *ionic a minore* foot in classical versification. The primary determinant should be the metrical position, but in doubtful cases the final determinant must be the sense – carefully considered – that results.

19 Except for the fact that, as British director Tim Carroll told me (and permits me to say), actors are wont to stress personal pronouns, especially 'I' and 'me', wherever they occur.

20 *OED* hail, v. 1: 2. *trans.*, gives this passage as an instance of the meaning, 'To pour down as hail; to throw or send down in a shower with considerable force like hail in a storm'. But it seems likely that in the context 'hail (down)' has also and first the sense and force of homophonic *hail* (v. 2), ' 3. To call or shout to (a ship, a person, etc.) from a distance, in order to attract attention'.

21 Alex Preminger and T. V. F. Brogan, eds, *The New Princeton Encyclopedia of Poetry and Poetics* (Princeton: Princeton University Press, 1993).

22 A term is available from classical prosody, *lēkythion*, but *heptasyllabics* is self-descriptive without detailed explanation. In *Shakespeare's Metrical Art*, George T. Wright says that the only successful form of trochaic metre in English is 'tetrameter – especially with catalexis, a truncated last foot, as in "Téll mĕ whére ĭs fáncў bréd"' (George T. Wright, *Shakespeare's Metrical Art* [Berkeley & Los Angeles: University of California Press, 1988], p. 185).

23 In *Dream* iambic octasyllabic-lines are more common than trochaic.

24 Wright says of these associations that the verses 'serve mainly to change the rhythm or to provide a verse mode more appropriate for certain kinds of characters', who 'signal their peculiar status (at least part of the time) through tetrameter couplets' (Wright, *Shakespeare's Metrical Art*, p. 114).

25 *The Tempest* is the last play of Shakespeare's sole authorship, and if any play – and epilogue – *sounded* like a farewell to the stage, this is it, and it would have been fitting.

26 As of 1 January 2009 the article had not yet been improved, evidently.

27 See the Bibliography for the four glossaries referred to, and for two theatre-orientated glossaries (Bátsford, Penguin), one of which gives the term thoughtful and less short shrift than the others (Batsford, ed. Hodgson).

28 Note that the Greek rhetorical figure hypallage expresses dysphasia, 'derangement in speech due to confusion or loss of ideas arising from affection of the brain' (*OED*).

29 The discussion of the Epilogue will use Stanley Wells, Gary Taylor, *et al.*, eds, *William Shakespeare: The Complete Works*, Oxford Shakespeare, 2nd edn (Oxford: The Clarendon Press, 2005).

30 The online *OED* has a particularly good entry on *Puck*, n.1 (revision of September 2008).

31 Cf. John Lennon's autobiographical *In His Own Write* (New York: Simon & Schuster, 1964).

32 See the chapter (4) on this production in Jay L. Halio's *Shakespeare in Performance: A Midsummer Night's Dream* and Jeremy Lopez's chapter in this volume.

33 Gabriel Egan seems to have put paid to the long-standing supposition (shared by me) that it was more common to *hear* a play than *see* it. In the LION database he found that in over 100 'example expressions [. . .]the preponderance of visual over oral phrasing is more than twelve to one' (332), and 'Nearly half (three-eighths) of the rare aural examples are by Shakespeare'. See 'Hearing or Seeing a Play? Evidence of Early Modern Theatrical Terminology', *Ben Jonson Journal*, 8 (2001), pp. 327–47. It is nevertheless noteworthy that the aural is more prominent in Samuel Johnson's 'Preface' to *Shakespeare's Works* (1765), where 'A dramatick exhibition is a book recited with concomitants that increase or diminish its effect' (p. 40).

CHAPTER FOUR

The Weaver's *Dream* – Mnemonic Scripts and Memorial Texts

Paul Menzer

A search for the age-old link between weaving and dreams leads quickly into realms of pseudo-history and crypto-myth. The thread runs from the Fates who spun the thread of life through Plato's notion that the world was woven through the weavers of classical myth through William Shakespeare's *A Midsummer Night's Dream* and unspools at Gary Wright's 1976 power ballad 'Dream Weaver' and an Adobe software product of the same name that enables its purchaser to spin their own 'web sites'.

Critics have long noticed that images of weaving-and-dreaming animate *A Midsummer Night's Dream* at both the explicit level of language and in its deeper narrative structure. But images of weaving can also govern our thoughts about the process of formation and fragmentation by which early modern plays came together for a moment – as script, as performance, as book – before unravelling once more. Considered as a craft, not an art, that is, weaving provides a clarifying analogy for the way that plays like *Dream* were put together by an ensemble of crafters working with dispersed, disparate and distributed material. For however diverse their trades might seem, early English playwrights, players and printers were all engaged in the same practice – they all worked something fractional into something whole; they all took something distributed and rendered it entire. As the script moved from the site of writing to the scene of reading, however, it became vulnerable to *mis*reading, as labourers in one trade tried to decipher writing systems designed by and for another. After all, playwrights wrote manuscripts for players to read, memorize and put aside. In other words a playscript was, fundamentally, a mnemonic aid to help an actor remember his lines. Printers then had to 're-purpose' that mnemonic aid, translate it into an artefact that memorialized performance: printed plays were, fundamentally, memorials to past performances. In short, printers had to translate mnemonic scripts into memorial texts, and this process was not invariably a seamless one.

A Midsummer Night's Dream is an unusually good example of this translation since it stages a rehearsal in which craftsmen struggle to make sense of the mnemonic scripts that enabled performance. Furthermore, *Dream*'s earliest printers apparently also struggled to interpret those scripts, since the first printed texts of *Dream* bear traces of uncertain translation. The following chapter therefore traces the fragmentation and consolidation process that governs the composition, rehearsal and printing of *A Midsummer Night's Dream* and focuses on the uneasy translation of mnemonic scripts into memorial texts. The intersection of shuttle and loom offers a compelling image of individual labour within a collective enterprise – an image that hovers over the junction of fragmentary part and collective whole that governs the labour practices of actors and ensembles across the ages.

Dream Weaving: Writing

Romantic notions of writing tend to fantasize the originality of the individual artist. Alone in his garret the dew-eyed poet communes with his muse, then delivers his labour to a waiting world. Such a notion badly mistakes the writing practices of early modern playwrights, however, which required efficiency, productivity, collaboration and appropriation. Indeed, the word play*wright*, with its emphasis upon writer-as-maker, is nowhere more appropriate than in the early Elizabethan period, when playwrights churned out plays to meet a hungry playhouse market. Late in life, the playwright Thomas Heywood claimed to have had a hand or at least 'a maine finger' in 220 plays.[1] Playwrights were craftsmen, analogous to, not distinct from, the period's tailors, tinkers and weavers.

Nor did the period's craftsmen consider their products and practices to be non-creative. An exemplary instance is outlined in a 1682 pamphlet entitled *The Triumphant Weaver: or, the Art of Weaving Discuss'd and Handled*, where the writer, 'R. C.', describes the superiority of weavers to the 'Painter, and Th'Imbroiderer'. 'Dost thou desire the shape of any Beast? | That in our work, by us can be exprest,' the weaver/writer asserts. 'Or any Fowl, or any Fish to see? | These also, easily can produced be. | Or any Tree, or Herb, or Flower? likewise, | We can present them all before your eyes'. Warming to his theme, R. C. closes with a sealing couplet: 'Or would you wear a Rose of *July*-flower? | To make you any lies in Weavings power'.[2] The pregnant duplicity of the phrase 'make you any lies' – where 'any' glances back at '*July*-flower' and forward to 'lies' – may be unintentional, but the fabricating practices of the weaver have proved a durable image for a range of creative practices, particularly writing, whose ends are to make you see something that is not *really* there. At any rate, it would be a mistake to imagine early modern playwrights and weavers (among other crafts) to traffic in utterly alien trades, the former 'artists' and the latter 'tradesmen'.

The analogy between the playwright's and the weaver's craft particularly obtains with Shakespeare's *Dream* – a play beholden to weaving on a number of levels. For instance, source studies of Shakespeare's *Dream* frequently use the terms of weaving to convey the process by which Shakespeare drew disparate literary and dramatic precedents together. Peter Holland refers to the play's '*net*work of comic contrasts' that Shakespeare made out of a '*tangle*' of lovers he found in Sidney's *Arcadia*; John Arthos cites the play's '*entangle*ments of humans'; Harold F. Brooks describes *Pyramus and Thisbe* as an example of how Shakespeare '*weaves* [. . .] together' material from a whole series of sources'; R. A. Foakes commends the play's '*web* of meanings' that Shakespeare '*wove* inextricably together to our lasting delight'.[3] Whether prompted by weaving's common association with dreams or with *Dream*'s preoccupation with a weaver, source studies frequently draw out the weaver/writer analogy to characterize Shakespeare's treatment of source material.

However, despite the image of weaving so frequently deployed to characterize *Dream*, the play hardly presents a seamless fabric. *Dream* displays a flagrant disregard for the rough seams between its three main plots (fairies/craftsmen/lovers) and the settings they inhabit. After all, the trade unions of Athens were probably not choked with men named Nick, Peter and Snug. Nor was Theseus a 'duke' or Hippolyta a 'duchess'. The play's ostentatious hetero-geneity reaches an absurd peak in Act V, where a group of early English craftsmen present the classical tale of *Pyramus and Thisbe* for a duke and duchess at their Athenian palace, after which a rural English fairy named 'Robin Goodfellow' sweeps up before craving the audience's forbearance.

Ultimately, the (il)logic of dreams helps these disparate parts cohere and frustrates any Thesean attempts to rationalize the disorder.[4] After all, dreams, like woven textiles, also 'present' images 'all before your eyes', and the play discreetly links dreams with weaving throughout. The First Fairy banishes 'weaving spiders' from the side of his sleeping queen (II.i.20) but more pertinent is the 'Hempen Homespun' Bottom, who upon waking from his 'rare vision' (which was not a dream, precisely) wishes instantly to memorialize the experience in an act of writing, which will be 'Bottom's Dream'. Throughout the play, the homely image of weaving grounds its more abstract associations between dreams and creativity and somehow fuses the play's fragments into a seeming, transient whole, no more yielding than a dream.

While source studies necessarily treat the process by which writers wove together a variety of material, images of textiles can also prompt a re-evaluation of the solidity of the 'finished' product. Andrew Murphy, for one, has considered the way the period's dramatists refashioned existing materials while he emphasizes the woven permeability of the playtext itself:

> The Renaissance playtext often functions as a kind of composite of materials configured and reconstituted into a new entity. One thinks, for instance, in the case of the Shakespeare canon, of the passages from Plutarch refashioned into iambic pentameter; of chronicles mined for material for the histories; of classical stories reworked into new plays; of the recycling of materials and themes already treated by contemporary fellow writers and dramatists, whether English or European. The Renaissance playtext is thus not a bounded, unique, singular entity, but rather is permeable, often having other texts woven through its fabric.[5]

In these terms, the fact that 'text' and 'textiles' are cognates can inform the production of early modern dramatic plays at both the literal and figurative level, for both the composition of plays and the production of printed playbooks.

It may be too much to call *Dream* an extended meditation on Shakespeare's own writing practices, but the play is unusually preoccupied with forms of creative making. We witness a play rehearsed, a prologue commissioned, a ballad plotted and an extended riff on the connection between lunatics, lovers and poets. *Dream*, of course, is hardly unique even among Shakespeare's canon for its reflectivity on writing practices. The play does, though, feature Shakespeare's most explicit representation of a rehearsal, a scene in which players translate script into performance. The scene is a riot, but also revealing, for just as the seams show between some of Shakespeare's sources, the play's rehearsal scene shows the fissures that can develop when players attempt to mesh their parts into a seamless whole. Rehearsal, above all, occasions a script's transition from the initial site of writing to its primary scene of reading, where, in a weaver's terms, a shuttle-full of individual threads meet to spin a whole-cloth fabric.

Bottom's Up: Rehearsal/Performance

First rehearsal on the early English stage was, among other things, an acid test of the mnemonic system that turned solitary composition into collaborative playing. There, 'theatre takes over writing and turns to play' in Scott McMillin's words.[6] Indeed, first rehearsal may have borne more weight then than now because first rehearsal may have also been the last. For while it is unclear precisely how many group rehearsals companies normally held in the period, theatre historian Tiffany Stern believes that players often limited themselves to 'one general rehearsal'. Some contemporary sources hint at more. William Prynne, for one, complains about how 'hours, evening, halfe-dayes, dayes, and sometimes *weekes are spent by all the Actors* (especially in solemne academicall Enterludes) *in copying, in conning, in practicing their parts*, before they are ripe for publike action'.[7] To be sure, Prynne singles out non-professional, academic plays and his anti-theatrical zeal makes this statement dubious evidence. Less specific but probably more reliable is Thomas Heywood, who writes in *An Apology for Actors* that plays were often 'rehearsed, perfected, and corrected before they come to public view'.[8] Theatre owner Philip Henslowe's playhouse 'diary' presents tantalizing but ultimately exasperating evidence. In some cases, days and weeks passed between the company's acquisition of a playscript and its onstage premiere. How many rehearsals took place between receipt and performance of a script is ultimately uncertain, though it seems safe to conclude that players today devote more time to rehearsal than their early modern predecessors.

We might agree that even a single group rehearsal would give the players a chance to work out muddled cues. As is well known, in the English Renaissance each actor received a manuscript scroll that included his lines, a few stage directions, and the two-to-four word cues that prompted him to speak. And that is all. A scribe or scribes had divided the playwright's script into its constitutive parts, one per player. First rehearsals presented then a moment of textual reassembly, where players would gather together the sundered parts (perhaps literally: in *Dream* the players seem to have parts on hand during rehearsal). As such, group rehearsal tested a playwright's skill because the occasion tried a writer's ability to deploy the mnemonic system that enabled ensemble performance. Furthermore, since cues affect at least two players – giver and receiver – group rehearsal provided an opportunity to negotiate changes that affected or altered cues. First rehearsal was therefore the first collective re-membering of a play, where warp met woof, as a company of players wove individual parts into a collective whole.

Dream's rehearsal scene stages just such an event and explicitly exhibits the operating system that made performance possible on the early modern stage – and, of course, its potential for failure. Some caution is necessary: *Dream* is a play not a documentary, and the dictates of drama not verisimilitude shape its contours. The failure of Flute and Bottom to manipulate the part-and-cue system may be a gross exaggeration of the scenarios that occurred in early modern rehearsal. Nevertheless, the rehearsal sequence in *Dream* is a tantalizing comic dilation on rehearsal practice in the period and revelatory of the *kinds* of problems that attend when a playscript moves from writing, to re-membering, to playing.

While it is easy to ascribe Flute's and Bottom's mistakes to their amateur incompetence, the part-and-cue system obtained across *all* ranges of dramatic activity in the period – amateur, academic, professional, English and continental. Indeed, the cuing system is at least one dramatic characteristic shared by a diversity of dramatic presentations under a wide range of auspices in the English Renaissance. The joke in *Dream* is that Bottom and Flute – despite being 'thought fit through all Athens' to play before Theseus and Hippolyta (I.ii.5) – are so inexperienced that they have never encountered parts and cues before, despite the system's ubiquity. In other words, Shakespeare exploits the comic potential of a breakdown in one of the period's most widely shared performance technologies. The satiric target of *Dream*'s rehearsal scene is not just the incompetence of amateur players, then, but rather the potential confusions caused by a common playhouse practice. In a play saturated with images of weaving and webs, Shakespeare stages a moment where warp and woof clash rather than mesh.

It is telling here that a comic treatment of a bungled rehearsal does not focus upon a failure of *memory* – the player's recurrent nightmare – but a failure of *mnemonics*. To Quince's dismay, Flute reads 'all [his] part at once, cues and all' (III.i.93–94), ploughing through without pause, failing to understand the format of parts. Flute's problem, that is, is not with his memory or articulation. He does not, in Hamlet's well-known critique, 'mouth it' (III.ii.2–3) or speak 'more than is set down for' him (III.ii.39). Flute speaks *precisely* what is set down for him. It is not a failure of acting, it is a failure of reading. In other words, Flute's failure is not personal but technical: he cannot operate the writing system that re-membered individual parts into a collective whole. What apparently seemed comic to Shakespeare was not so much an individual's personal failure – though Flute is chiefly to blame – but his failure to master the collaborative mechanism upon which ensemble playing depended. Flute the craftsman, the bellows-mender, cannot decipher the operating system of another craft – playmaking.

Flute fails to understand the fundamental textual apparatus that turned writing into playing, that re-joined the sundered parts. To speak 'all your part at once, cues and all' is an interpretative failure, a failure to *read* correctly. (Snug has a related concern: being 'slow of study' he requests a written transcript of his part; he wants to read it rather that perform it 'extempore' [I.ii.64] – the implication that parts were not invariably written out is intriguing.) While Bottom's failure to 'come upon his cue' may be seen as a lapse in a system of orality – in which information is conveyed via voice and ear – Flute's mistake belongs to the world of literacy, in particular his unfamiliarity with a textual system designed to enable oral performance.

Although it would be too much to claim that the scene mirrors the period's fabled negotiation between oral and literate cultures, it does depict a breakdown precisely at the point of friction between the 'author's pen and the actor's voice' – to borrow Robert Weimann's phrase.[9] Shakespeare writes a scene that may well have replayed itself with some regularity in rehearsals; even seasoned actors may have encountered frustration operating the mnemonic system of cues and parts. To summarize, the comedy here is not merely a comedy of amateur ineptitude but a comedy of frustration about the literary material that enabled the transition between radically different modes of articulation – writing and playing.

The failure to successfully *use* the part-and-cue system is, in *Dream*, the players' fault, but writers could share the blame if they failed to anticipate the division and re-membering of their scripts. In fact, *Dream*'s comic riff on repeated and premature cues is compounded by the fact that the scene in parts – the parts of *A Midsummer Night's Dream*, that is, not the 'parts' of *Pyramus and Thisbe* – itself contains a welter of complicated cues. For instance, in III.i, Flute gives Bottom's entrance cue, '– never tire' at line 90; Quince gives the cue again at line 95 when he corrects Flute; and, finally, Flute gives Bottom his 'real' cue ('– never tire') at line 97 at which point Bottom enters with an ass's head on his sconce. Potentially, the actor playing Bottom *could* attempt to enter twice – at line 90 and 95 – before his 'real' cue since Bottom's part would have read as follows:

> But hark, a voice. Stay thou but here a while
> And by and by I will to thee appear.
> [Exit]
>   *– would never tire*
> If I were fair, Thisbe, I were only thine.

The premature cues set up a potential gag where Bottom enters prematurely twice without the ass's head – prompted by the cue ' – never tire' at lines 90 and 95 – only to follow the comedic 'rule of three' by entering at line 97, ass-head-and-all, as the punchline to an elaborate joke. This sets up quite a complicated scenario, however: the Lord Chamberlain's Men at some point in the mid-1590s rehearsed a play with repeated and premature cues that contains a 'rehearsal' of a 'play' that contains 'repeated and premature cues'. Surely it took a rehearsal of the 'rehearsal' to clarify the repetition of cues, sort out the real cues – of *A Midsummer Night's Dream* – from the fake ones – of *Pyramus and Thisbe* – and block the business for maximum comic impact. The multiplying confusions for the Lord Chamberlain's Men in the successful rehearsal of an 'unsuccessful rehearsal' may be unavoidable. It might be impossible to write a scene about 'premature' cues without using premature cues. When each player has but partial access to the complete script, the point of transition from writing to playing will always present a possible scene of misreading, as players work to join the sundered parts.

The mechanicals' amateur status certainly increases the rehearsal's plausibility, but Shakespeare's choice of tradesmen can also prompt us to reconceive the practice of playmaking in the period as more craft than art, collaborative labour in which an ensemble of men render a product from re-purposed stuff – scripts, clothing, properties etc. Tellingly, Bottom calls the 'scrip' (I.ii.3) of *Pyramus and Thisbe* a 'good *piece* of work' (I.ii.13), and indeed the script is but one 'piece' of the final, entire 'work'. Players make performance – the final 'work' – out of bodies, costumes, voice, properties and a number of ancillary documents that supplement the 'scrip' that we anachronistically and misleadingly refer to as 'the play'. For the 'scrip' was far from the only literary material necessary to stage a play. In the comic banter of I.ii alone – previous to even the first rehearsal of *Pyramus and Thisbe* – we hear from Quince of a 'scroll of every man's name which is thought fit through all Athens to play in our interlude' (I.ii.4–5); the 'parts' that he desires his fellows to 'con [. . .] by tomorrow night' (I.ii.93–93); and 'a bill of properties' (I.ii.97) that he will draw up. Later, a prologue (in 'eight and eight') will supplement these materials. The players' individual scripts – their dialogue – will work in concert with other written materials – property lists, backstage plots, songs, prologues, epilogues, letters, the entire playbook – within a system of distributed literacy designed to enable oral performance by an ensemble of craftsmen, none of whom individually possesses the entire written 'work'. None of them have all of it, but all of them have enough. (The lone man who might claim to possess the whole work would be the backstage bookkeeper, who holds some form of an 'executive text'; ironically, he is meant to stay off stage since the theatre disguises the writing systems that enable it.) The play is quite literally the sum of its parts.

Dream's handicraft men are, then, aptly chosen for the labour required to render multiple parts into a solitary whole. Tailors, joiners and weavers, at least, are trades devoted to the fabrication of end products from pieces of the work. As the principal among these craftsmen, Bottom the Weaver's trade offers particularly apt homologies to the processes of playwriting, playmaking and play printing. It is therefore aptly ironic that Bottom the Weaver puts the most pressure upon the ensemble of Athenian craftsmen as they work on *Pyramus and Thisbe*. It is not just Bottom's failure to operate the mnemonic system of cues, however – Flute is more liable to this charge – but his ambition to play all the parts that threatens the seamless intersection of individual labour within a collective enterprise. Bottom has a kind of monomania best displayed by his desire to turn an ensemble performance into a one-man show. He recites, at one point, both Thisbe's lines and his own, which converts dialogue into monologue: 'An I may hide my face, let me play Thisbe too. I'll speak in a monstrous little voice: "Thisne, Thisne!" – "Ah Pyramus, my lover dear, my Thisbe dear and lady dear"' (I.ii.47–50). While benign and comic, Bottom is an entrepreneur within an ensemble, a one-man gang whose greed for more work disrupts the collaborative nature of distributed labour.

Comedies routinely distribute punishments and rewards to their characters and invite the audience to ask why certain behaviours are celebrated and others condemned. Within *Dream*'s jurisprudence, it seems, Bottom is singled out for comic punishment for usurping Quince's literary and theatrical authority. While it is not clear whether Quince represents the writer or the bookkeeper of *Pyramus and Thisbe* (or both), his authority resides in his possession of the 'scrip' or 'scroll' as well as the parts. His authority is textually vested, and Bottom immediately asserts the countervailing rights of the player. Quince calls the first meeting to order, but Bottom closes it by dismissing the players – 'Enough; holde, or cut bowstrings' (I.ii.104). By the mechanicals' second meeting, Bottom calls the shots – 'Are we all met' (III.i.1) – makes dramaturgical adjustments to the play and demands rewrites of Quince. 'Bully Bottom' indeed (III.i.7). As the scene suggests, collaboration between playwright and players – between text and performance – might not always be an entirely cooperative affair, with authority happily passed from writer to players.

Bottom the Weaver's name and trade help reveal the logic of his punitive transformation. Puck prefers things 'that befall pre-post'rously' (III.ii.121–22) and with Bottom he is as good as his word. Since 'Bottom' aspires to be on top, he is 'translated' through a series of preposterous inversions. Puck makes an ass out of Bottom's top and triggers a fathomless chiasmal pun: Puck puts an ass's head on the top of Bottom the Weaver (Bottom the Weaver 'preposterously' is 'Weaver's Bottom', the English vernacular for *ischial bursitis*, a medical condition suffered by weavers – in other words, a 'pain in the ass', which Bottom certainly is). Bottom's preposterous transformation is an apt punishment – though a comic one – for his disruption of the distributed authority of ensemble playing – and his usurpation of the 'playwright' Quince's gentle sway.

The first and last cues on Bottom's part telegraph the character's disruption of and re-absorption by his fellows. Bottom's first cue and first lines prompt the player to divide the 'company' into its individual members:

> – *all our company here?*
> You were best to call them generally, man by man according to the scrip.

> (I.ii.1–3)

Quince opens the rehearsal with an emphasis on corporation ('Is all our company here?'), which Bottom quickly divides. He challenges Quince's 'company' and directs him to call forth the actors 'man by man', a roll-call that Bottom continually disrupts by asserting his own desire to turn the labour of many into the labour of one – namely himself. As argued above, the play will punish Bottom for his self-assertion within the economy of company labour, and, in fact, Bottom's 'part' ends with a mirror image of his first cue-and-response:

> – *Ay, and a wall too.*
> No I assure you, the wall is down that parted their fathers.
> Will it please you to see the epilogue or to hear a bergamask
> dance between two of our company?
>
> (V.i.344–48)

Whereas Bottom's first cue cites unification ('– all our company'), his final cue cites a partition ('– a wall too'). But Bottom ends where he began, with a preposterous (in)version of his opening division of Quince's 'company': Bottom's final lines reincorporate 'two of our company' within the harmonizing discourse of collaborative dance. Indeed, by the final performance of *Pyramus*, Bottom has mastered the writing system that he and Flute earlier struggled mightily to comprehend: he tells the duke that ' "Deceiving me" is Thisbe's cue. She is to enter now...' (V.i.183). Chastened by the play, transformed by his 'rare vision', Bottom ends up on top.

A Midsummer Night's Dream is a play unusually preoccupied with the unification of divided parts.[10] As argued earlier, in its fictional depiction of early modern rehearsal practice, the play explicitly stages the work it takes to turn parts into a whole. Furthermore, Bottom's comic disruption of the collaborative process stages the possible frictions when players wove individual lines into the collective fabric of a play, bound by the temporal duration of its performance. The pressure that a strong, ambitious actor can apply to the group work of playmaking is a durable comic theme, but in *Dream* the dynamic of part and whole provides a resonant context for Bottom's disruption of, and reincorporation by, the ethos of company work.

Ultimately, the III.i rehearsal scene manifests the tension between written drama and orality that, remarks Erika Fischer-Lichte, characterizes western theatre. For Fischer-Lichte this tension exists because:

> Drama, with its fixed, written text, [...] consists exclusively of homogenous linguistic/written signs, and even complex signs (such as character and plot) arise through the combination of linguistic/written signs, [while] performance is made up of heterogenous signs which may be verbal or nonverbal (mime, gesture, proxemics, mask, costume, props, set, sounds, music).[11]

As this section has explored, the part-and-cue system was the point of contact between literacy and orality: rehearsal concentrated on converting the one into the other. However, Fischer-Lichte's formulation of a 'fixed [...] homogenous' written text seems governed by the orthodoxy of print. It certainly overstates the unity and autonomy of dramatic texts (both written and printed) in the early modern period. As the next section explores, while print may seem to offer the ultimate fixity, where 'piece[s] of work' definitively solder into an unbreakable whole, the process of fragmentation and consolidation has no bottom.

The Misinterpretation of *Dreams*: Printing

While players may have occasionally struggled to read and re-member their written parts, they had the advantage of doing so within the labour context for which playwrights designed the scripts. That is, playwrights knew their finished scripts would be parted and recollected and so, presumably, worked to facilitate that process. Printers, on the other hand, read playscripts within an alien labour context, in that playscripts were not primarily designed to facilitate printing. If players struggled to translate writing into playing, the printer's translation of written script to printed text could be exponentially more difficult, for they were, in essence, re-purposing mnemonic scripts into memorial texts.

In tangible terms, early modern printers − no less than their contemporaries in the weaver's livery company − re-purposed raw textile material into an end product that unified disparate parts into an autonomous artefact that, at the same time, worked to disguise those constituent parts. The printing of an early modern play would, then, seem to represent the ultimate fabrication of a dramatic script's parts into an interwoven whole. Script yields to codex, and instability stabilizes. But the fixity of print is an illusion. Indeed, the word 'book' implies an anachronistic sense of a bound, 'closed' object, secured between covers, despite the fact that bookbinding was a separate industry from print, a site of customization for the early modern buyer of a printed text. The transition from play*script* to play*book* was by no means a seamless one; nor did the printing of a dramatic manuscript impose final fixity − or closedness − upon the work. Again, *Dream* is an exemplary text in this regard, for both the first imprints of the play and its subsequent textual and theatrical history demonstrate the way that flux continues even after the script deserts playhouse for printhouse.

For starters, the first imprint of an early modern play required the 'translation' of a mnemonic system into a memorial one, and printed texts often bear the marks of that translation. For whatever manuscript(s) a compositor worked from, those manuscripts were originally designed to complement other mnemonic materials – plots, parts, property lists, etc. – that enabled the onstage, script-less animation of a play's written text. By contrast, printers produced 'memorial' texts, whose primary function was to memorialize performance, not enable it. For example, dramatic title pages in the period frequently advertise the playing occasions the text is explicitly meant to recall. The first quarto of *A Midsummer Night's Dream* advertises a text 'As it hath beene sundry times pub-*lickely acted, by the Right honoura*-ble, the Lord Chamberlaine his *servants*'. The text is a manifest memory of performative occasions. The printhouse is then a site of translation and potential misreading, no less – and, in fact, probably much more so – than the first rehearsal of a play.

As with the earlier transaction between writers and players, the transition from players to printers exposed the text to potential misreading since, in the printhouse, labourers from one craft – printing – had to decipher signs intended for use by labourers in another – playing. Scripts were designed, after all, to enable performance, not books. Just as the amateur actors in *Dream*'s rehearsal struggle to translate literacy into orality, compositors evidently struggled to translate scripts designed to enable orality into the ultimate form of literacy: the book.

The early printed texts of *Dream* offer several sites of misreading, and to study those particular cases a brief review of the play's textual history is necessary. The consensus on the textual history of *Dream* may be summarized as follows: the 1600 quarto (Q1) was set from Shakespeare's own foul papers; the second quarto (Q2; dated 1600 on the title page but actually printed in 1619) is an unauthorized reprint of the first quarto; and the 1623 *Folio* text (F1) was set from a copy of Q2, though one supplemented by some form of a backstage script (possibly the 'book' of the play in early modern theatrical terms).[12] F1 departs from Q1/Q2 largely in its treatment of stage directions, which supplement (sometimes redundantly, sometimes confusingly) those found in the earlier quartos. The opening of Act V in the F1 *Dream* also substantively departs from the quarto(s) and is considered in detail below. The textual state of *Dream* is, then, relatively simple, and scholars have reached a rare consensus, particularly for a play with multiple texts that show some sign of manuscript revision behind them.

Still, the early texts of *Dream* offer a number of sites of 'misreading'. For instance, the compositor of F1 *Dream* at one point misinterprets dialogue as a stage direction: he or they mis-set Titania's Q1 summons of the four fairies as a stage direction and eliminate the relevant Q1/Q2 line: '*Enter* Pease-blossome, Cobweb, Moth, Mustard-seede, *and four* Faries' (III.ii.154). Furthermore, all three early texts set I.i's '*Stand forth Demetrius*' and '*Stand forth Lysander*' (I.i.24,26) as stage directions that interrupt Egeus's opening suit to Theseus. Since Nicholas Rowe's 1709 edition, however, editors have set the two 'directions' as part of Egeus's plea. As Rowe noticed, the 'stage directions' complete blank verse lines, which suggests that the 'directions' were intended to be dialogue spoken by Egeus. Like Francis Flute the bellows-mender – who speaks his part 'cues and all' – the Q1/Q2/F1 compositor(s) who set this dialogue as stage directions are not inept or 'slow of study'. If anything, they, like Flute, are overly precise in printing everything that is set down for them. But they, again like Flute, simply do not know how to decipher the working documents of a different craft.

The setting of the F1 *Dream* is of particular interest, since the compositor(s) was working from two very different kinds of 'source' material – a printed quarto (Q2) *and* a playhouse manuscript of some sort. Furthermore, no early modern dramatic printing venture served more explicitly memorial functions than the Shakespeare *First Folio* (1623). Indeed, the memorial apparatus that previews the plays in the *Folio* nearly effaces the original use of the texts that appear thereafter. A substitution of a *corpus* for a corpse, the massive *Folio* commemorates the work of an individual (though one who functioned within a company economy). It eliminates any mention of Shakespeare's co-writers and praises the pristine manuscripts he delivered to his fellows. For all that, the *Folio* plays frequently display more signs than the earlier quartos of the agglutinative manuscripts from which the *Folio* texts were set. After all, the *Folio* appeared 30 years after Shakespeare composed his earliest plays, and the collection was assembled by his playhouse intimates. The manuscripts they had to hand may well have been backstage scripts worked over by variant hands on variant occasions. For all of its memorial retail, the F1 *Dream* bears the marks of its mnemonic origins and exhibits the way that fragmentation and partiality lie close beneath the uniform fabric of the printed play.

As discussed in the last section, the regime of part division and reassembly required playwrights to take care with repeated and premature cues lest they trigger a stutter of repetition, but scripted repetition could dizzy printers as easily as players. An innocuous error in the *Folio* demonstrates the way repetition threatens not just theatrical continuity but also the serial representation of a play's dialogue. In the *Folio*, Bottom's III.i introduction to the fairies is set as follows:

> *Bot.* I cry your worships mercy hartily; I beseech
> your worships name.
> *Cob. Cobweb.*
> *Bot.* I shall desire you of more acquaintance, good
> Master *Cobweb.* if I cut my finger, I shall make bold
> with you.
> Your name honest Gentleman?
> ***Pease. Pease Blossome.***
> *Bot.* I pray you commend me to mistresse *Squash,*
> your mother, and to master *Peascod* your father. Good
> master *Pease-blossome*, I shal desire of you more acquain-
> tance to. Your name I beseech you sir?
> *Mus. Mustard-seede.*
> ***Peas. Pease-blossome.***
> *Bot.* Good master *Mustard seede*, I know your pati-ence
> well: ...
>
> (F1.TLN 996–1011; bold-face added)[13]

The repetitive structure of the query-and-replies presents potential difficulties in rehearsal/performance, and Shakespeare has varied the cues Bottom delivers to his fellow actors each time to avoid premature prompting: '– your worships name' (TLN 997); '– name honest Gentleman?' (TLN 1002); '– I beseech you sir?' (TLN 1007). The script anticipates confusion at the moment of reassembly and takes steps to head it off. In short, the script works actively to ensure seamless reassembly. The repetition, however, was enough to throw off the *Folio* compositor. It is impossible to know precisely how the error occurred, but at TLN 1010 he gets caught up in a loop, resetting '*Peas. Pease-Blossome*' from TLN 1003. (The repetition does not appear in either the first or second quarto.) Critics frequently censure *Dream*'s F1 compositor: Greg calls him 'fussy but incompetent'; Foakes claims that 'he did not read the dialogue attentively'; Brooks accuses him of 'demonstrable negligence and clumsiness'.[14] (The pathology behind these libels is a subject for another essay.) As with the confusion of dialogue for stage directions, however, the error is not one of incompetence, or negligence, or clumsiness, but rather an unfamiliarity with cues designed to ensure theatrical – not print – continuity. In other words, this moment in *Dream* was easier to perform than to print.

Understandably less alert to repetition than a playwright or a player, the compositor's 'miscue' is a function of his craft. Printers are trained to mind their q's, not their cues.

As mentioned above, the opening of Act V in the *Folio* offers a particularly tangled instance where a compositor or compositors had to weave multiple sources into a single text. All three texts of *Dream* mislineate the verse in Theseus's 'lovers and madmen' meditation, which has led scholars to assume that the copy text included rewrites or revisions. W. W. Greg summarizes the textual tangle thus: 'There is no escaping the conclusion that in this we have the original writing, which was supplemented by fresh lines crowded into the margin so that their metrical structure was obscured'.[15] In this case, the 'inattentive' *Folio* compositor set precisely what he found in Q2; this, then, is not exactly a case of misreading but rather an example of the difficulty print confronts when – in Jerome McGann's terms – it turns a process into an object.[16] Print turns manuscriptural mess into typographical tidiness. The multiplicity of hands on a manuscript disappear into the uniformity of type, which imposes coherency upon the chaos of a manuscript that has collected amendments, revisions and alterations over the course of time and occasions. Nevertheless, the *Folio* text of *Dream* does disclose some of these processes even while attempting to bury them beneath the standardization of print.

In addition to translating the multiple intentions of the manu-script – collapsing process and object – the start of Act V in the *Folio* may also preserve another scene of misreading, as the compositor struggled to decipher theatrical shorthand. The *Folio* text transfers the reading of the 'brief' of 'how many sports are ripe' (V.i.42) from Theseus to Lysander – or, at least, to '*Lis.*' as the *Folio* speech prefix has it. In Q1/Q2, Philostrate hands the 'brief' to Theseus who both reads and responds to the range of extraordinary entertainments. The manuscript behind F1 eliminates Philostrate (though not entirely, for a ghost prefix, '*Phi.*' appears at TLN 1874, a seeming residue of an imperfectly revised scene), and calls for Egeus to hand the brief to Theseus who then seems to hand it to Lysander to read (*seems* to, since no stage direction indicates the action):

> *The.* Say, what abridgement haue you for this eue-ning?
> What maske? What musicke? How shall we beguile
> The lazie time, if not with some delight?
> *Ege.* There is a breefe how many sports are rife:
> Make choise of which your Highnesse will see first.
> *Lis.* The battell with the Centaurs to be sung

By an Athenian Eunuch, to the Harpe.
The. Wee'l none of that. That haue I told my Loue
In glory of my kinsman Hercules.

(F1.TLN.1835–44)

At TLN 1839, Egeus seems to present the 'breefe' to Theseus, yet it is 'Lis' who reads it at 1841. Critics have had to construct arguments to explain why it is more appropriate for 'Lysander' to read the prospective entertainments than Theseus (or Demetrius or Helena or Hermia or Hippolyta, for that matter). Oddly, the *Folio* text abbreviates 'Lysander' as 'Lis.'. 'Oddly' because it has set his name as 'Lys.' throughout the entirety of the preceding text and will do so for the rest of the play immediately following the recitation of entertainments. Certainly, the manuscript (or, possibly, an anno-tated quarto) from which the compositors worked may have set 'Lysander' as 'Lisander' (or 'Lys' as 'Lis'), and the compositors broke their own habit to precisely transcribe the manuscript (although, according to editorial tradition, the compositors were incompetent, clumsy and negligent). The shift from 'Lys.' to 'Lis.' leaves a mark, at any rate, that draws attention possibly not to a successful transcription but to, potentially, an errant translation.

It is possible that the manuscript read 'list' or 'lis' before each entry that Theseus was meant to read, which the compositors mistranslated as a character prefix. 'Brief' is synonymous with 'list' (*OED*, 6), and the manuscript from which F1 was set may here have signalled Theseus that he is reading from a 'list' (another example of the literary ephemera used within the playhouse). A similar feature may be observed throughout the *Folio* when letters or songs are preceded by '*the letter*' or '*the song*', and typography erupts into italics and lineal alteration. The *Folio* compositor of *All's Well* may have faced ambiguous copy precisely at a point where a character was meant to 'quote' from a 'letter', and Act V of *Dream* presents an analogous circumstance.

The suggestion may be fanciful, but it would explain the Egeus-to-Theseus-to-Lysander paper trail, the oddity that Lysander reads the brief, and the *Folio*'s abrupt but temporary shift into 'Lis.' as a speech prefix for a character it everywhere else refers to as 'Lys.'. For the purposes of this argument, it would represent another scene of misreading, as printhouse compositors mistook theatrical language, due not to a lack of diligence but rather a lack of familiarity with the shorthand of another craft. Just as a play-within-a-play might disrupt rehearsal practice, text-within-a-text might trouble the printing of plays. After all, plays-within-plays and text-within-text rely upon playhouse negotiations among practitioners with shared experience and expertise. The playhouse, in other words, contained everyone and everything it needed to overcome textual and performative challenges. The printhouse was also home to experienced and expert tradesmen, but they were experienced and expert at different *things* from the players. To some extent, compositors were faced with some of the same reading challenges as the players at first rehearsal, but were radically unequipped by their training to successfully surmount those challenges. (This is no slight; we can only imagine what a group of players pressed to print a Bible might produce.)

As a profoundly memorial project, the 1623 *Folio* might be thought to terminate the textual flux set in motion by Shakespeare's hand. The 1623 *Dream* is the last printed text of the play set from either a playhouse or authorial manuscript, the last text with direct living contact with the 'author's hand'. The fixity of print, however, is an illusion. As so often happens, history had the last laugh. Bottom's ambition to sing 'Bottom's Dream' – to wrest title authority from Shakespeare's *Dream* – was realized in 1661 with the performance and publication of the *Merry Conceited Humors of Bottom the Weaver*, a 'droll' that pruned away Theseus, Hippolyta and the lovers to centre on the comic antics of Bottom and his crew. Indeed, the theatrical history of *Dream* in performance is one of further fragmentation. As Peter Holland points out, 'the theatre history of *A Midsummer Night's Dream* is almost entirely one of fragmentation and abbreviation, a continual reflection of the sheer difficulty of assimilating the disparate parts of the text'.[17] Even the uniformity of print was not enough to fix the play's parts into an unbreakable whole.

Ultimately, in its composition, performance and printing, *A Midsummer Night's Dream* discloses and disguises forms of making shared by a range of early modern trades. As such, it exhibits the process by which early modern makers fabricated whole cloth products from multiple skeins. For all that they shared, however, playwrights, players and printers each had their own expertise. Fascinatingly, at divergent times, on disparate occasions, they all handled the same material object: the playscript. For each, this 'piece of work' was a means to a different end, and those various ends shaped and transfigured the material object in its handling.

Among the weavers of early modern England, a 'bottom' was the spindle about which thread was spooled. In performance, Bottom may for two hours or so seem to gather the play's disparate elements. But the play's history, both in performance and in print, suggests that fixity is loosely configured and *A Midsummer Night's Dream* is a play constantly on the verge of unravelling.

Notes

1   G.E. Bentley, *The Profession of Dramatist in Shakespeare's Time, 1590–1642* (Princeton, NJ: Princeton University Press, 1971), p. 27.

2   R. C., *The Triumphant Weaver: or, the Art of Weaving Discuss'd and Handled* (London: J. Deacon, 1682), pp. 20, 21.

3   William Shakespeare, *A Midsummer Night's Dream*, ed. Peter Holland (Oxford: The Clarendon Press), p. 47; John Arthos, *Shakespeare's Use of Dream and Vision* (London: The Bodley Head Ltd, 1977), p. 89; William Shakespeare, *A Midsummer Night's Dream* [1979] (London: Thomson Learning, 2004), introduction, p. lxxxv; William Shakespeare, *A Midsummer Night's Dream*, ed. R. A. Foakes (Cambridge: Cambridge University Press, 1984), pp. 5, 12.

4   On the subject of dream logic in *A Midsummer Night's Dream*, see Peter Holland's edition, pp. 1–112.

5   Andrew Murphy, 'Texts and Textualities: A Shakespearean history', in *The Renaissance Text: Theory, Editing, Textuality* (Manchester: Manchester University Press, 2005), pp. 191–210, p. 195.

6   Scott McMillin, *The Elizabethan Theatre and The Book of Sir Thomas More* (Ithaca, NY: Cornell University Press, 1987), pp. 35–36.

7   Tiffany Stern, *Rehearsal from Shakespeare to Sheridan* (Oxford: The Clarendon Press, 2000), pp. 76 and 60–61.

8   E. K. Chambers, *The Elizabethan Stage*, 4 vols (Oxford: The Clarendon Press, 1923), IV, p. 252.

9   Robert Weimann, *Author's Pen and Actor's Voice: Playing and Writing in Shakespeare's Theatre* (Cambridge: Cambridge University Press, 2000).

10 See Stephen Booth 'A Discourse on the Witty Partition' in *Inside Shakespeare: Essays on the Blackfriars Stage*, ed. Paul Menzer (Selingsgrove, PA: Susquehanna University Press, 2006), pp. 216–22.

11 Erika Fischer-Lichte, 'Written Drama/Oral Performance', in *The Show and the Gaze of Theatre: A European Perspective* (Iowa City, IA: University of Iowa Press, 1997), p. 317.

12 The most concise account of *Dream*'s printing history up to 1623 may be found in Stanley Wells and Gary Taylor, with John Jowett and William Montgomery, *William Shakespeare: A Textual Companion* (London: W.W. Norton, 1997), pp. 279–87.

13 All through line numbers (TLN) refer to Charlton Hinman, ed. *The Norton Facsimile: The First Folio of Shakespeare* (New York: W.W. Norton & Company 1968).

14 W. W. Greg, *The Shakespeare First Folio* (Oxford: The Clarendon Press, 1955), p. 246; Foakes's edition, p. 140; Brooks's edition, introduction, p. xxxi.

15 Greg, *The Shakespeare First Folio*, p. 242. See also Robert K. Turner, Jr, 'Printing Methods and Textual Problems in A Midsummer Night's Dream Q1', *Studies in Bibliography* 15 (1962), pp. 33–55, esp. pp. 46–47.

16 Jerome McGann, *The Textual Tradition* (Princeton, NJ: Princeton University Press, 1991), p. 183.

17 *A Midsummer Night's Dream*, ed. Holland, pp. 98–99.

CHAPTER FIVE

Spirits of Another Sort: Constructing Shakespeare's Fairies in *A Midsummer Night's Dream*

Matthew Woodcock

After Oberon witnesses the implications of the misapplied love-juice and instructs Puck on how they should set about resolving the night's confusions, the latter pauses both to provide a temporal marker for the audience and to suggest that the fairies' very nature requires them to conclude their actions by daybreak:

> My fairy lord, this must be done with haste,
> For night's swift dragons cut the clouds full fast,
> And yonder shines Aurora's harbinger,
> At whose approach ghosts, wand'ring here and there
> Troop home to churchyards; damned spirits all
> That in cross-ways and floods have burial
> Already to their wormy beds are gone,
> For fear lest day should look their shames upon.
> They wilfully themselves exile from light,
> And must for aye consort with black-browed night.
>
> (III.ii.378–87)[1]

Puck immediately paints a very dark picture of fairy-kind through associating them with the ghosts of those who had damned themselves by committing suicide. Puck's infernal vision of fairies is not without foundation and draws on a wider tradition that identifies fairies with consciously evil and malicious aspects of the supernatural. Oberon, however, is quick to dispel this image and disassociates fairies from accursed nocturnal creatures by declaring

'But we are spirits of another sort' (III.ii.388) and advertising his ability to sport by day and night. The exchange has great metadramatic comic potential that resonates with the mechanicals' sub-plot as we see a figure who appears to be momentarily unsure about what sort of character he is. Puck asks effectively, 'aren't we supposed to be the bad guys here?' Oberon's reply assures him that they are not *that* particular kind of fairy. This episode is rarely played for laughs but has traditionally been read instead to support the view, developed by nineteenth- and early twentieth-century fairy lore scholars, that the literary representation of fairies changed irreparably following *A Midsummer Night's Dream* and that Shakespeare is responsible for establishing the dominant character-istics of fairies found in subsequent literature and artwork. Shakespeare is chiefly lauded for having ameliorated fairies: divesting them of any negative associations found in medieval or early modern texts and folklore and presenting them as diminutive, innocuous creatures, the forerunners of the gauzy, winged fairies seen in Victorian and Edwardian poetry and painting.[2] Spirits of another sort indeed. As we shall see, this thesis and causal narrative oversimplifies Shakespeare's handling of fairy lore and is now widely contested. It should be added here – if only to amend from the outset the picture of fairies one may still have in mind – that early modern representations of fairies never imagine them as winged creatures, despite Puck's claim that he can circle the earth at fantastic speed (II.i.175–6). Winged fairies do not properly appear until the nineteenth century, with some of the earliest examples found in Thomas Hood's *Plea of the Midsummer Fairies* (1827) and Sara Coleridge's *Phantasmion* (1837).

Rather than using Oberon and Puck's exchange to evaluate whether we should view Shakespeare's fairies in *A Midsummer Night's Dream* as either good or bad, playful or malicious, innovative or traditional, this chapter treats the episode at face value: as an interpretative fault-line, a point prompting further, bigger questions derived from the fact that there are alternative ways of reading fairies in the play as a whole. The episode is one of many moments in *A Midsummer Night's Dream* where Shakespeare foregrounds the fairies' ambiguity and acknowledges that his audience may have had several different, seemingly conflicting, conceptions of the creatures in their minds when watching the play, not least because he himself constructs his fairies from multifarious source materials. This chapter will examine the causes and aesthetic function of fairies' interpretative ambiguity in *A Midsummer Night's Dream*; discuss the different sources of Shakespeare's fairies, and how they inform the fairies' presentation in the play; and also consider how *A Midsummer Night's Dream* responds to the literary and political vogue for fairies during the 1590s. Shakespeare's fairies are still often seen as static, fully-formed and unproblematic entities but this chapter highlights how the playwright uses the hermeneutic challenges integral to fairy mythology as a means of engaging and asking questions of his audience. Interpretative ambiguity, it will be argued, is a conscious, constitutive aspect of Shakespeare's fairies, a fundamental part of how we relate and react to *A Midsummer Night's Dream*.

From the moment of their first appearance at the start of Act II uncertainty and confusion abound concerning the exact nature and ontological status of fairies. The initial exchange between Puck and the nameless fairy assumes an interrogatory form, partly as a dramatic expedient that acquaints us with the rudiments of the fairy world, its rulers and their quarrel over the changeling boy. But this also has the effect of compounding the ambiguity and enigmatic quality of fairies. The fairy wonders whether she/he may have momentarily mistaken Puck's shape, and asks further questions derived from rumours and popular fears about his trickery. Puck's shifting nature is further suggested by the multiple names by which he is known – 'Hobgoblin' and 'Sweet Puck' (II.i.40), one carrying malign connotations, the other sounding more benign – and by the character's own admission of his shape-shifting abilities (II.i.45–54). Further indications of a rich, yet ill-defined back-story about fairies emerge upon Oberon and Titania's entrance and the glancing allegations of the royal pair's amorous liaisons with figures from classical pastoral and epic, Phillida and Theseus. Oberon accuses Titania of similar shape-shifting or mimicry as that practised by Puck in III.ii when she led Theseus 'through the glimmering night' to ravish a series of subsequently abandoned lovers (II.i.77–80); Titania's retort is that this is merely 'the forgeries of jealousy' (II.i.81). The stage history of this scene, and by extension of Shakespeare's fairies as a whole, demonstrates how both delightful and more sinister interpretations of fairies may already be drawn from the text. While Victorian productions repeatedly presented a balletic, musical and often childlike fairy world, twentieth-century stagings increasingly experimented with the boundary between mischief and malice and also emphasized the more aggressively sexual aspects of fairydom.[3] Further questioning is prompted as Titania reveals that contention between the fairy rulers blights the mortal realm (II.i.82–117): they are the unseen cause of a human misery matched for the play's first audiences by the foul weather, failing harvests and pestilence of 1594–96.[4] This is not to say that Shakespeare's audiences would have seen the play as somehow offering a credible rationalization of their present plight, but Titania's speech attempts to connect the playgoers' experience with that of the Athenians. For both groups, fairies provide a causal explanation, however contrived and provisional, for seemingly arbitrary actions or events: fairies exist if only as a theory or narrative solution. The difference in *A Midsummer Night's Dream* is that the audience now gets to see through the veil of invisibility (signalled by Oberon in II.i.186–87) that still obscures fairies to the Athenians. Theatre manager Philip Henslowe mentions 'a robe for to goo invisibell' listed in an inventory for the Admiral's Men in 1598, and a similar prop may have provided a sartorial cue for Oberon's magical concealment.[5]

Fairies' doubleness, or more exactly the role fairies play in *A Midsummer Night's Dream* to signal or insinuate doubleness, can also be seen in the descriptions of Titania's bower. Oberon evokes an exotic, fragrant *locus amoenus* (II.i.249–54) and yet the fairies' lullaby sung there implies that snakes, newts and insects could easily be one's bedfellows, and that the place for sweet dreams could potentially be one of nightmares (II.ii.9–30). In a similar fashion, Puck's exchange with Oberon in III.ii (discussed above) suggests the possibility of fairies' darker associations, which although corrected by the fairy king at the time are later implied again in IV.i.94–95 as the royal couple are prompted to retire upon hearing the morning lark. In V.i.362–78 Puck seems determined initially to preserve a sinister vision of 'fairy time' as he again collocates fairies with ghosts, though a few lines later we see him in the role of a potentially benevolent domestic spirit about to sweep Theseus's palace. Oberon and Titania then enter and bestow their own beneficence upon the Athenian couples. Even here E. Talbot Donaldson has identified a cynical edge to their perceived altruism since in blessing the ducal marriage Oberon and Titania 'are doing a very special favour to a couple that has shared their own promiscuity'.[6] Shakespeare makes it very difficult, therefore, to draw definitive conclusions about the fairies concerning either their form or moral status by the close of the play.

The difficulty that one faces in trying to pin down, deconstruct or otherwise get to the bottom of the fairies is demonstrated in the play itself by both the lowest and highest mortal characters. Bottom's attempts to translate his oneirological experience into communicable, rational language repeatedly fail:

I have had a most rare vision. I have had a dream past the wit of man to say what dream it was. Man is but an ass if he go about t'expound this dream. Methought I was – there is no man can tell what. Methought I was, and methought I had – but man is but a patched fool if he will offer to say what methought I had. The eye of man hath not heard, the ear of man hath not seen, man's hand is not able to taste, his tongue to conceive, nor his heart to report what my dream was. I will get Peter Quince to write a ballad of this dream. It shall be called 'Bottom's Dream', because it hath no bottom, and I will sing it in the latter end of a play, before the Duke.

(iv.i.201–13)

The best Bottom can offer is a misremembering of 1 Corinthians 2.9–10, where Paul writes of God's wisdom and the Holy Ghost, a garbled analogous evocation of a spirit of another sort altogether. The essence of 'Bottom's Dream' should surely be his amorous liaison with Titania and yet he laments that 'it hath no bottom': it lacks foundation or any kind of explanatory centre that forestalls the need for further interpretation or questions. The audience might momentarily place themselves in a privileged position since we indeed saw Bottom with Titania, but then we are once more faced with questions concerning the exact nature of fairies. Evoking Titania as the answer to (or 'bottom' of) Bottom's dream merely risks deferring explanation to yet another ambiguous concept. What exactly is a fairy queen? Each time one attempts to resolve what fairies are or mean we are led on to other texts, stories or versions of events. Fairies are thus 'playful' in a Derridean sense: they raise the possibility that we might apprehend a centre with which to understand them – be it an allegorical interpretation, a belief system or a textual tradition – but this always transpires to be a stimulus for further interpretation.[7] Appropriately (perhaps thankfully), Bottom never produces the promised elucidatory ballad. In the following scene, as Theseus contemplates the lovers' reports, there is a brief suggestion that the young couples detected an otherworldly presence in the night's affairs through the duke's dismissive reference to 'fairy toys', which he duly ascribes to overactive imaginations (v.i.2–3). Again the temptation as an audience member is to scorn Theseus's scepticism and limited worldview since we have seen the fairies at work. Yet Theseus immediately then reminds us of the nature of what we have been watching, and of the creative and constructive process that constitutes the poet and playwright's art:

The poet's eye, in a fine frenzy rolling,
Doth glance from heaven to earth, from earth to heaven;
And as imagination bodies forth
The forms of things unknown, the poet's pen
Turns them to shapes, and gives to airy nothing
A local habitation and a name.

(v.i.12–17)

Theseus's reference to a 'local habitation and a name' propounds the sense of the provisional and subjective nature of poetic creations. Despite Hippolyta's proposal that the multiple testimonies suggest something of 'great constancy; | But howsoever, strange and admirable' (v.i.26–7), Theseus has further complicated how we read fairies in the play by drawing attention back to the presence of the poet's imagination and pen, and implying that fairies may be little more than airy nothings that might indeed easily dissolve should we try and examine them too intently. Puck's epilogue similarly intimates that he and his kind might easily be rejected as an idle dream should they cause offence (v.i.414–19). Rather tellingly, Theseus and Hippolyta's discussion is never resolved as they are interrupted by the laboured artistry of the mechanicals' show, a further example of a play that reveals its own workings. As we can see, Shakespeare's fairies raise a number of contradictions and interpretative problems even before one takes into account the multiple associations that fairies had for his early modern contemporaries.

Critics have often noted how *A Midsummer Night's Dream* is full of disjunctures and juxtapositions between the different source materials and registers that Shakespeare brings together,[8] and this is demonstrated comprehensively through the construction of his fairies. Earlier generations of scholars were convinced that Shakespeare presents the most accurate and comprehensive realization of early modern fairy belief. But Shakespeare's fairies are drawn from a wide and eclectic range of sources and texts including popular lore concerning fairy rituals and Robin Goodfellow, medieval and early modern romance, and Elizabethan panegyric and entertainments that used fairy mythology to celebrate the queen. Shakespeare appears to go out of his way to bring together as many different motifs and images from fairy mythology as he possibly can within the play: changelings; fairy hunts or 'rades' (II.i.24–25); a sexualized fairy queen; a proclivity for dancing; diminutive stature; associations with nature, fertility, and generation; an exotic, Indian provenance; fairies' invisibility; and an apparent freedom from spatial constraints ('I'll put a girdle round about the earth | In forty minutes' [II.i.175–76]). Different kinds of fairy can also be distinguished: the regal, human-sized Oberon and Titania; the mischievous and potentially sinister hobgoblin Puck; and the named and unnamed attendant fairies whose tiny size is mentioned periodically. The ambiguity of Shakespeare's fairies derives both from the juxtaposition of different source traditions used and from within each tradition itself.

It is notoriously difficult to reconstruct patterns of early modern popular fairy belief since one is almost wholly reliant on literary and textual sources in which fairy myths and rituals may be more a record of something remembered rather than actively observed, or they are evoked only to be dismissed in sixteenth- and seventeenth-century witchcraft trial accounts and demonological treatises. Popular belief in fairies was certainly waning by the time Shakespeare composed *A Midsummer Night's Dream*, though there remained vast differences between urban and rural interactions with fairy lore, and in the way it functioned between social classes. The sceptic Reginald Scot in *The Discoverie of Witchcraft* (1584) maintained that fairy beliefs were now a thing of the past and that eventually belief in witchcraft would similarly decline: 'heretofore Robin goodfellow, and Hob gobblin were as terrible, and also as credible to the people, as hags and witches be now: and in time to come, a witch will be as much derided and contemned, and as plainlie perceived, as the illusion and knaverie of Robin goodfellow'.[9] Contemporary literary sources offer a refracted picture of how fairies were once experienced as a social reality through rituals of appeasement such as leaving out pails of water for fairy baths, keeping a clean home and through maintaining a code of good moral and sexual conduct.[10] As Regina Buccola discusses, fairy stories – not to be confused here with fairy tales – were thus rooted primarily in a domestic, predominantly female sphere, despite the fact it was often male spirits, like Robin Goodfellow, performing the duties.[11] For this reason fairy stories were often seen as the purview of marginal social groups such as female servants, old women and children. Scot assigns fairies, changelings and hobgoblins to a copious list of 'vaine apparitions' with which 'in our childhood our mothers maids have so terrified us'.[12] Protestant demonologists also cast fairies as the remnants of pre-Reformation ignorance and superstition, further compounding their transgressive connotations.[13] As Samuel Harsnet wrote in *A Declaration of Egregious Popish Impostures* (1603): 'What a world of hel-worke, deuil-worke, and Elue worke had we walking amongst vs heere in England, what time that popish mist had befogged the eyes of our poore people'.[14]

At the heart of popular fairy belief was their capacity to both reward and punish. To those who respected their codes, fairies offered a fantasy of social empowerment through provision of riches, favours and magical aid with domestic labours; Theseus's palace receives such a blessing at the close of *A Midsummer Night's Dream*. To those who violated their taboos or who simply fell foul of malicious whim, fairies could administer a sharp pinching (as Falstaff suffers at the hands of the 'fairies' in *The Merry Wives of Windsor* [v.v.90–102]), they could kill cattle and they had the power to abduct or slay mortals. It is this lingering potential for malice and punishment that informs the ambiguous presentation of fairies throughout Shakespeare's plays. The confusions of Ephesus in *The Comedy of Errors* lead Dromio of Syracuse to conclude that he is in fairyland and in imminent danger of being pinched black and blue (II.ii.191–5). Marcellus in *Hamlet* has a similar conception of fairies as Puck and connects them with the nocturnal hours when spirits walk abroad and witches practice their art (I.i.138–45). The darker connotations to which Puck and others allude have their foundations in contemporary associations between fairies and the dead, the devil and angels or demons.[15] Early modern witchcraft treatises make frequent references to individuals and buildings being 'fairy-haunted' and to the theory that fairies are departed souls of the dead.[16] This overlaps with the view of fairies found in works of Protestant demonology such as King James I's *Daemonologie* (1597), where it is argued that fairies are merely one of the demonic forms with which the devil interacts with mortals, a diabolic yet pleasing illusion played upon the senses.[17] There is also a sinister element to some changeling stories in which the fairies' abduction of human children is occasioned by a need to pay the levy of a child sacrifice, known as the 'tiend', to the devil. Fairies and fairyland are often physically located in an uneasy liminal space between heaven and hell, as in the romance of *Thomas of Erceldoune* and its ballad adaptations, which makes them especially hard to place on a moral spectrum.[18] As Winfried Schleiner reveals, Puck himself has a potentially diabolic provenance that overshadows pre-Shakespearean references to him as merely a trickster figure, since his name appears to derive from 'pook' or 'pouke', another term for the devil or a demon, as found in William Langland's *Piers Plowman* (c. 1378) and Edmund Spenser's 1595 *Epithalamion*.[19]

Fairies also appear in contemporary English and Scottish witchcraft reports and trial records, which are less a source for

Shakespeare but a vital context for understanding how his audiences may have interpreted the fairies. In some cases fairies are identified either by interrogators or the accused as demons or witches' familiars. Bessie Dunlop, who was executed in Edinburgh for witchcraft in 1576, claimed visits from the 'Queen of Elfame' herself, who left a fairy guide to support her during a time of postpartem adversity.[20] This hardly sounds malevolent but was interpreted reductively by the court as a form of iniquitous traffic with demonic spirits, and thus felonious. English judicial sources tell a similar story of men and women accused of witchcraft due to some form of interaction with what are described as fairies. In Exeter in 1566 John Walsh's witchcraft cross-examination centred on his 'book of circles' detailing the raising of spirits and communication with fairies.[21] Rituals for summoning fairies are found in contemporary printed sources such as Scot and in several extant early modern conjuration manuscripts.[22] Puck's declaration that fairy-kind run by the team of 'triple Hecate' (V.i.375), who has affinities with the underworld in her aspect as Proserpina and associations with classical sorceresses such as Medea, does little to dispel the infernal characteristics of fairies outlined above.[23] Shakespeare's first audiences may also have read about how fairy mythology was used as a deliberate veil for charlatans in a pamphlet published in 1595, *The Brideling, Sadling and Ryding, of a Rich Churle in Hampshire, by the subtill practise of one Judeth Philips, a professed cunning woman or Fortune teller*. The victim was duped into paying large amounts of money for the promise of meeting the fairy queen, only to be robbed and ritually shamed.[24] Fraud at the hands of those playing fairy queens is also evoked in Falstaff's taunting in *The Merry Wives of Windsor* and the scene in Ben Jonson's *The Alchemist* where Dapper is gulled by the disguised Dol Common. As Thomas observes, fairies' inherent elusiveness made them perfect vehicles for confidence tricksters.[25]

Efforts to get to the bottom of active fairy belief, in both popular and elite contexts, are further complicated by issues of textual transmission: no text exists from the sixteenth century that solely or directly addresses either popular fairy belief or intellectual and theological positions on fairy, in the same manner as is found for contemporary interactions with witchcraft or ghosts. The nearest work approximating a direct account, Robert Kirk's *Secret Common-Wealth of Elves, Fauns and Fairies*, was only completed in 1691, and its usefulness and relevance are obscured both by its date – one would never consider using Dryden's approximately contemporaneous works to elucidate Shakespeare – and by authorial and editorial idiosyncrasies. Kirk also filters his accounts of Scottish fairies through ideas from learned authorities such as Pythagoras, Plato, Dionysius Areopagite and Cornelius Agrippa. Attempts to access the extra-textual reality of early modern fairies continually lead us on to other texts. The same is seen with *A Midsummer Night's Dream*; although we can imagine that Shakespeare drew on memories of Warwickshire folklore when writing the play, many of his references to fairies and Robin Goodfellow are taken from Scot's *Discoverie*, in which he would also have found a puckish charm to 'set an horsse or an asses head upon a mans shoulders'.[26] Shakespeare is equally as bookish when choosing his fairy rulers' names. He takes 'Oberon' from the romance *Huon of Burdeux* and, as with Spenser's 'Tanaquill', looks to classical sources when naming his fairy queen. 'Titania' is used several times in Ovid's *Metamorphoses* to refer to both Diana the moon-goddess and Circe the shape-shifting sorceress; Shakespeare uses aspects of both figures in his play. The Dianic associations of fairy can also be sourced to early modern demonological texts including both Scot and James.[27] Classical mythology also lay behind the presentation of Puck, whose trickery and wanton matchmaking have been compared to the sportive Cupid of anacreontic lyric verse that was popular during the later sixteenth century.[28] Fairies were consistently represented in early modern dictionaries and translations from classical works as native analogues to Greek and Roman deities and demigods.[29] It should also be noted that 'fairies' and 'elves' are generally synonymous by Shakespeare's day, and he shows little interest in drawing ontological distinctions between fairies, elves and hobgoblins.

Sixteenth-century fairy belief – or its textual trace – furnished Shakespeare with a rich yet potentially problematic conception of fairydom, that becomes complicated further through his use of Chaucer and medieval romance. It is from Chaucer's 'Merchant's Tale' that Shakespeare appears to have derived his conception of the bickering king and queen of fairies who get involved in human amorous affairs. Chaucer's tale may look back to the fourteenth-century romance *Sir Orfeo*, which presents a version of the Orpheus story adapted to native folklore and sees Herodis captured by the fairy king and taken to his subterranean domain. Shakespeare could also have had Chaucer's *Sir Thopas* in mind when contriving Titania's liaison with Bottom, although this is but one of many printed romances available in the sixteenth century that portray a fairy mistress wooing a mortal lover.[30] John Bourchier, Lord Berners's translation of *Arthur of Little Britain* (printed 1560), for example, sees the eponymous hero put through a rigorous testing process by a fairy queen where her own ardent advances actually present one of the greatest obstacles to completing the quest. As Carolyne Larrington discusses, the amorous attentions of a fairy mistress often lead to what amounts to a form of thrall or captivity – as Bottom discovers in III.i.143–44 – and the attendant spectre of emasculation or dehumanization, which the hapless weaver also experiences, albeit temporarily.[31]

No less enigmatic is the original fairy king, Oberon, who first appears in a thirteenth-century French romance, *Huon of Burdeux*, expanded and adapted into prose in the fifteenth century and translated into English by Berners in 1534. Shakespeare may also have known a now lost stage adaptation of the romance of 1593–94 and Robert Greene's play *James IV* (c. 1590), in which a character named Oberon acts as an expositor figure.[32] Shakespeare passes over several prominent features of the romance, such as Oberon's stature – he is 'but of iii. fote, and crokyd shulderyd',[33] the result of a fairy curse – and the fact that there is no mention of a fairy queen. Shakespeare does, however, pick up on associations in *Huon* between fairyland and the wondrous East or 'Inde', a term used in medieval and early modern topography to denote not simply what we might equate with modern India but a larger, imaginatively contrived geographic extremity located beyond the boundaries of the known world.[34] Margo Hendricks constructs an elaborate postcolonial argument addressing why Shakespeare has Oberon and Titania fight over a specifically *Indian* boy[35] but the answer is relatively straightforward: fairies in *Huon* and *A Midsummer Night's Dream* are denizens of Inde, a liminal space that has far greater potential to evoke wonder and strangeness as an imaginative blank canvas than as a fixed, cartographically identifiable location. Once again fairies seem evasive, even when we attempt to point to them on a map.

There was also a third fairy tradition that would have informed Shakespeare's thinking as he conceived the play's central characters, and inflected the experience of his audience as they watched: the use of fairy mythology in Elizabethan celebratory verse and entertainments. Spenser's romance epic *The Faerie Queene* (1590, 1596) is the best known exemplar of this tradition and centres around a governing conceit that the fairy queen, Gloriana (also called Tanaquill), is an allegorical figure for Elizabeth.[36] Individual books chart the quests of Gloriana's knights but these are set within the framing narrative of Prince Arthur's search for the fairy queen who appears to him in an amorous dream, then disappears and continues to elude him for the rest of the (unfinished) poem. Spenser's fairy knights possess few of the characteristics of those found in earlier romances like *Huon* or *Sir Orfeo* and are a breed apart from the fairies and trickster Puck of popular folklore. At one point Spenser embeds a chronicle in the text setting out the lineage of fairy kings that starts with Elfin, who – like the romance Oberon – 'all India obayd', and closes with a transparent allegory of the Tudors.[37] Spenser's use of fairy mythology to represent Elizabeth remains highly ambiguous, however, since we never really get to see Gloriana, other than via Arthur's fleeting, oneiric vision, and she exists throughout the poem as a powerful yet distant figure portrayed solely in stories and images. As I argue elsewhere, Gloriana appears to be consciously presented as a problem to be solved, inviting an interrogation of the whole process of representing and mythologizing Elizabeth.[38]

Fairy mythology had been used to celebrate the queen for over 15 years by the time *A Midsummer Night's Dream* and Spenser's poem appeared, and it was but one aspect of the multi-media discourse now commonly termed the cult of Elizabeth that saw the queen fashioned variously as the goddess Astraea; the biblical heroines Esther, Judith and Deborah; the virgin queen; and the chaste Diana or Cynthia figure.[39] The fairy queen figure had been employed at several of the elaborate entertainments with which Elizabeth was greeted during royal progresses to the provinces and visits to her aristocratic subjects.[40] At Woodstock in 1575 the fairy queen greeted Elizabeth as a friend and fellow monarch, while at Norwich in 1578 Thomas Churchyard designed a show in which boys dressed as fairies performed a dance for the queen that conjoined fairy lore with classical mythology.[41] At one point Churchyard's fairies emerged from a concealed hole in the ground, perhaps the original of the sawpit from which Evans's fairies are instructed to leap and pinch Falstaff in *The Merry Wives of Windsor* (IV.iv.51–54). In 1591 the Earl of Hertford staged an elaborate entertainment at Elvetham that again cast Elizabeth as the fairy queen's friend and favourite. The fairy queen, Aureola, dwells underground with Auberon the fairy king and nightly praises Elizabeth's name in a Dianic prayer.[42] It used to be thought that Oberon's vision of Cupid shooting his arrow at 'a fair vestal throned by the west' (II.i.155–65) was a veiled allegory of the 1575 Kenilworth festivities, where the Earl of Leicester attempted (unsuccessfully) to court Elizabeth,[43] but it is more likely that if the passage indeed evokes a royal entertainment it was the relatively recent water pageantry of Elvetham and the lunar associations of its fairy queen. At Ditchley in 1592 Sir Henry Lee reprised the use of fairy mythology initiated at Woodstock, although the fairy queen never actually appeared. Elizabeth only heard of her 'just revengefull' powers and the control she has over her subjects, of her capacity to reward the favoured and punish the disobedient.[44] The Ditchley entertainment perfectly illustrates how apposite fairy mythology is for representing the doubleness, unknowability and potential ruthlessness of royal power.

Each of the traditions discussed above engender lingering uncertainties about the form, location, moral orientation and powers of fairies that could shape an audience's experience and understanding of Shakespeare's play. The question remains: what did an early modern audience see, or believe they saw, when watching the fairies of *A Midsummer Night's Dream*? Are they the re-imagined vestiges of popular folklore; the momentarily benevolent manifestations of potentially malicious (perhaps infernal) spirits; the dramatized adaptation of characters from medieval romance; or a burlesque reworking of a mythological scheme used to represent and celebrate Elizabeth? Or has Shakespeare brought all of these elements together, but in such a fashion that we can still see the joins, the inconsistencies, the re-patchings? Fairy stories of every kind – in popular lore, medieval romance, trial records or demonological treatises – are always in some way about uncertainty and ambiguity, and possess a peculiar, though enduring resistance to any form of absolutes, be it concerning appearance, ontology or moral value. Shakespeare appears to embrace this point in *A Midsummer Night's Dream* and revels in how fairies may be misread and misinterpreted, and the fact that this really does not matter. The clash of different conceptions of fairydom has great comic potential, as discussed above. Shakespeare also makes a dramatic and aesthetic virtue of the questions fairies may raise, just as he does with the interpretative activity initiated by the ghost in *Hamlet* and the witches in *Macbeth*; in both plays the plot sees the protagonist test the accuracy and legitimacy of supernatural agency and knowledge. In *A Midsummer Night's Dream* we are encouraged to enjoy the playfulness of multiple interpretations – for example, the possibility that the fairies might turn nasty (again) – and follow a plot that demonstrates the fairies' characteristic capacity to both reward and punish that concludes, not with any gesture of their being irrevocably ameliorated or disarmed, but with a demonstration of *one* aspect of their nature: the benevolence shown to recipients of their favour.

A Midsummer Night's Dream demonstrates that fairies can not only be misread, or read in different ways, but that they can also be rewritten and reapplied, again with great comic – though also subversive – potential. The ambiguities, uncertainties and taboos concerning how fairies appear and what they can achieve offered Shakespeare and his contemporaries an imaginative framework for both representing Elizabeth and interrogating the forms and imagery through which she appeared and ruled. As Louis A. Montrose writes, Shakespeare's appropriation of the fairy queen in *A Midsummer Night's Dream* not only draws on contemporary royal myth-making but continues to reproduce and manipulate those cultural forms.[45] Shakespeare thus responds to the literary and political vogue for fairies with an entertainment about royal entertainments. The audience – whether they were guests at an aristocratic wedding or paying playgoers – are entertained both by the mechanicals' show that diverts the Athenians during the dilatory prenuptial period, and by the pranks performed by Puck for Oberon. Puck's epilogue invites identification between his role as a 'shadow', meaning a form of spirit, and its contemporary use as a term denoting an actor. From his initial appearance Puck casts himself as Oberon's entertainer and hands-on master of revels all rolled into one as he explains that all of the mischiefs for which he is notorious in popular lore are not performed arbitrarily or the product of personal caprice, as critics frequently assume.[46] Puck stresses that he works by royal command, or at least under royal aegis: 'I jest to Oberon, and make him smile | When I [. . .]' (II.i.44–45): he then lists his mirthful tricks. Oberon at one point fears that Puck exceeds his office and is operating of his own accord as he reproaches him: 'Still thou mistak'st, | Or else committ'st thy knaveries wilfully' (III.ii.345–46). It is as if Puck has been deviating from the script.

Shakespeare creates his own version of an entertainment featuring a fairy queen that is far less stately than the aristocratic shows. He subverts the motif of a fairy queen taking a mortal lover that lies at the heart of Spenser's – by no means unproblematic – panegyric text, and exposes to ridicule one of Elizabeth's mythical avatars. This is not to say that Titania should be read automatically as Elizabeth, since direct identification with the queen is not implied in every entertainment, but Shakespeare certainly refashions a popular scheme of Elizabethan political imagery, demonstrating its potential for burlesque and that the raw materials of Elizabethan myth-making can be rewoven or, to mix the metaphor, reprogrammed to produce different effects from those conceived by the authors of the earlier entertainments.[47] Fairy power still wins the day in the play but it is Oberon who emerges from the night's devices having achieved his goal and obtained the Indian boy while

Titania was distracted 'seeking sweet favours' for Bottom (iv.i.48). Once awake she asks on two occasions why she finds herself asleep with mortals but receives no answer from Oberon, who merely declares that they are 'new in amity' (iv.i.86), and there is no further mention of the boy. While Titania holds the weaver in delightful thrall, she in turn is the victim of Oberon's machinations. For Montrose this reverses the royal power dynamic within which Shakespeare's work is implicitly located:

> In the triangulated relationship of Titania, Oberon and Bottom, a fantasy of masculine dependency upon woman is expressed and contained within a fantasy of masculine control over woman. And, more specifically, the social reality of the Elizabethan players' dependency upon Queen Elizabeth is inscribed within the imaginative reality of a player-dramatist's control over the Faery Queen.[48]

Fairy mythology thus affords Shakespeare an imaginative, transformative space where, albeit only for the play's duration, a playwright may script a queen, turn a queen into a subject. And yet – as Puck signals in the Epilogue – the airy, insubstantial subject matter of the play offers perfect deniability should offence be found or caused:

> If we shadows have offended,
> Think but this, and all is mended:
> That you have but slumbered here
> While these visions did appear;
> And this weak and idle theme,
> No more yielding but a dream
>
> (v.i.Epilogue.414–19)

Whereas Spenser in the proem to Book II of *The Faerie Queene* apologizes for his use of fairies by disavowing the role of the imagination in their construction, claiming that 'Of faery lond yet if he more inquire | By certein signes here sett in sondrie place | He may it fynd',[49] Shakespeare does exactly the opposite. His fairies may be dismissed in the time it takes to wake from a dream, or in the time it takes to remove and stow a stage property like a 'robe for to goo invisibell'.

Shakespeare's fairies are not, however, as easy to dispel or dismiss as he might have liked or expected and this chapter would not be complete without addressing an issue raised at the outset: the legacy of Shakespeare's fairies. The resilience of his portrayal of fairies was noted long ago by the folklorist Alfred Nutt: 'Shakespeare's vision stood by itself, and was accepted as the ideal presentment of fairydom, which, for two centuries at least, has signified to the average Englishman of culture the world depicted in the *Midsummer Night's Dream*'.[50] Shakespeare certainly made a great contribution to the late Elizabethan vogue for fairies that was given renewed energy and currency by Spenser's *Faerie Queene* and the royal entertainments of the early 1590s. The association of Elizabeth with the fairy queen, and her realm with fairyland, even features in several of the elegies produced upon the queen's death in 1603. John Fenton, author of *King Iames His Welcome to London*, refers to God 'Yeelding the Scepter to Elizaes charge, | Who whiles she sway'd it sway'd it with like hand, | As did Titania sway the Fairie land'.[51] Puck appears to have been a particularly popular element in *A Midsummer Night's Dream* and features subsequently in several ballads and chapbooks – such as *Robin Goodfellow; His Mad Pranks, and Merry Jests* (1628) – that both feed on the same folklore that Shakespeare used and borrow heavily straight from the play.[52] By the early seventeenth century Robin Goodfellow had become largely detached from his roots in native folklore and his character was now more of a literary figure of fun to be enjoyed by the book-buying middle classes, part of a wholesale commodification of rural popular culture.[53]

It is much harder to identify the legacy of specifically and exclusively Shakespearean fairies, despite the claims of earlier scholars who argue that *A Midsummer Night's Dream* established the tradition and literary model for ameliorated and diminutive fairies. As has been demonstrated along the way in this chapter, Shakespeare's fairies are by no means entirely denuded of their negative, darker potential. Katharine Briggs and Harold Brooks have also shown at length that Shakespeare was not the first to present diminutive fairies, and each marshal illustrative examples of such creatures found in medieval chronicles and English and Welsh folklore.[54] He may also have known the far more recent instance found in Greene's *James IV* where Oberon 'lookest not so big as the king of Clubs'.[55] But Shakespeare in fact already mocks the kind of literalist readings of the stage that underlie attempts to measure fairies when we observe the preparations for, and reception of, the mechanicals' play. Snout and his fellows' worries that the lion will frighten the ladies of the audience (III.i.25–42) and Theseus's pernickety jibe about Starveling's depiction of moonshine ('the man | should be put into the lantern. How is it else the man | i'th'moon?' [V.i.241–43]) anticipate much of the pedantic farce involved when trying to apply a tape-measure to airy nothings. As C. S. Lewis writes of fairy measurement: 'solemn discussions as to whether they are merely dwarfish, or Lilliputian, or even insectal, are quite out of place [...] the visual imagination of mediaeval and earlier writers never for long worked to scale'.[56] Diminutive creatures that clearly hearken back to *A Midsummer Night's Dream* and the Queen Mab speech from *Romeo and Juliet* were nevertheless a characteristic fixture in many examples of seventeenth-century fairy poetry, including William Browne's *Britannia's Pastorals* (1613), Michael Drayton's *Nimphidia* (1627) and *Muses Elizium* (1630), and Robert Herrick's *Hesperides* (1648). But the fairies of all three poets' works can only be justly termed 'Shakespearean' in that they are the product of exactly the same kind of syncretic constructive method as that employed in *A Midsummer Night's Dream*. All traces of the original dramatic Oberon, Titania and their retinue are now blended together with elements drawn from Spenserian poetry, royal panegyric, classical mythology and the pastoral tradition. Much the same is seen in the fairies of Thomas Dekker's play *The Whore of Babylon* (1607), which portrays the fairy queen Titania ruling over a fairyland based on Spenserian allegory, and of Jonson's masque *Oberon* (1611). As we have seen above, fairy stories are good at signalling that they have an origin elsewhere, outside and beyond the text we have before us. It is this sense that in order to fully understand or get to the bottom of Shakespeare's fairies we have to become a little lost amongst other texts and stories that continues to make *A Midsummer Night's Dream* a source of both intrigue and delight.

Notes

1   William Shakespeare, *A Midsummer Night's Dream*, ed. Peter Holland (Oxford: The Clarendon Press, 1994).

2   Minor White Latham, *The Elizabethan Fairies: The Fairies of Folklore and the Fairies of Shakespeare* (New York: Columbia University Press, 1930), pp. 176–96; Roger Lancelyn Green, 'Shakespeare and the Fairies', *Folklore* 73 (1962), pp. 89–103.

3   Trevor R. Griffiths, *A Midsummer Night's Dream*, Shakespeare in Production (Cambridge: Cambridge University Press, 1996), pp. 114-24.

4   *A Midsummer Night's Dream*, ed. Harold Brooks (London: Methuen, 1979), p. xxxvii.

5   *Henslowe's Diary*, ed. R. A. Foakes and R. T. Rickert (Cambridge: Cambridge University Press, 1961), p. 325.

6   E. Talbot Donaldson, *The Swan at the Well: Shakespeare Reading Chaucer* (New Haven, CT: Yale University Press, 1985), p. 47.

7   Jacques Derrida, *Writing and Difference*, trans. Alan Bass (London: Routledge, 1978), p. 280.

8   *Dream*, ed. Brooks, p. lxxxv; Thomas Moisan, 'Antique Fables, Fairy Toys:

Elisions, Allusion, and Translation in *A Midsummer Night's Dream*', in *A Midsummer Night's Dream: Critical Essays*, ed. Dorothea Kehler (New York: Garland, 1999), pp. 275–98.

9 Reginald Scot, *The Discoverie of Witchcraft*, ed. Brinsley Nicholson (Wakefield: E. P. Publishing, 1973), p. 105.

10 Latham, *The Elizabethan Fairies*, pp. 111–47; Keith Thomas, *Religion and the Decline of Magic* (Harmondsworth: Penguin, 1973), pp. 728–32.

11 Regina Buccola, *Fairies, Fractious Women, and the Old Faith: Fairy Lore in Early Modern British Drama and Culture* (Selinsgrove, PA: Susquehanna University Press 2006), pp. 41–42.

12 Scot, *The Discoverie of Witchcraft*, p. 122.

13 Latham, *The Elizabethan Fairies*, pp. 62–63; Matthew Woodcock, *Fairy in The Faerie Queene: Renaissance Elf-Fashioning and Elizabethan Myth-Making* (Aldershot: Ashgate, 2004), pp. 16–20; Buccola, *Fairies, Fractious Women, and the Old Faith*, pp. 55–57.

14 Samuel Harsnet, *A Declaration of Egregious Popish Impostures* (London, 1603), sig. S3^v.

15 Katherine Briggs, *The Anatomy of Puck: An Examination of Fairy Beliefs Among Shakespeare's Contemporaries and Successors* (London: Routledge, 1959), pp. 117–45.

16 George Gifford, *A Dialogue Concerning Witches and Witchcrafts* (1593), ed. S. F. Davies (Brighton: Puckrel Publishing, 2007) p. 6; Harsnet, sig. D3^r.

17 Lawrence Normand and Gareth Roberts, *Witchcraft in Early Modern Scotland: James VI's Demonology and the North Berwick Witches*, (Exeter: Exeter University Press 2000), pp. 418-19; Woodcock, *Fairy in The Faerie Queene*, pp. 24-7.

18 *The Romance and Prophecies of Thomas of Erceldoune*, ed. James A. H. Murray, EETS OS 61 (London 1875), p. 12; Helen Cooper, *The English Romance in Time: Transforming Motifs from Geoffrey of Monmouth to the Death of Shakespeare* (Oxford: Oxford University Press, 2004), pp. 179–80.

19 Winfried Schleiner, 'Imaginative Sources for Shakespeare's Puck', *Shakespeare Quarterly* 36 (1985), pp. 65–68.

20 Diane Purkiss, *Troublesome Things: A History of Fairies and Fairy Stories* (Harmondsworth: Penguin, 2000), pp. 105–8; Buccola, *Fairies, Fractious Women, and the Old Faith*, pp. 58–60.

21 *Witchcraft*, ed. Barbara Rosen (London: Arnold, 1969), pp. 68–69.

22 Scot, *The Discoverie of Witchcraft*, pp. 338–42; *Illustrations of the Fairy Mythology of A Midsummer Night's Dream,* ed. James Orchard Halliwell (London: Shakespeare Society, 1845), pp. 229–34.

23 *Dream*, ed. Brooks, p. 125.

24 Rosen, *Witchcraft*, pp. 213–18.

25 Thomas, *Religion and the Decline of Magic*, p. 734.

26 Scot, *The Discoverie of Witchcraft*, pp. 257–58; *Dream*, ed. Brooks, pp. lxxxii–iii; Purkiss, *Troublesome Things*, pp. 158–63.

27 Ernest Schanzer, 'The Moon and the Fairies in *A Midsummer Night's Dream*', *University of Toronto Quarterly* 24 (1955), p. 241.

28 Purkiss, *Troublesome Things*, pp. 167–70.

29 Latham, *The Elizabethan Fairies*, pp. 48–55.

30 Helen Cooper, *The English Romance in Time: Transforming Motifs from Geoffrey of Monmouth to the Death of Shakespeare* (Oxford: Oxford University Press, 2004), pp. 211–16.

31 Carolyne Larrington, 'The Fairy Mistress in Mediaeval Literary Fantasy', in *Writing and Fantasy*, ed. Ceri Sullivan and Barbara White (London: Longman, 1999), pp. 41–43.

32 For further discussion of both *Huon of Burdeux* and Greene's *James IV*, see Annaliese Connolly's chapter in this volume.

33 *The Boke of Duke Huon of Burdeux, done into English by Lord Berners*, edited by S. L. Lee, EETS ES 40, 41, 43, 50 (London, 1882–87), p. 63.

34   Mary B. Campbell, *The Witness and the Other World: Exotic European Travel Writing, 400–1600* (Ithaca, NY: Cornell University Press, 1988), pp. 47–57; Iain Macleod Higgins, *Writing East: The 'Travels' of Sir John Mandeville* (Philadelphia, PA: University of Pennsylvania Press, 1997), pp. 2–6.

35   Margo Hendricks, ' "Obscured by Dreams": Race, Empire, and Shakespeare's *A Midsummer Night's Dream*', *Shakespeare Quarterly* 47 (1996), pp. 37–60.

36   Woodcock, *Fairy in The Faerie Queene*.

37   Edmund Spenser, *The Faerie Queene*, ed. A. C. Hamilton, 2nd edn (London: Longman, 2001), pp. 259–60.

38   Woodcock, *Fairy in The Faerie Queene*, pp. 107–8.

39   E. C. Wilson, *England's Eliza* (Cambridge, MA: Harvard University Press, 1939); Roy Strong, *The Cult of Elizabeth: Elizabethan Portraiture and Pageantry* (London: Thames & Hudson, 1977).

40   Matthew Woodcock, 'The Fairy Queen Figure in Elizabethan Entertainments', in *Elizabeth I: Always Her Own Free Woman*, ed. Carole Levin, Debra Barrett-Graves and Jo Eldridge Carney (Aldershot: Ashgate, 2003), pp. 97–118.

41   Thomas Churchyard, *A Discourse of the Queenes Maiesties Entertainment in Suffolk and Norfolk* (London, 1579), sigs. G2^r–G4^r.

42   Jean Wilson, *Entertainments for Elizabeth I* (Woodbridge: Brewer, 1980), pp. 115–16.

43   *Shakespeare: The Critical Tradition: A Midsummer Night's Dream*, ed. J. M. Kennedy and Richard F. Kennedy (London: Athlone, 1999), pp. 137–41.

44   Wilson, *Entertainments for Elizabeth I*, p. 131.

45   Louis Adrian Montrose, ' "Shaping Fantasies": Figurations of Gender and Power in Elizabethan Culture', in *Representing the English Renaissance*, ed. Stephen Greenblatt (Berkeley, CA: University of California Press, 1988), pp. 31–64.

46   Mary Ellen Lamb, 'Taken by the Fairies: Fairy Practices and the Production of Popular Culture in *A Midsummer Night's Dream*', *Shakespeare Quarterly* 51 (2000), p. 310; Purkiss, *Troublesome Things*, p. 167.

47   Lisa Hopkins, 'The Dark Side of the Moon: Semiramis and Titania', in *Goddesses and Queens: The Iconography of Elizabeth I*, ed. Annaliese Connolly and Lisa Hopkins (Manchester: Manchester University Press, 2007), pp. 117–35.

48   Montrose, ' "Shaping Fantasies" ', p. 235.

49   Spenser, *Faerie Queene*, p. 158.

50   Alfred Nutt, 'The Fairy Mythology of English Literature: Its Origins and Nature', *Folklore* 8 (1897), p. 31.

51   I[ohn]. F[enton]., *King Iames His Welcome to London* (London, 1603) sig. B2^r.

52   Halliwell, *Illustrations of the Fairy Mythology of A Midsummer Night's Dream*, pp. 120–70; Purkiss, *Troublesome Things*, pp. 171–74.

53   Lamb, 'Taken by the Fairies', p. 300; Wendy Wall, *Staging Domesticity: Household Work and English Identity in Early Modern Drama* (Cambridge: Cambridge University Press, 2002), pp. 106–12.

54   Briggs, *The Anatomy of Puck*, pp. 45–46; Brooks's edition, pp. lxx–xxv.

55   Robert Greene, *The Scottish History of James the Fourth*, ed. J. A. Lavin (London: Benn, 1967), p. 7.

56   C. S. Lewis, *The Discarded Image: An Introduction to Mediaeval and Renaissance Literature* (Cambridge: Cambridge University Press, 1964), p. 127.

CHAPTER SIX

Shakespeare and the Fairy King: Re-viewing the Cultural and Political Contexts of *A Midsummer Night's Dream*

Annaliese Connolly

Recent work on the fairies of *A Midsummer Night's Dream* reflects a critical trend in early modern scholarship which has examined the uses of fairylore on the early modern stage and has utilized a range of primary material, including contemporary accounts of witch trials and superstition to develop our understanding of the sociopolitical and religious uses of fairy belief. These studies focus upon figures popular in fairylore such as Puck and the different manifestations of a fairy queen.[1] This chapter seeks to complement work in the field by offering several important shifts in focus. Firstly, the subject of the chapter will be Oberon, the fairy king, whom Shakespeare would have found, not amongst the oral traditions of fairylore or the popular pamphlets which recorded the activities of Robin Good-fellow, but in the prose romance *Huon of Burdeux*.

Secondly, this chapter will argue that critics who have contented themselves with identifying the similarities and differences between Shakespeare's Oberon and the portrait of the fairy king found both in *Huon of Burdeux* and in other plays which also used the prose romance as their source such as Greene's *The Scottish History of James the Fourth* and the anonymous *The Tragical History, Admirable Atchievments and various events of Guy Earl of Warwick* have overlooked an important difference between the depiction of Oberon in these plays and prose and in Shakespeare's *Dream*. Shakespeare is unique in providing Oberon with a wife and this development in the depiction of the fairy king marks a defining moment in the cultural mythography of Oberon in Tudor, and particularly Elizabethan, literature. Since the translation of *Huon de Bordeux* (c. 1534) Oberon was used to offer a flattering analogue for Henry VIII and this mythical persona was developed by subsequent poets and dramatists such as Edmund Spenser in *The Faerie Queene* and Thomas Dekker in *The Whore of Babylon* into an elaborate genealogy for the Tudors to underline the myth of descent. In the context of this genealogy Oberon provided a number of attractive attributes, including his ability to designate his heir by a process of adoption and his own single status: Oberon is able to overcome those aspects of the body politic and the body natural which had complicated Henry's own dynastic ambitions. Within the parameters of this mythical family tree, Elizabeth as Tanaquil is presented as the daughter of Oberon and his true heir. When Shakespeare provides Oberon with a fairy queen he undertakes a deliberate process of re-evaluation, using both the female-dominated fairy world of the play and the childless marriage of Oberon and Titania to articulate concerns about female rule, and through the scope of Oberon's magic the play offers a pointed assessment of the achievements of the Tudor dynasty.

That *Huon of Burdeux* is the source for Shakespeare's Oberon has long been recognized by scholars of the play. The fairy king first appears in English literature when Sir John Bourchier, Lord Berners translated the French *Huon de Burdeux* into English (c. 1534). Here the fairy king appears as the protector and surrogate father of the eponymous hero, a French nobleman and subject of the emperor Charlemagne. Huon's story concerns the quest he is sent upon by Charlemagne to atone for mistakenly killing the emperor's son. Huon is sent to Babylon to fulfil a list of seemingly impossible tasks which include killing the fearsome admiral Gaudys and returning with four of his teeth and a handful of hair from his beard. Fortunately, Huon is befriended by Oberon the fairy king who provides him with a magical horn whose powers enable Huon to succeed. Oberon's attachment to the nobleman is such that he designates Huon his heir, so that he will rule the fairy kingdom of Monmur upon Oberon's death.

During the twentieth century, discussion of Shakespeare's sources for the fairy king tended to identify the parallels between Oberon in *Huon of Burdeux* and *A Midsummer Night's Dream*. In each case, for example, Oberon is willing to use his magic to help those mortals he encounters in the wood and he has influence over the weather. Shakespeare's Oberon, like his romance counterpart, is careful to differentiate between himself and his followers and other kinds of supernatural spirits. These points of similarity are summarized by Harold Brooks:

Shakespeare would know of Oberon from several sources, but it is in *Huon of Burdeux* that he is fairy king of a wood where travellers are bound to lose themselves and encounter his magic power; this, too, is an Oberon who distinguishes himself from evil creatures of the supernatural world, as Shakespeare's does with 'we are spirits of another sort', and whose assistance (as he tells Huon) is indispensable to a happy outcome.[2]

Peter Holland also pinpoints those corresponding features of the prose narrative and the play:

> Fully described and actively involved in the action of the colossal romance *The Book of Duke Huon of Burdeux* [...] this fairy king who controls the wood 'full of the Fairy and strange things' shares with Shakespeare's Oberon a delight in hunting and great magical power (particularly the ability to conjure up the illusion of extremely localised storms). This Oberon is only three feet high but this is solely the result of his growth having been halted by a curse.[3]

Oberon's diminutive size in *Huon of Burdeux*, in contrast with his adult size in *Dream*, has tended to be the only point of difference remarked upon by critics in the treatment of the fairy king and here critics have suggested that the prose romance played its part in offering Shakespeare another instance of child-sized fairies: 'What precedent, if any, had Shakespeare for his diminutive fairies? Small fairies were the rule: but small meant the size of a three-year-old child, or the two foot tall goblins of Paracelsus, or in *Huon of Burdeux*, Oberon's stature as a three-foot dwarf'.[4]

Geoffrey Bullough in his discussion of *Huon of Burdeux* as a source for Shakespeare's Oberon argues that the references to the griffin at several points in *Dream* provide further evidence that Shakespeare was familiar with the romance and in particular the episode when Huon is carried off by a griffin, but eventually fights and kills the bird and its offspring.[5] The first mention of the mythical creature in the play comes at II.i.232 when Helena imagines her pursuit of Demetrius in the wood, and the second is during the discussion of the mechanicals concerning the part of the lion when Bottom describes how 'there is not a more fearful wild fowl than your lion living'.[6] Here Bullough, in attributing these references to *Huon*, follows the first Arden editor of *Dream*, Henry Cunningham, who suggested that Bottom's description of the lion invokes the story from *Huon* where the griffin is described as 'a crewell fowle [. . .] ferfull it was to beholde'.[7]

In addition to *Huon of Burdeux* Shakespeare may also have found portraits of the fairy king in other plays by his contemporaries that had also used the prose romance as their inspiration. The popularity of prose romances as sources for the Elizabethan stage is demonstrated by the number of romances adapted for performance during this period as well as those plays which capitalized on the popularity of the genre by including characters and motifs associated with it in their plays. Between 1593 and 1603, for example, Henslowe's *Diary* records entries for performances or payments for at least eight plays which dramatized stories from the romance tradition, including *Huon of Burdeux* (1593), *Uther Pendragon* (1597), *The Life of King Arthur* (1598), *Valentine and Orson* (1598), *Brutus* (1598), *Tristram of Lyons* (1599), *Seven Wise Masters* (1600) and *The Four Sons of Aymon* (1602-3).[8] While the *Diary* only records three performances of *hewen of burdoche* or *burdockes* in late December and early January 1593–94,[9] the story of Huon and its dramatic potential can be seen through its influence upon a number of contemporary plays. One such play is Robert Greene's *The Scottish History of James the Fourth* which is also a likely source for Shakespeare's fairy king. The play was entered in the Stationers' Register on 14 May 1594 and the first quarto was published in 1598, but it is likely that the play was written much earlier since Greene was dead by 1592. In terms of Greene's own canon of dramatic works *James the Fourth* is considered to be his last play after *Friar Bacon and Friar Bungay*, which has been dated 1589–90, so *James the Fourth* is likely to have been written c. 1590.[10] While the play's title suggests that it is a history play, the action situates it squarely within the prose romance tradition. The play begins with the dynastic marriage between James IV and Dorothea, the daughter of the King of England, but James has designs upon Ida, the daughter of the Countess of Arran and with the help of his adviser Ateukin, James plots to have Dorothea murdered. This narrative is framed by the commentary of two choric figures: Bohan, a misanthrope, and Oberon the fairy king. Oberon favours the misanthrope and his two sons, Slipper and Nano, who become servants to Ateukin and Dorothea respectively, and he intervenes in the action of the play to save Slipper from the gallows.

Greene's depiction of Oberon in his play follows *Huon of Burdeux* in a number of respects: firstly, the fairy king's diminutive size is established in the opening scene of the play as Bohan the misanthrope remarks upon Oberon's stature: 'Thou lookest not so big as the King of Clubs, | nor so sharp as the King of Spades, nor so fain as the King a Daymonds'.[11] This concurs with the account given by Huon's companion of Oberon: 'he is of heyght but of iii fote, and crokyd shulderyd, but yet he hath an aungelyke vysage, so that there is no mortall man that seethe hym but that taketh gret pleasure to beholde his fase' (*Huon of Burdeux*, p. 63).

Secondly, Greene uses Oberon's role as a presenter and external observer to indicate his capacity to intervene in the action of the play. Here Oberon fulfills his role as the champion of Bohan's sons, specifically Slipper, whom he favours, which recalls his comparable role as the protector of Huon. Oberon blesses Nano and Slipper with the following gifts:

> for their sport I will give them this gift: to the dwarf I give a quick wit, pretty of body, and awarrant his preferment to a prince's service [. . .] to loggerhead your son I give a wandering life, and promise he shall never lack.
>
> (0.i.98–103)

In *Huon of Burdeux* Oberon explains to the hero that in order to fulfil his quest he will need to call upon Oberon's power and protection and gives him a magic horn which will enable him to summon the fairy king and a thousand men to his side:

> I wyll gyue the a ryche horne of ivorey, the whiche is full of grete vertu the whiche thou shalt bere with the it is of so grete vertu that yf thou be never so farre fro me, as soone as thou blowest the horne I shal here the and shall be incontenenent with the with a .C thousande men of armes for to socoure and ayed the.
>
> (pp. 77–78)

Greene, like Lyly, takes advantage of the king of the fairies and his attendants to provide instances of stage spectacle, particularly dancing, to indicate his mythical qualities and his power.[12] In *James the Fourth* Oberon first appears accompanied by music and an antic:

> *Music playing within. Enter after OBERON, King of Fairies, an Antic, who dance about a tomb placed conveniently on the stage; out of the which suddenly starts up, as they dance, BOHAN, a Scot, attired like a Redesdale man, from whom the Antic flies. Oberon manet.*
>
> (0.1.sd)

This spectacle has a purpose, which Oberon explains; since Bohan, the misanthrope, previously loved dancing Oberon brings him dancers as a mark of his favour and to remind him of his former life:

> Oberon, King of Fairies, that loves thee because thou hatest the world; and to gratulate thee, I brought those Antics to show thee some sport in dancing, which thou hast loved well.
>
> (0.1.76–79)

Despite Oberon's prominence within the play the critical responses to the fairy king in *James the Fourth* have been rather mixed. Early responses to the play tended to confine discussion to the explication of the allegorical nature of the work[13] and while some critics acknowledged the appearance of Oberon in the play[14] others have chosen to ignore or dismiss it. The Revels edition, for example, briefly discusses the play's full title: '*The Scottish Historie of James the Fourth, slaine at Flodden. Entermixed with a pleasant Comedie, presented by Oboram King of Fayries*', yet fails to address the question of Oberon's role in the play. The editor of the Revels edition, Norman Sanders, acknowledges that the source for Greene's play is the Italian novel *Hecatommithi* by G. B. Geraldo Cinthio, but does not consider what other sources Greene may have consulted for the figure of Oberon, which must have surely included *Huon of Burdeux* (p. xiii). Sanders concurs with the assessment of both Kenneth Muir and J. A. Lavin concerning Oberon's inclusion in the play. Muir argues that 'the induction and choric interludes between the acts are tedious and unnecessary', while Lavin regards them as 'an excuse for the introduction of inter-act jigs, hornpipes, and rounds, which are extraneous to the play'.[15] More recently Alexander Leggatt and Margo Hendricks have argued that Oberon's role is integral to our understanding of the play. Leggatt, for example, discusses the play's hybrid nature and suggests that its two presenters, Oberon and Bohan, are used to signal the play's generic binarism: 'Bohan is satiric, moralizing, finally despairing; he presides over the play as history and tragedy. Oberon is festive, comic, life-affirming; he presides over the play as comedy and romance'.[16]

Margo Hendricks discusses Greene's portrait of the fairy king in order to trace the association between Oberon and the East. In *Huon of Burdeux*, the hero encounters Oberon in a wood on his way to Babylon and here the king tells him that he is 'kynge of Momur, the whiche is a .iiii. C. Leges fro hense' (p. 74). The fairy kingdom seems to be located between Jerusalem, where Huon has just visited, and Babylon. Hendricks argues that subsequent depictions of Oberon in Elizabethan plays and poetry link him to the East and to India, the generic name given the Middle East during the medieval and Renaissance periods. Hendricks points out that Greene's play underlines this link through the three dumb shows which are presented by Oberon during the play featuring Queen Semiramis, Cyrus and Sesostris.[17]

Another play which also features Oberon and may have been a further potential source for Shakespeare's portrait of the fairy king is the anonymous work *The Tragical History, Admirable Atchievments and various events of Guy Earl of Warwick*. The play was first published in 1661, but despite this late publication date Helen Cooper has recently argued that it was probably written in the early 1590s, between 1593 and 1594. Part of the evidence for this dating relates to the inclusion of a section in Act II which refers directly to exploits of Huon and has an appearance by Oberon, neither of which appear in the popular accounts of the romance found in chapbooks or broadside ballads. Cooper argues that this material is included to cash in on the popularity of *Huon of Burdeux* on the stage.[18] The author of *The Tragical History*, like Greene, follows the details of *Huon of Burdeux* quite closely in their characterization and depiction of the fairy king's physical appearance, exploiting the comic potential of Oberon's diminutive size and the opportunity for stage spectacle afforded by his magical powers. Oberon's size provides the subject for the comic exchanges between Sparrow, the clown servant of Guy of Warwick, and the fairies. Sparrow begins by referring to the size of Oberon's fairy attendants: 'what fine little hop, O my Thumbs have you got here'.[19] As a comic coward Sparrow would rather play-fight the fairies than tackle the giant: 'Unch ye whoreson little pigpies, you i'le tickle ye ifaith' (sig.B4r). Sparrow fails to recognize Oberon, asking 'but master what is that same little gentleman's name?' (sig.C1v) and even when Guy introduces Oberon Sparrow fails to take seriously his identity as a king, firstly by confusing his name with that of the giant Colbron they are about to kill:

SPARROW: Little Gentleman is your name King Colbron?
OBERON: No Sir, my name is King Oberon.

(sig.C1v)

Sparrow continues to provide Oberon with epithets which emphasize his size, referring to him as 'King Muttonbone' (sig.C1v). While the plays might use Oberon's height to comic effect, *Huon of Burdeux* emphasizes the fairy king's majesty through his sumptuous clothing and magical powers. When Huon first sees Oberon in the wood he is described as wearing

> a gowne so ryche that it were marvayll to recount the ryches and faysyon thereof and it was so garnyshyd with precyous stones that the clerenes of them shone lyke the sone. Also he had a goodly bow in hys hands so ryche that it coude not be estymyde, and his arrows after the same sort.
>
> (p. 65)

The fairy king's appearance in *The Tragical History* is used to provide instances of stage spectacle, particularly feats of magic. Oberon rescues the hero from an 'Inchanter' at the castle of Donathar who has placed Guy in a 'hell bred slumber' (sig.B4v). Oberon is able to break the spell partly by the restorative effect of fairy music and dance:

> You harmlesse spirits of the flowry Meades,
> Nymphes, Satyres, Fawnes, and all the Fairy train,
> That waits on Oberon the Fairy King,
> Attend me quickly with your silver tunes;
> And in a circled Ring, lets compasse round,
> This sleeping knight that lies upon the ground.
>
> *Enter the Fairies with Musick, they Dance about him. Oberon strikes Guy with his Wand, he awakes and speakes.*
>
> (sig.B4 v)

Oberon explains here that he favours Guy and has rescued him because of his love for Huon of Burdeux and rewards him with a magic wand:

> I am the Fairy King that keeps these Groves,
> For Huon of Burdeaux sake, thy Warlike friend,
> The dear loved Minion of the Fairy King,
> Will I make Guy of Warwicks name be fear'd;
> For conquest of the Tower of Donathar,
> Here take this charming Wand, I give it thee,
> Which is of such great vertue if it touch,
> All the Inchantments in this spacious world,
> They all shall be dissolv'd immediately.
>
> (sig.B4r)

Oberon is presented in *Huon* as an exemplar of kingly virtues and emphasis is placed upon his status as both a mortal man and in distinguishing his magic from other kinds of dark magic. While Oberon can control the weather, calling up storms and conjuring castles in the air, his magic is located firmly in a Christian context. When he first encounters Huon in the wood and the knight refuses to speak with him for fear of his enchantments, Oberon addresses Huon and his men in the following terms:

> Ye xiiii men that passyth by my wood, god kepe you all and I desyre you speke with me, and I conjure you ther to by god almyghty, and by ye crystendome that ye have receyved, and by all that god hath made answer me.
>
> (p. 67)

Later Oberon explains that his power comes from God and shows Huon a magic cup which to the virtuous will be full of wine, but to the sinful will be empty; before Oberon passes it to Huon he makes the sign of the cross over it three times. The significance of this ritual recalls both the Last Supper and the actions of the priest during the consecration of the bread and wine during Mass. Oberon is cast in a Christ-like role as Huon's guide and protector. As detailed above, the Oberon of *James the Fourth*, *The Tragical History* and *A Midsummer Night's Dream* is also presented as a force for good in the ways in which he serves as the champion of Slipper, Guy and Helena. While these plays do not present Oberon directly addressing a Christian god, they do contrast Oberon with figures of evil or wrongdoing, including the 'Inchanter' or the King of Scotland and his villainous adviser Ateukin.

As this first part of the chapter has been suggesting, Shakespeare follows the portrait of Oberon found in *Huon of Burdeux* and in the plays of his contemporaries in many respects. Shakespeare's Oberon does, however, differ from the portrait of the fairy king found in the prose romance and in the dramatic manifestations on the Elizabethan stage in one significant respect: Shakespeare is unique in giving Oberon a wife.[20] In *Huon of Burdeux* Oberon is a solitary figure; he does not have a queen and governs his kingdom alone. Oberon's power is presented in terms of powerful family connections which focus upon his parents rather than the fairy himself and his role in consolidating that position through a dynastic marriage. Oberon explains to Huon that his mother was a fairy, the Lady of the Secret Isle, and that she gave birth to Neptanabus, King of Egypt, and that he in turn was the father of Alexander the Great. Oberon's father was Julius Caesar, who encountered the Lady of the Isle on his journey to Thessaly to defeat Pompey the Great (pp. 72–73).

The absence of a fairy consort for Oberon is underlined in the romance narrative by the strategy he employs to solve the problem of who will succeed to the throne of Momur. Oberon does not have an heir of the body and therefore designates Huon as his heir:

> I wyll gyve you my realme and all my dygnyte, the which I may lawfully do, for it lyeth in me to gyve it where as I thynke best, and bycause I love you so entyerly I shall set ye crowne on your hede, and ye shall be kyng of my realm.

> (p. 75)

In many ways the portrait of Oberon as a lone king underlines the masculine nature of the romance world. It is a place of fantasy where men can exist without women, where the roles of women as wives and mothers have been circumvented by the process of adoption. Oberon offers an attractive model of kingship and is an exemplar of a Christian king: powerful, God-fearing and able to transcend the more problematic aspects of the role, notably the issue of succession.

Matthew Woodcock has suggested that in translating *Huon of Burdeux* in c. 1534, Lord Berners may have intended Oberon as a flattering analogue for his king and patron Henry VIII.[21] Certainly the suitability of this comparison for Henry VIII is made explicit in literature of the Elizabethan period, specifically in Edmund Spenser's *The Faerie Queene*. In Book II of the poem, first published in 1590, Spenser signals the influence of *Huon of Burdeux* upon his poem by aligning Sir Guyon with knights from the romance tradition, including Huon himself.[22] Canto i describes how Guyon is knighted by Huon himself during a visit to Oberon's fairy kingdom:

> He was an Elfin borne of noble state,
> And mickle worship in his natiue land;
> Well could he tourney and in lists debate,
> And knighthood tooke of good Sir *Huons* hand,
> When with king *Oberon* he came to Faerie land.[23]

Later in Canto x when Guyon and Arthur read the histories of Britain and fairyland, Oberon reprises his role as a powerful figurehead in the chronicles of fairyland. Spenser's poem ostensibly celebrates the Tudor dynasty by offering an idealized portrait of Henry VIII. As Oberon's own genealogy indicates, he is associated with important empire builders and is reputedly the son of Julius Caesar and a mythical analogue for Henry. Oberon would lend weight to Henry's and England's claims to empire. As Diane Purkiss has remarked, 'Oberon is linked to the powerful dead, and in particular dead patriarchs, the conquerors and founders of nations'.[24]

The stanzas which recount the 'Antiquitee of Faery lond' in the final section of Canto x of *The Faerie Queene* begin by suggesting that Oberon's ancestors established a tradition of conquest:

> Of these a mighty people shortly grew,
> And puissant kinges, which all the world warrayd,
> And to them selues all Nations did subdew:
> The first and eldest, which that scepter swayd,
> Was *Elfin*; him all *India* obayd,
> And all that now *America* men call.
>
> (II.x.72)

Here the genealogy refers to the conquest of both India and America by Elfin, which draws upon the tradition of locating fairyland in the East and more specifically in India, while also calling upon ideas associated with the *translatio imperii* which sanctioned English claims to empire-building in the West based on their mythical decent from another great progenitor, Brutus. The final section of the fairy genealogy is a thinly veiled allegory of the Tudor dynasty with Elficleos used to figure Henry VII while Oberon represents his son, Henry VIII:

> The wise *Elficleos* in great Maiestie,
> Who mightily that scepter did sustayne,
> And with rich spoyles and famous victorie,
> Did high aduance the crowne of *Faery*:
> He left two sonnes, of which faire *Elferon*
> The eldest brother did vntimely dy;
> Whose emptie place the mightie *Oberon*
> Doubly supplide, in spousall, and dominion.

> Great was his power and glorie ouer all,
> Which him before, that sacred seat did fill,
> That yet remaines his wide memoriall:
> He dying left the fairest *Tanaquill*,
> Him to succeede therein, by his last will.
>
> (II.x.75–76)

In this fairy chronicle Spenser presents Henry as husband to Catherine of Aragon, but then smoothes over the difficult reigns of Edward and Mary by omitting them from this fairy genealogy. Henry's will, rather like Oberon's adoption of Huon of Burdeux, attempts to sidestep some of the difficulties of succession. The genealogy is double-edged, however, since the reference to Henry's will indicates that the king had recourse to other means to secure the succession. It also concludes with Tanaquil, which underlines the way in which the Tudor dynasty ends with Elizabeth.

Matthew Woodcock has suggested that the genealogy is ambiguous as it also allows 'the difficult question of Elizabeth's succession to remain in focus'.[25] One of the important functions of the family tree read by Guyon in Book II of Spenser's poem is the relationship it establishes between Henry as Oberon and Elizabeth as Tanaquil, Gloriana and the Faerie Queene. Oberon as an allegorical representation of Henry VIII depicts the relationship with Elizabeth as one of parent and child, a king and his successor, a queen and her father. It is this particular relationship established in *The Faerie Queene* which Thomas Dekker refers to in his allegorical play *The Whore of Babylon*, written c. 1606.[26] Here Dekker follows Spenser in figuring Henry VIII as Oberon and the father of Titania, the fairy queen, when the character of Florimell recounts the genealogy of the queen which serves once again as a thinly veiled account of the accession of the Tudors:

> for when great *Elfiline*
> (Your grandsire) fild this throne, your bowers did shine
> With fire-red steele, and not with Fairies eies,
> You heard no music then, but shriekes and cries,
> Then armed Vrchins, and stearne household Elues,
> Their fatall pointed swords turnd on themselues.
> But when the royall *Elfiline* sat crowned,
> These ciuill woes in their own depth lay drowned.
> He to immortall shades beeing gone,
> (Fames minion) great King *Oberon*,
> Titaniaes royall father, liuely springs,
> Whose Court was like a camp of none but Kings.
> From this great conquering Monarchs glorious stemme,
> Three (in direct line) wore his Diadem:
> A King first, then a paire of Queenes, of whom
> Shee that was held down-cast, by Fates doome,
> Sits now aboue their hopes: her maiden hand,
> Shall with silken thred guide Fairie land.[27]

Oberon is also used as a mystical figure with specifically Tudor associations in Ben Jonson's masque *Oberon, The Faery Prince*, written in 1611. In this particular entertainment the part of Oberon was written for Henry, Prince of Wales for performance at court. Henry deliberately fashioned an identity for himself which aligned him with the Elizabethan values of chivalry and those nobles associated with militant Protestant politics during the reign of Elizabeth, such as the Earl of Leicester, Sir Philip Sidney and the Earl of Essex. Henry was also particularly keen to emphasize a line of descent stretching from his namesake Henry V through to his Tudor forebears, particularly Henry VIII, and the choice of Oberon as a character for the prince to perform underlined this heroic genealogy.[28]

Both *The Whore of Babylon* and *Oberon, The Faery Prince* demonstrate the association between Oberon and Henry VIII and, more importantly for the purposes of my argument, they indicate that Oberon continued to be depicted as a king without a consort after Shakespeare's *A Midsummer Night's Dream* had been performed and published. This suggests that Shakespeare's decision to provide Oberon with a wife marked an important watershed in the portrayal of the fairy king. Shakespeare's decision to provide him with Titania as his fairy queen intensifies the scrutiny of the Tudors begun by Spenser in *The Faerie Queene*. Shakespeare's engagement with *Huon of Burdeux* therefore goes beyond simply transposing the figure from the romance to the stage and instead indicates the ways in which he reworks the figure of Oberon to re-evaluate his use as part of the Tudor myth of origin and Elizabeth's status as the last of that dynasty.

As I suggested earlier, *Huon of Burdeux,* in its depiction of the relationship between Oberon and the eponymous hero, offers a patriarchal fantasy where the bonds between men are unmediated by women. In *A Midsummer Night's Dream*, Shakespeare presents his audience with the flipside of this. By providing Oberon with a fairy queen, Shakespeare inverts the masculine world of *Huon of Burdeux* and the model of kingship exemplified by Oberon. This shift is signalled in the opening scene of the play as the masculine world of the romance gives way to the female-dominated sphere of Shakespeare's play, where the Athenian wood and landscape of faraway India are characterized by a variety of female relationships and female forms of power. In this way Shakespeare's play foregrounds contemporary cultural anxiety about female power and sexuality.

Critics such as Shirley Nelson Garner and Louis Montrose have argued that the marriages which mark the culmination of the play's action can only take place once the women of the play have submitted to patriarchal control and the bonds between them have been broken.[29] This pattern is established in the opening scene of the play with the preparations for Theseus's marriage to the Amazonian Queen Hippolyta. Hippolyta's identity as an Amazon immediately raises the vision of an alternative social order, a world where the tenets of patriarchy are inverted. Amazonian mythology was frequently employed in Elizabethan travel narratives to articulate encounters with the peoples of South America and Africa. In 1582 an account of an expedition to the Spice Islands recorded that:

> Near the mountains of the moon there is a queen, empress of all these Amazons, a witch and a cannibal who daily feeds on the flesh of boys. She ever remains unmarried, but she has intercourse with a great number of men by whom she begets offspring. The kingdom however, remains hereditary to the daughters and not the sons.[30]

Although Theseus reminds Hippolyta that he has 'woo'd thee with my sword', his impatience to be married is expressed through the equivalence between the waning of the moon and powerful female figures who serve as obstacles to his desire:

> Now, fair Hippolyta, our nuptial hour
> Draws on apace. Four happy days bring in
> Another moon – but O, methinks, how slow
> This old moon wanes! She lingers my desires
> Like to a stepdame or a dowager
> Long withering out a young man's revenue.
>
> (I.i.1–6)

Hippolyta, despite expressing her sympathy for Hermia's plight, remains an isolated and virtually silent figure in the play. The isolation of women is examined in the relationship between Helen and Hermia which is initially characterized by bonds of friendship established in childhood:

> And in the wood where often you and I
> Upon faint primrose beds were wont to lie,
> Emptying our bosoms of their counsel sweet,
> There my Lysander and myself shall meet.
>
> (I.i.214–17)

The love they experience for Lysander and Demetrius serves to undermine their friendship, however, with Helena prepared to break Hermia's confidence about the couple's plan to elope. Later Helena believes that Hermia has joined forces with Lysander and Demetrius to ridicule her friend's passion for Demetrius. Helena rebukes her friend for her unkindness, recalling their youth:

> Is all the counsel that we two have shared –
> The sisters' vows, the hours that we have spent
> When we have chid the hasty-footed time
> For parting us – O, is all quite forgot?
> All schooldays' friendship, childhood innocence?
>
> (III.ii.198–202)

Louis Montrose notes that:

> the maidens remain constant to their men at the cost of inconstancy to each other. If Lysander and Demetrius are flagrantly inconstant to Hermia and Helena, the pattern of their inconstancies nevertheless keeps them constant to each other [. . .] At the end of A Midsummer Night's Dream, as at the end of As You Like It, the marital couplings dissolve the bonds of sisterhood at the same time they forge the bonds of brotherhood.[31]

This pattern can also be discerned in the triangulated relationship between Oberon, Titania and the changeling boy. Titania's interest in the boy relates to her own relationship with the boy's mother and her desire to act as a kind of surrogate mother:

> His mother was a vot'ress of my order,
> And in the spicèd Indian air by night
> Full often hath she gossiped by my side,
> And sat on Neptune's yellow sands,
> Marking th' embarkèd traders on the flood,
> When we have laughed to see the sails conceive
> And grow big-bellied with the wanton wind,
> Which she with pretty and with swimming gait
> Following, her womb then rich with my young squire,
> Would imitate, and sail upon the land
> To fetch me trifles, and return again
> As from a voyage, rich with merchandise.

But she, being mortal, of that boy did die;
And for her sake do I rear up her boy;
And for her sake I will not part with him.

(II.i.123–37)

Oberon's desire for the boy has been discussed as an exploration of the ways in which masculine identity was defined in part through its dependency upon women. The female community established by Titania and her votaress establishes a family unit which does not require a male figurehead; Montrose remarks that, in her role as foster parent: 'Titania links the biological and social aspects of parenthood together in a wholly maternal world, a world in which the relationship between women has displaced the relationship between husband and wife'.[32]

Oberon not only finds that he is Titania's rival for the boy – he wants to take the boy and make him one of his henchmen, marking his transition from childhood to puberty – but he is also the boy's rival for the affection of his own wife since Titania has 'forsworn his bed and company' (II.i.62). By separating Titania from the changeling boy Oberon is able to re-establish his control over his wife and distance her from the female community of which she had been a part.

By making the action of the play pivot upon the quarrel between Oberon and Titania, Shakespeare is able to foreground the problems facing the fairy king which could arise within a marriage and which cannot necessarily be solved by magic, such as childlessness. In giving Oberon a fairy queen, the sobriquet used by Spenser to flatter Elizabeth in his poem, the play also indicates that the shift in Oberon from father to husband invites consideration of the issue of female rule. Titania does not present a very flattering portrait of a queen, since she dotes both upon the changeling boy and later upon Bottom. Critics such as Helen Hackett have argued that the infatuation with the child is a consequence of the childless marriage between Oberon and Titania, and that the queen treats Bottom not only as a substitute lover but also as a substitute child.[33] Oberon's use of the love potion as a means of restoring his control over his wife also invites a contemporary audience to consider the impact that such actions might have on responses to the king and his use of magic. In *Huon of Burdeux*, for example, Oberon's magic contributes to his majesty as a king, inspiring awe in those who see it, and it is used to overcome apparently impossible adversaries and situations during Huon's quest. In *Dream*, Puck's opening exchanges with Titania's fairy attendant establish Oberon as a potent figure and yet the context of this description is the wrangling between a husband and wife:

> Oberon is passing fell and wrath
> Because that she, as her attendant, hath
> A lovely boy stol'n from an Indian king.
> She never had so sweet a changeling;
> And jealous Oberon would have the child
> Knight of his train, to trace the forest wild.
> But she perforce withholds the loved boy,
> Crowns him with flowers, and makes him all her joy.
>
> (II.ii.20–27)

The bickering between Oberon and Titania concerning their mutual infidelities also serves to make both the fairy king and queen much more human and therefore much less impressive. The status of Oberon's magic and indeed of the king himself is reduced since he uses his magical powers to reassert control over his wife through a humiliating tryst with Bottom. The effect of this particular use of fairy magic is to demystify it and to demonstrate its limitations. While Oberon certainly succeeds in securing the boy and restoring his wife to himself by the end of the play, we see that the discord has been caused by the childless marriage between the king and queen and that perhaps Oberon's actions provide only a short-term solution to the problem.

The translation of *Huon de Burdeux* into English was crucial for the formation of a cultural mythography for Oberon the fairy king in English literature. The prose romance established a series of characteristics for the king which were then reproduced in Elizabethan and Jacobean poetry and plays, including his own status as an idealized king and his mythical lineage as the son of Julius Caesar. The deployment of Oberon as an allegorical representation of Henry VIII and the father of Elizabeth, the fairy queen, meant that these images of the Tudor dynasty were available to be appropriated and reworked by writers such as Spenser and Shakespeare. Shakespeare's decision to develop his source material and provide Oberon with a fairy queen, a title which had by the early 1590s acquired a specific cultural meaning in relation to Elizabeth herself, permitted a reassessment, not just of Elizabeth, but of the dynasty overall.

Notes

1   See for example, Mary Ellen Lamb, 'Taken by the Fairies: Fairy Practices and the Production of Popular Culture in *A Midsummer Night's Dream*', *Shakespeare Quarterly* 51 (2000), pp. 277–312; Wendy Wall, 'Why Does Puck Sweep?: Fairylore, Merry Wives, and Social Struggle', *Shakespeare Quarterly* 52 (2001), pp. 67–106; and Regina Buccola, *Fairies, Fractious Women, and the Old Faith: Fairy Lore in Early Modern British Drama and Culture* (Selinsgrove, PA: Susquehanna University Press, 2006).

2   William Shakespeare, *A Midsummer Night's Dream*, ed. Harold Brooks (London: Routledge, 1993), p. lix.

3   William Shakespeare, *A Midsummer Night's Dream*, ed. Peter Holland (Oxford: Oxford University Press, 1994), p. 31.

4   *Dream*, ed. Brooks, p. lxxi.

5   Geoffrey Bullough, *Narrative and Dramatic Sources of Shakespeare*, 6 vols (London: Routledge & Kegan Paul, 1966), I, pp. 72–75.

6   *Dream*, ed. Holland, III.i.29–30. All further quotations from the play will be taken from this edition and reference will be given in the text.

7   *The Boke of Duke Huon of Burdeux*, ed. S. L. Lee, 2 vols (London: Early English Text Society), I, p. 427. All further quotations will be taken from this edition and reference will be given in the text.

8   Ronald S. Crane, 'The Vogue of *Guy of Warwick* from the Close of the Middle Ages to the Romantic Revival', *PMLA* 30 (1915), pp. 125–94.

9   Henslowe's *Diary*, ed. R.A. Foakes, 2nd edn (Cambridge: Cambridge University Press, 2002), p. 20.

10 Robert Greene, *The Scottish History of James the Fourth*, ed. Norman Sanders (London: Methuen, 1970), pp. xxv–ix.

11 Greene, *The Scottish History of James the Fourth*, ed. Sanders, 0.17–19. All further quotations will be taken from this edition and reference will be given in the text.

12 See for example, John Lyly, *Endymion*, ed. David Bevington (Manchester: Manchester University Press, 1996), IV.iii.30–45.

13 See for example, Ruth Hudson, 'Greene's *James IV* and Contemporary Allusions to Scotland', *PMLA* 47 (1932), pp. 652–67 and Catherine Lekhal, 'The Historical Background of Robert Greene's *The Scottish History of James IV*', *Cahiers Élisabéthains* 35 (1985), pp. 27–45.

14 Early examples include: Felix Schelling, 'Some Features of the Supernatural as Represented in Plays of the Reigns of Elizabeth and James', *Modern Philology* 1 (1903), pp. 31–47 and H.W. Herrington, 'Witchcraft and Magic in the Elizabethan Drama', *The Journal of American Folk-Lore* 32 (1919), pp. 447–85.

15 Kenneth Muir, 'Robert Greene as Dramatist', in *Essays on Shakespeare and Elizabethan Drama in Honour of Hardin Craig*, ed. Richard Hosley (London: Routledge & Kegan Paul, 1963), pp. 45–54; J. A. Lavin, 'Introduction' to Robert Greene, *The Scottish History of James the Fourth* (London: Ernest Benn, 1967), p. xv.

16 Alexander Leggatt, 'Bohan and Oberon: The Internal Debate of Greene's *James IV*', *The Elizabethan Theatre* XI (1990), pp. 95–116, p. 98.

17 Margo Hendricks, '"Obscured by dreams": Race, Empire, and Shakespeare's *A Midsummer Night's Dream*', *Shakespeare Quarterly* 47 (1996), pp. 37–60, pp. 44–48.

18 Helen Cooper, 'Guy of Warwick, Upstart Crows and Mounting Sparrows', in *Shakespeare, Marlowe, Jonson: New Directions in Biography,* ed. Takashi Kozuka and J.R. Mulryne (Aldershot: Ashgate, 2006), pp. 119–38, pp. 123–24.

19 *The Tragical History, Admirable Atchievments and various events of Guy Earl of Warwick* (London: T. Vere and W. Gilbertson, 1661), sig. B4r. All further quotations will be taken from this edition and reference will be given in the text.

20 References are made to Oberon and his fairy queen in Caroline plays, where he

is paired either with Mab or Titania, including John Ford's *Perkin Warbeck*, published in 1634, Thomas Randolph's *Amyntas, or The Impossible Dowry*, published in 1638 and James Shirley's *The Gentleman of Venice*, published in 1655. The tradition among plays which feature Oberon between c. 1590–1611 is to present him without a consort, with Shakespeare's fairy king providing an interesting alternative to this trend.

21   Matthew Woodcock, *Fairy in The Faerie Queene: Renaissance Elf-Fashioning and Elizabethan Myth-Making* (Ashgate: Aldershot, 2004), p. 38.

22   For early discussion of the influence of *Huon of Burdeux* on *The Faerie Queene* see Jefferson B. Fletcher, '*Huon of Burdeux* and *The Faerie Queene*', *Journal of English and German Philology* 2 (1898–99), pp. 209–11, and John R. Macarthur, 'The Influence of *Huon of Burdeux* upon *The Faerie Queene*', *Journal of English and German Philology* 4 (1902), pp. 215–38.

23   Edmund Spenser, *The Faerie Queene*, ed. A.C. Hamilton, 2nd edn, revised (Harlow: Pearson Longman, 2007), II.i.6. All further quotations will be taken from this edition and reference will be given in the text.

24   Diane Purkiss, *Troublesome Things: A History of Fairies and Fairy Stories* (London: Penguin, 2000), p. 175.

25   Woodcock, *Fairy in The Faerie Queene*, p. 135.

26   For recent discussion of the play see Jean E. Howard, *The Stage and Social Struggle in Early Modern England* (London: Routledge, 1994); Susan E. Krantz, 'Thomas Dekker's Political Commentary in *The Whore of Babylon*', *Studies in English Literature* 35 (1995), pp. 271–291; and Regina Buccola, 'Virgin Fairies and Imperial Whores: The Unstable Ground of Religious Iconography in Thomas Dekker's *The Whore of Babylon*', in *Marian Moments in Early Modern British Drama*, ed. Regina Buccola and Lisa Hopkins (Aldershot: Ashgate, 2007), pp. 141–60.

27   Thomas Dekker, *The Whore of Babylon*, in *The Dramatic Works of Thomas Dekker*, ed. Fredson Bowers, 4 vols (Cambridge: Cambridge University Press, 1955), I.ii.25–42. All further quotations from the play will be taken from this edition and reference will be given in the text.

28   See Roy Strong, *Henry, Prince of Wales and England's Lost Renaissance* (London: Thames & Hudson, 1986) and Curtis Perry, *The Making of Jacobean Culture: James I and the Renegotiation of Elizabethan Literary Practice* (Cambridge: Cambridge University Press, 1997).

29   Shirley Nelson Garner, 'A Midsummer Night's Dream: "Jack shall have Jill; / Nought shall go ill"', in *A Midsummer Night's Dream*, ed. Richard Dutton (Houndmills: Palgrave, 1996), and Louis Adrian Montrose, ' "Shaping Fantasies": Figurations of Gender and Power in Elizabethan Culture', *Representations* 2 (1983), pp. 61–94.

30   Quoted in Montrose, 'Shaping Fantasies', p. 66.

31   Montrose, 'Shaping Fantasies', p. 69.

32   Montrose, 'Shaping Fantasies', p. 72.

33   Helen Hackett, '*A Midsummer Night's Dream*', in *A Companion to Shakespeare's Works: The Comedies*, ed. Richard Dutton and Jean E. Howard, 4 vols (Oxford: Blackwell Publishing 2005), III, pp. 338–57, p. 343.

CHAPTER SEVEN

Constructing Experiences and Charting Narratives: The Future in/of *A Midsummer Night's Dream*

Tripthi Pillai

Nearly a decade after it reared its ugly head, the crisis of theory within literary critical studies seems to be behind us. The result is that Shakespeare scholars, who as a rule have maintained an active interest in engaging the methodologies of diverse theories, are once again eager to locate and collaborate with new systems of knowledge. Be it Gabriel Egan's *Green Shakespeare: From Ecopolitics to Ecocriticism*, Douglas Bruster's *Shakespeare and the Question of Culture*, Ayanna Thompson's *Colorblind Shakespeare: New Perspectives on Race and Performance* or Richard Wilson's *Shakespeare in French Theory: King of Shadows*, the renewed enthusiasm for theoretical approaches to Shakespeare's drama and poetry is a positive indicator of the future of early modern scholarship.[1] But in what precise direction is this scholarship heading?

Lawrence Buell raises the important point that at present literary studies is missing a 'paradigm initiating statement like Edward Said's *Orientalism* (for colonial studies discourse) or Stephen Greenblatt's *Renaissance Self-Fashioning* (for new historicism)',[2] which defines and establishes a critical method that may then be emulated and appropriated by the field. (Buell's comment, as it happens, is made in the context of 'literatures of the environment', but his observation resonates with the general state of literary criticism.) This absence of a theoretical centre, however, need not be a frightening thing. If anything, it is symptomatic of the complex multiplicity that marks theory's future within literary criticism.

While no single theoretical approach stands out as a self-sufficient model, the interweaving of theories presents new ways of reading literature. Early modernists have begun to embrace this direction and already some interesting patterns are emerging. For instance, Garrett Sullivan's *Memory and Forgetting in English Renaissance Drama* is one among several texts that have set the tone for the discussion of Shakespearean literature in the context of temporality.[3] Lisa Hopkins's *Shakespeare on the Edge: Border-Crossing in the Tragedies and the Henriad* is similarly representative of the field's growing consciousness of the politics of geography,[4] specifically the disruption of spatial borders and boundaries by an increasingly global cultural economy. In their respective works, Sullivan and Hopkins combine the methods of new historicism with other philosophies to present their readers with new ways of reading time (remembering and forgetting, in the case of Sullivan) and space (the allegorization of landscape, in the case of Hopkins).

Intriguing as they are by themselves, the conjunction of temporal and spatial logics further enhances the possibilities of reading early modern literature. I will focus on this conjunction for the purpose of this chapter and will offer specifically a critical reading of *A Midsummer Night's Dream* that traces the complex intersections between desire and spatio-temporal relations in the play as they are manifested in characters who strive to construct alternative futures and identities for themselves or others. Futurity – which Derrida defines as 'the condition of all promises or of all hope, of all awaiting, of all performativity, of all opening towards the future'[5] – is a play of multiple desires that exist simultaneously within our present beings. Simply put, futurity is that condition of our present experience in which we want, need, wish, hope and plan for diverse objects and states to be realized in our future. *A Midsummer Night's Dream* essentially is a play about futurity, a text in which characters' processes of dreaming are scrutinized and, at certain points, transformed into their realities. The exercising of their desires (or dreams) leads the characters to conflicts within or between organized spaces of their bodies, kingdoms and territories. More-over, their imagination of the future collides with cultural sites of their memory, resulting in a powerful if transient stage of 'becoming'.

Of particular use to my reading are the theories of Deleuze and Guattari, who in their works encourage anti-memory as the site of 'becoming', which is not a fixed state of being but rather 'constitutes [...] a non-localizable relation' that 'sweeps up' the seemingly isolated structures or bodies that lock power within their beings.[6] By destabilizing and unfixing beings, becoming forces connections to form between them through ungoverned flows of energy or desire. It is these ungoverned flows that, the philosophers suggest, can transgress the limits of temporal sequence, of history, and thus free up human consciousness:

> [Becoming] is the opposite of macropolitics, and even of History, in which it is a question of knowing how to win or obtain a majority. [...] Unlike history, becoming cannot be conceptualized in terms of past or future. [...] [A]historical societies set themselves outside history, not because they are content to reproduce immutable models or are governed by a fixed structure, but because they are societies of becoming.
>
> (pp. 291–92)

Becoming works in conjunction with 'deterritorialization', another Deleuzian term that will be significant to our understanding of the conjunction of spatio-temporal logics within *A Midsummer Night's Dream*. Deterritorialization is a movement that 'indicates the creative potential of an assemblage' or structured body, and attempts to 'free up the fixed relations that contain' it.[7] Invariably the deterritorialized bodies are once again reterritorialized, when they either return to the original state of organization or formulate alternative bases of structuring power and energy. But it is the moment of flux that is the site of becoming. This moment, Deleuze asserts in an earlier work, 'does not tolerate the separation or the distinction of before and after, or of past and future'; rather, 'the essence of becoming [...] move(s) and [...] pull(s) in both directions at once'. Thus becoming is paradoxical because it encompasses

> the infinite identity of both directions or senses at the same time – of future and past, of the day before and the day after, of more and less, of two [*sic*] much and not enough, of active and passive, and of cause and effect'. [8]

In other words, the past is unfixed and appropriated in Deleuzian becoming and the body freed, so much so that the hold of the past no longer determines the infinite potential of the future. What is of interest to me in this interplay is the possibility of generating new ways of reading the mistimed, timely and untimely actions performed by characters in the play that René Girard suggests is Shakespeare's 'first mature masterpiece'.[9]

Locating Time and Timing Location: The Production and Appropriation of Bodies

A Midsummer Night's Dream hurriedly dislocates the dramatic centre of the play from the urban geography of Athens to the neighbouring wooded fairy realm where Oberon and Titania wage a war that is a cause for global concern. Titania believes that the couple's battle over 'a little changeling boy' has resulted in complete natural and social chaos on earth (II.i.120). In a speech conjuring images that eerily anticipate twenty-first century horrors of global climate change, the queen of fairies claims joint responsibility with Oberon for the various sea storms and floods that have ruined the crop and rendered useless the agrarian economy that depends on the systematic notion of seasons, which are the climatic representation of the passage of time:

> But with thy brawls thou hast disturbed our sport.
> Therefore the winds, piping to us in vain,
> As in revenge, have sucked up from the sea
> Contagious fogs which, falling in the land,
> Hath every pelting river made so proud
> That they have overborne their continents.
> The ox hath therefore stretched his yoke in vain,
> The plowman lost his sweat, and the green corn
> Hath rotted ere his youth attained a beard;
> The fold stands empty in the drownèd field,
> And crows are fatted with the murrain flock;
> [...]
> Therefore the moon, the governess of floods,
> Pale in her anger, washes all the air,
> That rheumatic diseases do abound.
> And thorough this distemperature we see
> The seasons alter: hoary-headed frosts
> Fall in the fresh lap of the crimson rose,
> And on old Hiems' thin and icy crown
> An odorous chaplet of sweet summer buds
> Is, as in mockery, set.
>
> (II.i.87–111)

It seems the clockwork that oversees the efficacy of the seasons and, more importantly, of farming, is dismantled by the violent tempers of the unearthly creatures. The result, claims Titania, is that '[t]he spring, the summer, | The childing autumn, angry winter, change | Their wonted liveries, and the mazèd world | By their increase now knows not which is which' (II.i.111–14). Indeed, Titania's repeated stress on the word 'therefore' in her speech presents the horrific transformation of the earth as the direct and undeniable consequence of untimely fairy intervention. Just as significant, her speech suggests that human experiences of temporality are in fact the result of unearthly agency. Moreover, earthly routines offer themselves as 'sport' to the fairies (II.i.87), the disruption of which is first and foremost on Titania's mind. Her implication is important because it discloses not only the power of the creatures such as herself, Oberon and Puck, but it also emphasizes the folly of characters who, despite believing they can successfully manipulate their own futures, are controlled by the eccentricities of atemporal agents that treat them as objects of play. Lysander and Hermia are two such characters, who take cheer in their potential to construct their own future. Determined to marry in spite of 'the ancient privilege of Athens' that permits fathers to 'dispose of' their children in a manner that best suits their own patriarchal interests (I.i.41–42), the two plan to elope to a far-away place, 'seven leagues' removed from Athens (I.i.159). In place of Egeus's wealth and their inheritance, the lovers hope to benefit from the economic security provided by Lysander's aunt, a woman who, being wealthy and widowed, poses a threat to early modern conceptions of patriarchy. Their plans for self-rule, however, are shattered just 'a league without the town' (I.i.165), where fairies meddle constantly with human agendas to transform their future courses.

Similar intersections of the mundane – activities that comprise human life – and the spectacular – fairy dispute – mark the many locations that, in the play, become sites of contestation. The fairies articulate their mutual discontent not in a private fairy realm that is inaccessible to human beings, but rather in 'the palace wood, a mile without the town' (I.ii.91), in a place that is frequented by the human subjects whose lives are the very matter that is at stake in the fight between Titania and Oberon. Let us consider the Indian boy who functions almost in the manner of territory over which the royal fairies dispute, forcing the intermingling of supernatural and human futures. Even the prehistory of the child is not without the traces of futurity that emerge at borderline spaces.

Refusing to surrender the child to Oberon's desire for dominance and continuity, Titania's claim to the boy is rooted in social and cultural history and a sense of inheritance – in short, in secured futurity:

His mother was a vot'ress of my order,
And in the spicèd Indian air by night
Full often hath she gossiped by my side
And sat with me on Neptune's yellow sands,
Marking th' embarkèd traders on the flood,
When we have laughed to see the sails conceive
And grow big-bellied with the wanton wind;
Which she, with pretty and with swimming gait,
Following – her womb then rich with my young squire –
Would imitate, and sail upon the land
To fetch me trifles, and return again
As from a voyage, rich with merchandise.
But she, being mortal, of that boy did die;
And for her sake do I rear up her boy,
And for her sake I will not part with him.

(II.i.123–37)

Titania's speech has been widely discussed by postcolonial and feminist scholars, who focus on the politics of the uneasy material conjunction of bodies and space.[10] In 'The Changeling in *A Dream*' William Slights argues that the Indian boy, a figure of great mystery but little matter, is an object interpreted variedly by those characters within the play that desire him.[11] Where Oberon boldly claims entitlement based on his desire for a 'henchman' (II.i.121), Titania clings to the child based on her sense of loyalty to a history of traffic that she shared with her votaress, a woman who may have been of royal, if human, descent. As critics have noted, Titania's nostalgic speech about her time spent in the company of the gossip is inundated with metaphors of pregnancy and mercantilism. Caroline Bicks, among others, suggests that, in keeping with the early modern female interactions of gossips and pregnant women, female friendship, as described in this scene, transcends socioeconomic barriers and temporarily evokes egalitarian homosociality.[12] Similarly, Slights notes the near conflation of the images and rhetoric of pregnancy and mercantilism that presents the women's relationship in terms of mirthful empathy. While the states of pregnancy and mercantilism share a sense of investment, anticipation and productivity, they also possess distinct elements of risk: merchants' ships foundered at sea and pregnant women died in childbirth; in both cases the future that is mobilized through these bodies is uncertain and unreliable. Thus, the votaress's body, which is intended to secure her king's sense of patriarchal futurity through the birth of a male heir, becomes a bundle of contradictions; dying in childbirth, she is an engine both of death (the end of temporal sequence) and life (the initiation of temporal experience). The limit of her own mortality prevents the woman from participating in her child's future. But her life, specifically her time spent with Titania on 'Neptune's yellow sands', also destabilizes the Indian king's future rights to his son.

Along with serving her king's sense of futurity, the votaress is a provider of material fulfillment for the fairy Titania. Like the ships whose movements she imitates, the Indian woman brings goods or 'trifles' back with her from her travels and gives them to her queen. Also like the ships, she is a vessel that carries within her 'rich [...] merchandise' in the shape of the 'young squire' whom she may only keep for the duration of her pregnancy but must inevitably give up to her king or the fairy queen – that is, surrender to someone of greater status and power.[13] Like her pregnancy, which is both a condition – a state of being – and a passing stage, the votaress's relationship with the queen of fairies is premised on impermanence and opportunity. After all, Titania's claim to her inheritance of the boy stems directly from his mother's death, the circumstance that accompanied his birth. Strangely, the politics of trade that the woman playfully mimics prior to her death on the Indian shores anticipates the multiple and mutable trades that take place upon her death between the members of fairy royalty. The transformation of the Indian votaress's jovial simulation of early modern economics into a tragically real transaction, in which she loses her life and the child, also anticipates Titania's bizarre transformation from the lyrical protector of the Indian boy to the foolish lover of a beast, to one who loses both the pretty child and her ferocious autonomy to Oberon.

Monsters: Making Them, Laughing at Them, Loving Them, Becoming Them

The fairies' relationships with the Indian mortals, which are all founded on principles of liminality and located on 'the narrow margin between sea and land' are defined by transience.[14] Titania and Bottom's erotic entanglement is similarly suspended in space and time. Seeking vengeance and cheap laughs, Oberon punishes his wife by casting a problematic spell upon her. For his magic to yield the results he desires, Titania must give in to a monstrous appetite and, blinded by her desire for the deformed Bottom, surrender the pretty boy to the king of the fairies. Much has been made of Titania's desire for the base human. For instance, Jan Kott, who famously visualizes the transformed Titania as 'a very tall, flat, and fair girl' of Scandinavian origin, insists that she forces Bottom to bed with her because '[t]his is the lover she wanted and dreamed of', although 'she never wanted to admit it, even to herself'.[15] In claiming that her actions are a direct product of her sexual appetite, Kott overlooks the fact that Titania's love and judgement have been perverted by none other than her husband and it is precisely because Oberon wills it so that Titania hankers after the ass-headed Bottom. While Kott sees in Titania's goblin train all the potent ingredients of 'the pharmacy of the witches' (p. 118), it is only Oberon who has access to the magical power contained within things such as the petals of love-in-idleness.

Moreover, it is Oberon, not Titania, who winds up a dangerous if musical charm while squeezing pansy juice onto his wife's eyelids:

What thou seest when thou dost wake,
Do it for thy true love take;
Love and languish for his sake.
Be it ounce, or cat, or bear,
Pard, or boar with bristled hair,
In thy eye that shall appear
When thou wak'st, it is thy dear.
Wake when some vile thing is near.

(II.ii.33–40)

Notably, Titania's train is wary of the negative effects of such charms as the one uttered by Oberon. Thus, in the lullaby for their queen intended as a prophylactic to protect her from perilous magic, they pray '[n]ever harm | Nor spell nor charm | Come [their] lovely lady nigh' (II.ii.16–18). But their song is powerless and fails to safeguard Titania against Oberon's more ominous spell.

If, as Kott suggests, the various animals listed in Oberon's spell 'represent abundant sexual potency, and some of them play an important part in sexual demonology' (p. 118), it is also perfectly clear that it is the fairy king who wishes to conjure up the deviant logic of desire and smear it upon Titania's eyes. Of course, where he wishes his wife only to suffer humiliation and ridicule, the fairy queen experiences a marvelous becoming before reterritorializing onto her position within the culture of royal patriarchy. What I identify here as a 'becoming', Philippa Berry calls 'a highly potent, combustible combination of phantasy and desire', which 'produces the midsummer night's dreaming', one that first 'reverses and then reorders the erotic preferences of the male lovers'.[16] Berry is right to point to magic's connection with masculine fantasy and to the eventual return of all characters' individual desire to the familiar coded locations of hierarchical heternormativity. But the nuances of some of the characters' desires remain secret. Chief among these is Oberon's, whose wish to debase his wife by animalizing her erotic exchanges at the same time implicates him in his own cuckoldry through his participation in a voyeuristic bestial sexuality.

In their chapter on the diversity of the experience of becomings, Deleuze and Guattari give particular importance to the connection between the human and animal, which they term 'becoming animal'. Their explanation of the phenomenon is important enough to be quoted at length:

> A becoming-animal always involves a pack, a band, a population, a peopling, in short, a multiplicity. [...] One may retain or extract from the animal certain characteristics: species and genera, forms and functions, etc. Society and the State need animal characteristics to use for classifying people; [...] But we are not interested in characteristics; what interests us are modes of expansion, propagation, occupation, contagion, peopling. [...] We do not wish to say that certain animals live in packs. [...] What we are saying is that every animal is fundamentally a band, a pack. That it has pack modes, rather than characteristics, even if further distinctions within these modes are called for. It is at this point that the human being encounters the animal. We do not become animal without a fascination for the pack, for multiplicity.
>
> (pp. 239–40)[17]

In this difficult yet fascinating passage, Deleuze and Guattari suggest that becomings in general but becoming-animal in particular entails multiple, complex networks of desire. The socially simplified and categorized being (the animal or the human) is bereft of its potential to articulate its multi-faceted desires, until it liberates itself from the limiting structures of state and initiates hitherto unthought-of collaborations.

The theorists go on to define becoming-animal in terms of 'unnatural participations' or 'unnatural nuptials' of human and animal. They ask:

> [w]ho has not known the violence of [...] animal sequences, which uproot one from humanity, if only for an instant, making one scrape at one's bread like a rodent or giving one the yellow eyes of a feline? A fearsome involution calling us toward unheard-of becomings.
>
> (p. 240)

The spread of unnatural nuptials does not result in production, reproduction, or filiation; rather it results in 'contagion' and 'epidemic'. Human and animal 'bands', Deleuze and Guattari argue, are like 'hybrids', which, 'being born of a sexual union that will not reproduce itself', are sterile. As a result, becoming-animal (banding through non-reproductive means) constantly confronts the newness of unions and 'begins over again every time, gaining that much more ground' (p. 241). Such a phenomenon 'is a far cry from filiative production or hereditary reproduction, in which the only differences retained are a simple duality between sexes within the same species, and small modifications across generations' (p. 242).

Deleuze and Guattari's philosophy may at first glance seem far-fetched in connection with the transformations triggered by Oberon in *A Midsummer Night's Dream*. However, their theories of unnatural participation echo the thoughts of several Renaissance scholars, particularly that of Ambroise Paré, who, in *On Monsters and Marvels*, presents the various (horrible) transformations that result from the combination of human and animal.[18]

First published in 1573, Ambroise Paré's *On Monsters and Marvels* provides an intriguing catalogue of monsters born of diverse unnatural causes. In a section on the birth of those monsters that result from the unnatural sexual union between human beings and beasts (the 'mixture or mingling of seed'), Paré writes that such creatures 'bring great shame to those who look at them or speak of them'. Although he hurries to inform his readers that the horror 'lies in the deed and not in the words'[19] that narrate or the eyes that witness the details of the monstrous result of bestiality (p. 67), his self-conscious articulation of guiltlessness betrays an urgent desire to justify his curiosity about what he presents to his readers as deviant sexuality. In fact, at the conclusion of the chapter he promises to

> refrain from writing [...] about several other monsters [...] which are so hideous and abominable, not only to see but also to hear tell of, that, due to their abominable loathsomeness I have neither wanted to relate them nor to have them portrayed.
>
> (p. 73)

Ironically, before reaching his conclusion, Paré provides his readers with six detailed illustrations of monsters that resulted from inter-species copulation; his brief chapter covers nothing short of nine cases of monstrosity.

Paré's declaration resonates through the speech and actions of

Oberon and Puck, who maintain their grim fascination for the monster Bottom's exchanges with Titania even as they judge her fairy bed to be a corrupt space. As discussed earlier, Oberon's spell articulates his wish to make his wife 'languish for [. . .] a vile thing'. But he also wishes to imagine his wife's monstrous dotage: 'I wonder if Titania be awaked; | Then, what it was that next came in her eye, | Which she must dote on in extremity' (III.ii.1–3). Puck too takes delight in announcing to Oberon that his 'mistress with a monster is in love' (III.ii.6). In fact, it is by means of their respective imaginations of the conjunction of Titania and a beast that Oberon and Puck experience their becomings. By magically imposing on his wife his own desire for an animal connection, the fairy king becomes quite like the sorcerer that Paré describes in his work:

> [N]o one can deny, and one should not deny, that there be sorcerers [. . .] who through subtle, diabolic and unknown means corrupt the body, intelligence, and health of men and of other creatures, [such] as animals, trees, grasses, *air*, *earth*, and *waters*.
>
> (p. 85; emphasis added)

Paré's words find a parallel early in *A Midsummer Night's Dream*, when Titania accuses her estranged husband of similar sorcery, of creating through his ill will an imbalance in nature.

Oberon's sorcery also finds parallels in Deleuze and Guattari. But unlike the early modern surgeon who views sorcery as merely a step away from the diabolical, Deleuze and Guattari celebrate the figure of the sorcerer as a fundamental agent of becoming. Indeed, to them the 'sorcerer' is the 'exceptional' or 'anomalous' individual with whom 'an alliance must be made in order to become-animal' (p. 243). Such sorcerers, they claim, are located 'at the edge of the fields or woods. They haunt the fringes. They are at the borderline of the village, or *between* villages' (p. 246). The theorists' description of sorcerers fits with Gail Paster and Skiles Howard's evaluation of Oberon's hybrid activity. They propose that 'Oberon, when he alters Titania's imagination and causes her quasi-amorous, quasi-maternal dotage upon the monstrous baby Bottom, may be said to participate in both traditions [. . .] of science and [. . .] of fairy lore'.[20] Not surprisingly, Oberon is also located on the geographical cusp of the city and the forest. His proximity to the human and the fairy is what enables him to work his magic equally on them.

While what Oberon ultimately wants is his wife's disempowerment, humiliation and subservience, at the same time in exercising his magical desires he problematizes the future of matrimony. Titania's loss of control and will can only come about if Oberon endangers his own patriarchal hold over his marriage bed. The deformation wrought by his spell, then, not only plays a cruel trick upon his wife and the Athenian weaver, but it also transforms – albeit tentatively – the sexual conventions of monogamist patriarchy. Eventually, conventional order is restored: Oberon acquires the Indian boy for whom he risked cuckoldry; Titania, having suffered embarrassment for her gross misjudgement, wishes only to separate herself from the mortals and dance the night away with her husband, whom she once again recognizes as her 'lord' (IV.i.98). In effect all characters reterritorialize onto the contemporary modes of patriarchal and hierarchical being. But through their inability completely to forget their suspended transactions with the other, and through their desire to narrate and expound upon their monstrous becomings or imaginations, they carry forward into the future remnants of their experiences. That the play ends on a conventional comedic note, in marriage and laughter, in no way alleviates the audience's disturbing recognition that all the marital arrangements in the play have resulted from Oberon's unnatural desire for a human mortal, and that all corrections or reformations of transgressive individuals have stemmed from not entirely forgotten intersections between human and fairy. The uneasy laughter at play's conclusion, then, is as much a result of potential for the resurrection of deformity as it is a product of the re-establishment of form (norm) in the present. But this uneasiness of comedy marks the entire play, not just its conclusion. Indeed in *A Midsummer Night's Dream* Shakespeare consistently unravels the murkiness of deviant laughter.

Andrew Stott's analysis of early modern representations of deformity is rooted in the period's theoretical preoccupations with genre, specifically comedy, but also in its ethical engagement with laughter.[21] Stott combines the influence of Sidney's discouragement in *Defence of Poetry* of the use of vulgar elements in comedy, those that do not produce a sophisticated sense of delight in readers or the audience but merely a raucous laughter, with the growing early modern appreciation for Hobbesian ethical objections to laughing at the deformed, in order to suggest that Renaissance intellectuals strove to reconfigure the terms of comic laughter. The politics of such a reconfiguration are represented in Shakespeare's shifting appeals to laughter in *A Midsummer Night's Dream*. The play prominently situates the rude mechanicals as worthy of 'loud laughter' (V.i.70). But it simultaneously positions them in the eyes of a few as pitiable subjects whose 'wretchedness' must not be 'o'ercharged' by the demands of pleasure-seeking aristocrats (V.i.85). This polarity of response that plays itself out in Philostrate's and Hippolyta's respective anticipations of the players' comic performance is remarkable especially because it is foreshadowed early in the play, both in the earthly and fairy realms.

Bottom's transformation into a deformed creature in Act III, scene i, produces a laughter that is at the heart of what David Cressy recognizes as the social power of ridicule. Indeed, Oberon expects and desires the production of merriment among those subjects who condemn the deformed body as one that is unworthy of dignity, much less romantic or erotic pursuit. The ass-headed Bottom, then, becomes funny specifically to those observers (Oberon, Puck, the audience) who expect the undrugged Titania to have better taste and sense than to fawn over a shallow 'thickskin' (III.ii.13). In the earthly realm Philostrate and the aristocratic men of Athens mimic Oberon's dominant ideology of laughter when they welcome as comic performance the 'simpleness' of the 'hardhanded' Athenian labourers (V.i.83, 72). The 'tragical mirth' of the play of *Pyramus and Thisbe* brings 'merry tears' to Philostrate (V.i.57, 69). For Theseus, Demetrius and Lysander the mechanicals' drama becomes the occasion for the witty offstage performance of their repartee about the beastliness of the actors. (Notable among these are Demetrius's reference to the actors as 'asses' and Theseus's suggestion that the poor men are all 'beasts', fox-like and goose-like in their performance [V.i.153, 216, 233]). But this is only half the story. While popular early modern responses to disability and deformity combined social contempt with laughter, a powerful minority pressed for a revision of the terms of merriment. In *A Midsummer Night's Dream*, Hippolyta presents the minority position among the mortals; her objection to the comedy of the rude mechanicals is as much to the production of laughter at them as it is to their inadequate sense of theatrical production.

The most immediate result of this shift in the dynamic of laughter is the inversion of the perception of the laugher. That is, the hitherto secure position of the individual laughing at the lowly or deformed body begins to be challenged when the object of contempt is relocated from the physically monstrous to the morally pitiless. In short, it is now the turn of the scorner to be the scorned. This is best exemplified by the transformed Bottom's initial exchange with his fairy mistress. As opposed to Oberon and Puck's contemptuous laughter at their reshaping of Bottom, Titania's erotic longing and love for the deformed creature problematizes the earlier comic moment by

injecting into it a mesmerizing lyricism that counters the vulgar if
alliterative sounds of laughter. In place of Puck's 'hempen homespuns'
(III.i.72), Titania presents an alternative vision of the mechanical whose
'fair virtue's force' moves the queen of the fairies 'to swear' that she
loves Bottom (III.i.133–34). Moreover, instead of inflicting fear on the
lowly humans and extracting a cruel laugh at the expense of their
physical terror – Puck's 'I'll be [...] a headless bear, sometimes a fire'
speech comes to mind (III.i.103–4) – Titania appeals to Bottom's desire
for both material fulfillment and absolute immateriality:

> I am a spirit of no common rate.
> The summer still doth tend upon my state,
> And I do love thee. Therefore, go with me.
> I'll give thee fairies to attend on thee,
> And they shall fetch thee jewels from the deep,
> And sing while thou on pressèd flowers dost sleep.
> And I will purge thy mortal grossness so
> That thou shalt like an airy spirit go.
>
> (III.i.145–52)

Titania enacts Oberon's wishes by playing the fool in love; indeed,
she takes Bottom for her 'true love', just as her husband wishes her
to when he casts a spell upon her eye, and she languishes for the
beastly creature's 'sake' (II.ii.34–35). Through the monstrous
appropriation of Bottom, Oberon successfully acquires a child –
the sweet Indian boy – whom he doubtless will tailor to suit his own
principles of futurity.

It is important to note that Oberon and Titania (and Puck, who is
the king's spritely minion and representative) are interested in
dominating their relationships with the human. But where the male
fairies choose the established – if jaded – methods of comic scorn to
control Bottom, Titania relies on mystical seduction to do the same.
Consequently, her command to her minions to '[t]ie up [her] lover's
tongue' and 'bring him silently' to her 'bower' (III.i.191,187)
resembles the erotic violence that accompanies the sadomasochistic
dynamic which, Deleuze would argue, may be interpreted as a 'path
of mutation precipitated through the actualisation of connections
among bodies that were previously only implicit' and which unravel
'new powers in the capacities of those bodies to act and respond'.[22]

On one level, the image of a tied-up Bottom feeds into the
carnivalesque violence of *charivari*, which often involved crude re-
enactments of the inversion of gender and power within matrimony.
That the bossy Titania manages to silence two male figures in the

play, one of them her husband and the other her proposed lover, surely makes her a ripe candidate for social punishment; an early modern audience may well have been aware of this potential as they watched the fairy queen order her minions to disempower Bottom. But the tongue-tied Bottom also conjures up the Deleuzean image of the masochist who relies on a ' "cold" oral mother' to provide 'an alternative source of psychosexual authority to the father' and thus expels 'the phallic power of the paternal' from his universe.[23] Titania's silencing of Bottom, then, 'is in reality a transmutation of cruelty from which the new man emerges'.[24] Bottom's enslavement to Titania, if it can be called that, leads to his experience of becoming. In his transformative stage not only is he freed from the scornful interventions of the likes of Puck and Oberon, actions that resemble the early modern social devices of shaming, but while with Titania and her train of fairies he is also capable of transcending the limits of temporality.

When he awakens at the end of Act IV, scene i, Bottom's speech suggests that he has not skipped a beat in the mechanicals' rehearsal of *Pyramus and Thisbe*. Finding himself alone in the woods, abandoned by his friends, he confronts what he can at best construe as his dream-like experience. He tries in vain to articulate it to/for himself and soon defers the task of narration to an unimaginable or 'bottomless' future:

> Man is but an ass if he go about to expound this dream. Methought I was – *there is no man can tell what Methought I was* – and methought I had – but man is but a patched fool if he will offer to say what methought I had. The eye of man hath not heard, the ear of man hath not seen, man's hand is not able to taste, his tongue to conceive, nor his heart to report what my dream was. *I will get Peter Quince to write a ballad of this dream*. It shall be called 'Bottom's Dream,' because it hath no bottom.
>
> (IV.i.203–12, emphasis added)

His promise is obviously funny. It is also disturbing because of its impossibility; for how is Peter Quince to give artistic salience to his friend's becoming when Bottom himself cannot intelligently articulate it? When he is reunited with his friends in the city, Bottom is unable to give words to his wondrous experience, even though he promises his companions that he is 'to discourse wonders' (IV.ii.26). The alternation between his recognition of the impossibility of narrative to explain becoming and his desire to 'tell [...] everything' is best understood through Deleuze's explanation in *The Logic of Sense* of Alice's experience of becoming when in Wonderland (IV.ii.28):

> It is language which fixes the limits [...], but it is language as well which transcends the limits and restores them to the infinite equivalence of an unlimited becoming. Hence the reversals which constitute Alice's adventures: the reversal of becoming larger and smaller [...]; the reversal of the day before and the day after [...]; the reversal of more and less [...]; the reversal of cause and effect.[25]

Narration cannot contain Bottom's experience, thereby rendering 'unlimited' his becoming. However much he struggles to articulate his experience, it is clear that he has not forgotten it, just like the young lovers, who recall in a haze their experiences within the fairy-laden forest.

Demetrius first attempts to give some shape to his experiences of becoming by referring to them as 'these things' that 'seem small and undistinguishable, | Like far off mountains turnèd into clouds' (IV.i.186–87). Hermia, on the other hand, believes that, owing to her transformed vision, 'everything seems double' (IV.i.189). As with Deleuze's Alice, who cannot determine 'which way' to turn because her travels take her 'always in both directions at the same time', so it is with the Athenian lovers, whose efforts at narrativizing their respective becomings fail because of the paradoxical tension within the experiences (*Logic of Sense*, p. 3). But unlike Bottom, who hopes in future to transcend through art (specifically 'a ballad') the limitations of language and express the 'infinite equivalence of an unlimited becoming', the young couples, on returning to the organized space of the city, quickly reterritorialize onto the established codes of marriage (*Logic of Sense*, p. 3). Their refusal to question the process of the renewal of their romantic entanglements, which has once again enabled the lovers to partake of the socioeconomic fruits of Egeus and Theseus's approval of their marriages, makes them subjects of 'regulated transformation', which, as Elizabeth Grosz explains in *Becomings*, is in direct opposition to the truly new experiences of identity:

> Predictable, measurable, regulated transformation seems a social prerequisite; but upheaval, the eruption of the event, the emergence of new alignments unpredicted within old networks seem to threaten to reverse all gains, [...] to place chaos and disorder at the heart of regulation and orderly progress.[26]

Keen to gain predictable social acceptance through their revised relationships, then, the Athenian lovers discard even the hazy recollections of their wild (culturally new) experiences. Their burden of inexplicable waking dreams is taken up by Bottom, who alone refuses to let go of his wild experiences but promises to share them with others. Although Theseus claims to the 'fair lovers' that he of their 'discourse [. . .] more will hear anon' (IV.i.176–77), he makes it perfectly clear to Hippolyta that he does not want to engage in such 'forms of things unknown' that only a 'poet's pen' can translate or 'name' (V.i.15–17). Similarly, after their initial confusion regarding their own consciousness, the lovers agree that they 'are awake' and will nostalgically 'recount' their past 'dreams' to each other en route to the temple. However, when they speak again, the lovers do not mention their experiences in the woods, but, along with Theseus the duke, ridicule the mechanicals' performance of *Pyramus and Thisbe*. Notably, we only hear from Demetrius and Lysander, even though Hermia and Helena are present at the performance. Doubly reterritorialized, the two female friends seem not only to have left behind their twinned experience of childhood friendship when they were '[l]ike to a double cherry, seeming parted, | But yet an union in partition' (III.ii.209–10), but, being married, they also embrace a chaste silence that distances them from their hitherto autonomous identities as mobile and articulate lovers. Ironically, the women's earlier state of mobility coincided with their willingness to explore fearlessly new realms of identity. When Demetrius finds himself plagued by Helena, he warns her against rape, the necessary consequence of her romantic exploration and wandering:

> You do impeach your modesty too much
> To *leave the city* and commit yourself
> Into the hands of one that loves you not,
> To trust the opportunity of night
> And the ill counsel of *a desert place*
> With the rich worth of your virginity.
>
> (II.i.214–19, emphasis added)

But the as yet unmarried Helena is unfazed by the Athenian's beastly threat of rape or death at the hands of 'wild beasts' (II.i.228). Instead, she embraces the opportunity to shift contemporary politics and the rhetoric of erotic chase. 'The story shall be changed' (II.i.230), she informs Demetrius, when she will successfully rewrite the dynamic between Apollo and Daphne to cast the nymph in the body of the pursuer, the Greek god as the object of her pursuit. The myth that Helena chooses to appropriate in her 'story' is central to her physical location at the moment of her utterance – in the woods outside Athens.

In Ovid's first book of *Metamorphoses*, Apollo, cursed by Cupid's arrow, follows Daphne through the woods in the hope that she will reciprocate his love. But the young god's desire for the nymph is quickly frustrated, as he learns that the object of his love has an untamable, independent spirit that is far removed from patriarchal heternormative modes of being:

> In woods and forrests is hir joy, the savage beasts to chase,
>   [. . .]
> Unwedded Phebe doth she haunt and follow as hir guide,
>   [. . .]
> Full many a wooer sought hir love, she lothing all the rout,
> Impacient and *without a man walkes all the woods about.*
> And as for Hymen, or for love, and wedlock often sought
> She tooke no care, they were the furthest end of all hir thought.[27]

Penaeus, the river god and father to Daphne, reminds his daughter of her duty to the patriarch of marrying and bearing him male heirs to carry forward his lineage (Book I, p. 584). But the nymph, 'hating as a haynous crime the bonde of bridely bed' (Book I, p. 585) pleads with her father to grant her a wish that would secure her maidenhood. Penaeus reluctantly gives in to Daphne's transgressive desire, but simultaneously warns his child that her chastity will eventually be threatened by her beauty, the limit of her own form. Penaeus's words come true all too soon. Driven by his desire for the beautiful lover of woods, Apollo catches up with Daphne and courts the maiden by assuring her that he is neither 'Carle nor countrie Clowne' but the son of '[t]he king of Gods' (Book I, pp. 623, 630–31). Daphne, however, is not charmed by Apollo's bloodlines or even his divine powers, and sneaks away from the scene, famously leaving the young lover in mid-sentence. Unfortunately for her, the violent god chases her down, 'even as when the greedie Grewnde doth course the sielie Hare' (Book I, p. 649). Exhausted and unable to withstand Apollo's gaze or his erotic pursuit, Daphne seeks her father's help and prays to him to transform her shape, so she may escape possession. Peneaeus once again gives in to his daughter's wish and transforms her into a tree that, even while its leaves and branches adorn Apollo's 'golden lockes' or '[q]uyver' (Book I, pp. 685–86), remains sexually impervious to the bellicose god.

Helena's reimagination of Daphne's transformation is consistent with her over-arching desire to effect a change in the politics within the play. As early as Act I, scene i, she wishes to 'to be [...] translated' so as to experience Demetrius's love through her friend Hermia's eyes (I.i.191). Recognizing the power of love, which can 'transpose' monstrous objects to 'form and dignity' (I.i.233), she plans accordingly to alter the future course of her romantic career. Helena divulges to Demetrius the secret of Hermia and Lysander's elopement and, confident that he will pursue the object of his love into the woods, decides to 'transpose' contemporary gender roles by adopting the role of pursuer and feasting her eyes upon her own lover, chasing him 'thither and back again' (I.i.251). Her wilful mobility is astonishing, specifically because she hopes as author to document the means through which she will bring about a change in women's position in the arena of romantic courtship. Despite changing the roles of Apollo and Daphne in her appropriated tale, Helena retains the sexual dynamic of the mythical figures; Daphne remains female, even as she hunts down her lover. Thus, in the future that she envisions for all her 'sex' women will actively 'fight for love as men may do' (II.i.240–41). Propelled by her authorial intent, Helena traps her lover 'within the wood' outside the realms of civil, patriarchal society (II.i.192), so that she may 'speed to catch' him (II.i.233). In the process, the woods, the site where Demetrius earlier states he 'shall do [...] mischief' to Helena, suddenly become the space where the young woman may experiment with her dangerous and subversive desire – in short, the location of her becoming. But as with all other moments of becoming in the play, this one is also reterritorialized. Promised Demetrius as reward for her return to the city (and its accompanying order of subservience), Helena promptly falls into line with patriarchal ideology, happily and silently following the figures of authority to the temple, the site of reterritorialization.

While Titania's return to her marriage is not accompanied by a perfect silence, her language is meek, her verse finally humbled to a recitation de-fanged of aggression and pride, the very qualities that marked her early speeches in the play. Although she retains her musicality, a characteristic that, as I have suggested above, the queen mobilized effectively to woo Bottom, her much abbreviated verse is now merely a part of Oberon's general magical scheme, her words sandwiched between the fairy king's authorial chant (V.i.382–413). The patriarchs of the earthly and fairy realms manage to assert through their respective articulations the direction of their subjects' futures. With an 'iron tongue' Theseus sends off the newly married couples 'to bed' (v.i.354–55); Oberon orders 'every fairy' to 'bless' the marriage beds of the mortals so that 'Never mole, harelip, nor scar | Nor mark prodigious such as are | Despisèd in nativity | Shall upon their children be' (v.i.402–7). Clearly, the leaders are eager to pave the way for heternormativity and patriarchally secured reproduction, to establish biological futurity as the fundamental means of imprinting the self onto the future. In fact, Oberon's spell specifically targets the prevention of such monstrous births as are 'the blots of nature's hand' (v.i.400). Instead he certifies the future as a time of 'sweet peace' in a space of 'safety' (v.i.409, 411).

In spite of his organizing chant, there is some unfinished business at the conclusion of *A Midsummer Night's Dream*. Bottom's troublesome memory that he wishes to eternalize in song, Titania's eagerness to learn about her recent experiences with the other, and the Athenian lovers' enchanted marriages are all remnants of becoming, aspects of uncertainty that even Puck's magic broom cannot sweep under the carpet. To varying degrees, the characters' 'demand to remember [. . .] aspires to define the present and prescribe the future' in ways that cannot be determined or controlled by Theseus and Oberon.[28] Their reordering of characters' desires, then, may all come to naught. The last words of the play, spoken by the troublemaker Puck, offer no resolution but instead plunge us into the vagaries of equivocation, and this anticipates the ungovernable and unpredictable movement that is integral to the experience of becoming. With the prospect of further becomings lurking in the shadows and applying a paradoxical force to the seemingly stabilized relations in the play, the future in *A Midsummer Night's Dream* is as uncertain and unassuring as Puck's honesty.

Notes

1   Gabriel Egan, *Green Shakespeare: From Ecopolitics to Ecocriticism* (London: Routledge, 2006); Douglas Bruster, *Shakespeare and the Question of Culture: Early Modern Literature and the Cultural Turn* (New York: Palgrave Macmillan, 2003); Ayanna Thompson, ed., *Colorblind Shakespeare: New Perspectives on Race and Performance* (New York: Routledge, 2006); Richard Wilson, *Shakespeare in French Theory: King of Shadows* (London: Routledge, 2007). By contrast, David Kastan's *Shakespeare After Theory* (New York: Routledge, 1999) or Tom McAlindon's *Shakespeare Minus Theory* (Aldershot: Ashgate, 2004) are representative texts that emerged from the cynical period in the marriage of literary studies and critical theory. Jonathan Culler and Kevin Lamb, eds, *Just Being Difficult? Academic Writing in the Public Arena* (Stanford, CA: Stanford University Press, 2003) offers a collection of essays that address similar anxiety about theory across the literary fields.
2   Jean Arnold, Lawrence Buell *et al.* 'Forum on Literatures of the Environment', *PMLA* 115 (October 1999), pp. 1089–104, p. 1091.

3   Garrett A. Sullivan, *Memory and Forgetting in English Renaissance Drama: Shakespeare, Marlowe, Webster* (Cambridge: Cambridge University Press, 2005).

4   Lisa Hopkins, *Shakespeare on the Edge: Border-Crossing in the Tragedies and the Henriad* (Aldershot: Ashgate, 2005).

5   Jacques Derrida, *Archive Fever: A Freudian Impression* (Chicago: University of Chicago Press, 1996), p. 68.

6   Gilles Deleuze and Félix Guattari, *A Thousand Plateaus: Capitalism and Schizophrenia* (Minneapolis, MN: University of Minnesota Press, 1987), p. 293. All further references will appear parenthetically in the text.

7   Adrian Parr, *The Deleuze Dictionary* (Edinburgh: Edinburgh University Press, 2005), p. 67.

8   Gilles Deleuze, *The Logic of Sense* (New York: Columbia University Press, 1990), pp. 1, 2. All further references will appear parenthetically in the text.

9   René Girard, *A Theater of Envy: William Shakespeare* (South Bend, IN: St Augustine's Press, 2004), p. 29.

10 For recent scholarship on the play that focuses on this speech, see Thomas Frosch's 'The Missing Child in *A Midsummer Night's Dream*', *American Imago: Psychoanalysis and the Human Sciences*, 64 (winter 2007), pp. 485–511, and Jill Ehnenn's '"An Attractive, Dramatic Exhibition"?: Female Friendship, Shakespeare's Women, and Female Performativity in 19th-Century Britain', *Women's Studies: An Interdisciplinary Journal*, 26 (1997), pp. 315–41. For postcolonial and materialist readings of this scene, see especially Margo Hendricks's '"Obscured By Dreams": Race, Empire, and Shakespeare's *A Midsummer Night's Dream*', *Shakespeare Quarterly*, 47 (spring 1996), pp. 37–60, and Ania Loomba's 'The Great Indian Vanishing Trick – Colonialism, Property, and the Family in *A Midsummer Night's Dream*', in *A Feminist Companion to Shakespeare*, ed. Dympna Callaghan (Malden: Blackwell Publishers, 2000), pp. 163–87.

11 William Slights, 'The Changeling in *A Dream*', *Studies in English Literature 1500–1900*, 28 (1988), pp. 259–72.

12 Caroline Bicks, *Midwiving Subjects in Shakespeare's England: Women and Gender in the Early Modern World* (Aldershot: Ashgate, 2003).

13 Titania's emphasis on the word 'rich' in her speech about her votaress's wealth is crucial to our understanding of her investment in the woman. This sense of investment is only heightened when it is coupled with the queen's indication of her entitlement to the Indian boy: her votaress's womb, Titania claims, is 'rich' not with the mortal's own child, but rather with the fairy queen's 'young squire' (II.i.131).

14 Stevie Davies, *The Feminine Reclaimed: The Idea of Woman in Shakespeare, Spenser, and Milton* (Lexington, KY: University of Kentucky Press, 1986), p. 26.

15 Jan Kott, 'Titania and the Ass's Head', in *A Midsummer Night's Dream: Critical Essays*, ed. Dorothea Kehler (New York: Garland, 1998), pp. 107–25, pp. 118, 119. All further references will appear parenthetically in the text.

16 Philippa Berry, 'Nomadic Eros: Remapping Knowledge in *A Midsummer Night's Dream*', in *Forgetting in Early Modern English Literature and Culture: Lethe's Legacies*, Routledge Studies in Renaissance Literature and Culture, ed. Christopher Ivic and Grant Williams (New York: Routledge, 2004), pp. 137–50, p. 138.

17 Deleuze and Guattari, *A Thousand Plateaus*, pp. 239–40.

18 Ambroise Paré, *On Monsters and Marvels*, ed. and trans. Janis Pallister (Chicago: University of Chicago Press 1982). All further references will appear parenthetically in the text.

19 Janis Pallister points to the sixteenth-century French medical community's opposition to Paré's publications. The faculty of medicine was in part appalled by Paré's unification in his writing of the fields of medicine and surgery. But they were also concerned that his books, published in French and not Latin or

Greek, made medical secrets cheap, readily 'available to anyone and everyone who could read' (Paré, *On Monsters and Marvels*, trans. Pallister, p. xxiv). Whereas Pallister clearly interprets Paré's cataloguing of monsters as one conducted in 'the spirit of critical investigation' (p. xxv), his contemporaries and even some of his early translators (notably Malgaigne) identified a carnivalesque delight in his work.

20   Gail Kern Paster, and Skiles Howard, *A Midsummer Night's Dream: Texts and Contexts* (Boston, MA: Bedford, 1999), p. 301.

21   Andrew Stott, ' "The Fondness, the Filthiness": Deformity and Laughter in Early Modern Comedy', *Upstart Crow*, 24 (2004), pp. 15–24.

22   Parr, *The Deleuze Dictionary*, p. 145. Deleuze suggests that even though sadism and masochism are fundamentally different, they are both invested in the invention of 'new ways of feeling and thinking' (Ronald Bogue, *Deleuze on Literature* [London: Routledge, 2003], p. 15).

23   Nick Mansfield, *Masochism: The Art of Power* (Westport, CT: Praeger, 1997), p. 70.

24   Gilles Deleuze and Leopold von Sacher-Masoch, *Masochism: An Interpretation of Coldness and Cruelty: Together with the Entire Text of Venus in Furs* (New York: Braziller, 1971), p. 12.

25   Deleuze, *The Logic of Sense*, p. 3.

26   Elizabeth A. Grosz,, 'Thinking the New: Of Futures Yet Unthought' in *Becomings: Explorations in Time, Memory, and Futures*, ed. Elizabeth A. Grosz (Ithaca, NY: Cornell University Press, 1999), pp. 15–28, p. 28.

27   Ovid, *Metamorphoses*, ed. John Frederick Nims, trans. Arthur Golding (Philadelphia, PA: P. Dry Books, 2000), Book I, pp. 573–80; emphasis added. All further references will appear parenthetically in the text.

28   Sullivan, *Memory and Forgetting in English Renaissance Drama*, p. 10.

CHAPTER EIGHT

A Survey of Resources

Adrienne L. Eastwood

Uses in the Classroom

A Midsummer Night's Dream has enjoyed a multi-faceted critical history as well as a consistently vigorous performance history. The play seems continually to inspire interpretative shifts and provide the basis for increasing nuances in understanding. Other chapters in this volume discuss current and historical trends in detail; this chapter is designed to provide an overview of the available resources on the play for students interested in broadening their study beyond close work with the text.

The thematic richness of *Dream* is manifested by the variety of approaches to the text in the university classroom. The play's relatively uncomplicated plot line and the universal and trans-historical appeal of the love-potion comedy make it accessible; the variety of ways it has been discussed by literary critics and historical scholars give it theoretical depth. Since the early 1980s, scholars have noticed that the central conflict in the play involves the replacement of female relationships with ones that conform to patriarchal norms.[1] Therefore, professors and lecturers are likely to approach the play through an examination of the process of female containment in marriage, focusing most centrally on the idea that love (like writing plays or acting) is not spontaneous, but rather involves the imagination: 'Love looks not with the eyes, but with the mind' (I.i.234).[2] However, the imagination, as Theseus reminds us, can be fooled: 'How easy is a bush supposed a bear!' (V.i.22). Marriage, and the gender hierarchy it depends upon, is similarly conditional. So in my classes, for example, I tend to examine the various ways in which this play undermines the multiple marriages that are celebrated in Act v. Since the marriage of Theseus and Hippolyta frames the play, instructors and tutors may well focus on the character of the displaced Amazonian queen, to whom Shakespeare gives some of the blandest lines in the play. Does Hippolyta, essentially a prisoner of war, actually *want* to marry Theseus? A good discussion could revolve around the possibilities for her characterization that might be accessed through performance – such things as gesture and costume – that could cast a doubtful light on this central relationship. Since Amazonian myths during Elizabeth's reign take on an ambiguous quality (either as positive symbols of female power or as elicitors of male anxieties about female power)[3] this character could be read as similarly paradoxical.

Responding to those critics who, following Jan Kott, interpret *Dream* more darkly, instructors also might discuss Theseus and Hippolyta's fairy counterparts. The argument between Oberon and Titania that provides a central conflict for the play is a probable point of focus, the resolution of which could be viewed as tenuous. Both Hippolyta and Titania are ultimately denied options; they are forced – by sword or drugs – into compliance with patriarchal control. Instructors might present this idea as a way to encourage students to begin to see the play as more complicated on the topic of gender and marriage than the simple plot line suggests.

The acceptance of socially prescribed gender roles – by no means a given either in Shakespeare's day or our own – is a topic that instructors and tutors employ to help students to bridge the historical and cultural gap between sixteenth-century England and today. Robert Lublin, for example, combined the use of performance in the classroom with a discussion of feminist history. Lublin had students memorize II.ii (the scene in which Lysander tries to convince Hermia to have sex with him) and then led them, through discussion, to appreciate how much is at stake for Hermia in maintaining her virginity. Linking her anxiety with the relentless construction of patriarchal gender norms that seems to be advocated by the play, Lublin provocatively questions the ethics of using such a text in the classroom. He concludes that by teaching students about 'historically determined definitions of gender and sexuality', they might begin to interrogate their own, similarly historically determined, understanding of these categories.[4]

Performance can also be employed to further students' appreciation of Shakespeare's use of language and stagecraft to convey meaning. John Wilders describes a workshop he conducted in which he had students consider how the plays are divided into acts and scenes, emphasizing that these divisions are not consistent in quarto and *Folio* versions of the play.[5] By having the students enact various scenes from the play, he was able to help them discover how Shakespeare constructs 'visual as well as verbal impressions on the audience'.[6] Patricia Parker focuses on an editorial inconsistency in the printing of the *Pyramus and Thisbe* episode that derives from differences between the 1600 and 1619 quarto versions and the *Folio* edition of *Dream*.[7] Parker and her students then productively compared Shakespeare's usage with that of Ovid's *Metamorphoses* (in Golding's translation). Parker was able to get her students to uncover a complex instance of wordplay that they then connected back to the play.

Survey of Critical Resources

This section provides an overview of the various available editions of *Dream* and resources, both in print and online, that you might use as starting points for further research.

Survey of editions

Most of the recent editions of Shakespeare's *Dream* include detailed and informative introductions that contain either referenced footnotes or a bibliography, both of which can be plumbed for further reading. The Oxford World's Classics edition (general editor Stanley Wells) has a thoroughly researched and annotated introduction by Peter Holland that breaks the play into thematic categories, for example: Dreams, Fairies, Robin Goodfellow, Theseus and Hippolyta, The Lovers and *Pyramus and Thisbe*. The footnotes refer liberally to articles from a variety of critical perspectives – from psychoanalytic articles to new historical texts. Similarly, the Arden edition, edited by Harold F. Brooks, has an informative and detailed introduction that provides commentary on style, plot, themes, characters and setting.

A more recent edition, published by Bedford St Martin's Press (edited by Gail Kern Paster and Skiles Howard), responds to advances in new historicist research trends by including a 'Contextual Readings' section with excerpts from relevant texts also printed in the sixteenth century. These are presented with informative headnotes that provide a useful context for, and analysis of, the primary texts.

The New Cambridge Shakespeare, edited by R. A. Foakes, has been newly updated to include a discussion of selected theatrical productions of the play and a consideration of recent scholarship.

Foakes's edition has a revised reading list with a broader scope than earlier editions.

Companions to Shakespeare

Other great sources for beginning research are the 'companion' texts distributed by several of the larger publishing houses. Cambridge University Press's *Companion* series is probably the most comprehensive. Cambridge publishes a general *Companion to Shakespeare* edited by Margreta de Grazia and Stanley Wells. This book provides students with a detailed overview of Shakespeare's culture and works, but it also includes essays by prominent scholars on topics pertinent to the plays themselves, such as genre, the court and the city, gender and sexuality, London's 'outsiders' and English history. The *Companion* also features essays about the ongoing, global reception of Shakespeare today on stage and in film. Perhaps most useful to students is the section that summarizes twentieth-century criticism and the following chapter on reference books and available complete editions of the plays and poetry.

The *Cambridge Companion to Shakespeare* is an excellent resource for general information, but the series includes several other *Companion* texts for the student who wishes to research a more specific topic. The following are some of the available topics published by Cambridge that might assist you with further research on *Dream*. *Shakespeare on Stage*, edited by Stanley Wells and Sarah Stanton, which is a thorough account of Shakespeare in performance across time and around the globe. *Shakespearean Comedy*, edited by Alexander Leggatt includes essays on Shakespeare and the comic mode by top scholars in the field. This book provides a solid grounding in the comic tradition and offers a clear contexualization of Shakespeare's contribution to it. *Shakespeare and Popular Culture*, edited by Robert Shaughnessy is a collection of essays that discuss various interpretations – and appropriations – of Shakespeare's texts by television, film, fiction, and 'samplings' of Shakespeare in these, and other, media.

Blackwell Publishing offers a *Companion to Shakespeare* as well, edited by David Scott Kastan. This volume provides an exhaustive historical context for the study of Shakespeare, featuring contributions from some of the top scholars in the field. The topics provide students with a thorough grounding in the political thought and social structure of Elizabethan England.

The *Feminist Companion to Shakespeare*, edited by Dympna Callaghan, is also published by Blackwell. The collected essays in this text cover a wide range of topics relevant to feminist inquiry including sexuality, race and ethnicity, queerness, politics, economics and the body. The essays in this volume provide an important foundation for much of the twenty-first-century scholarship in feminist Shakespeare studies.

The *Bedford Companion to Shakespeare*, edited by Russ McDonald, is particularly valuable since, like the separate edition of *Dream* discussed above, it also includes excerpts from relevant early modern texts that illuminate aspects of Shakespeare's life and culture.

Guide to web-based resources

As most students and scholars of Shakespeare are aware, there are a host of internet sources available on the world-wide web. In fact, there are so many that finding something one needs online can be a daunting (and time-consuming) process. This section provides a guide to the more useful and reputable sources.

Study guides

Much to the chagrin of many professors, most students know how to access 'Cliff's Notes' (www.cliffnotes.com) and 'Spark Notes' (www.sparknotes.com) online. These sites are useful in that they provide plot summaries of the plays as well as general character and thematic analyses. The main problem with such sites is that the analyses tend to be reductive, superficial and devoid of critical or historical context. They might help with the basics, but students should not rely on them too greatly.

Several of my students have mentioned the helpfulness of 'No Fear Shakespeare' (www.nfs.sparknotes.com), a site that offers side-by-side 'modern translations' of Shakespeare's poetry into contemporary English.

Research-centred sites

There are some online study guides that do provide some analytical depth and historical background.[8] 'Shake Sphere: A Comprehensive Study Guide for the World of William Shakespeare' (www.cummingsstudyguides.net/xShakeSph.html), created and maintained by Michael J. Cummings (a writer and college instructor in Williamsburg, PA), offers a searchable site containing study guides for each of the plays and long poems that includes a discussion of themes and characters, as well as study questions and essay topics for each text. This site also includes information on Shakespeare's life and times, the early modern theatre scene, and available editions and concordances (including links to searchable websites like the eminently useful 'Open Source Shakespeare', www.opensourceshakespeare.org) of Shakespeare's works. 'Shake Sphere' also includes links to free, full-text versions of each of the plays and poems, but unfortunately, these are not annotated. One unique feature of the site is a list of all the DVDs of Shakespeare films that are available from Amazon.com, organized by play.

Terry A. Gray's site, 'Mr. William Shakespeare and the Internet' (http://Shakespeare.palomar.edu/criticism.htm) is a comprehensive, well-organized collection of links to other sites about Shakespeare and Elizabethan and Jacobean culture. Wikipedia[9] links to each of the plays are available here, and there is also a link to 'Shakespeare Quartos', furnished by the British Library, that offers information on the creation of the plays, sources and publication information on each of the extant versions. For example, two quartos exist for *A Midsummer Night's Dream*, and the British Library, which owns these texts, has posted information about each. Links to essays and short articles on Shakespearean topics, as well as links to other primary texts from the period, are also available.

Exploring any of these sites might give you ideas for further research, but the 'Shakespeare Oxford Library' (www.shakespear-e_oxford.com/sos/libry.htm) is particularly useful in this regard. This site, put up and maintained by the Shakespeare Oxford Society, is heavily dedicated to the authorship debate, but it has also collected a number of links to digital versions of other early modern primary texts, reviews of scholarly books, book reviews and links to journals, periodicals and some electronically available articles.

If, like many students, you want to get a better sense of Shakespeare's culture, The Folger Shakespeare Library has an excellent website (www.folger.edu/) dedicated to showcasing their collection and providing teachers, students and other scholars with resources about Shakespeare. This site offers lesson plans for teachers, as well as a fascinating 'Discover Shakespeare' section you might explore to get more information on Shakespeare's life and works, and publications about Shakespeare. It also has a fascinating section on 'Shakespeare in American Life' that addresses the often contentious reception of Shakespeare's plays in America and the effect of the plays on the construction of the American national identity. The site has links to other sites of interest as well as relevant podcasts.

Because Shakespeare is often only fully realized through performance, there are an increasing number of online resources available that focus on stage productions. 'Internet Shakespeare Editions' (http://internetshakespeare.uvic.ca/index.html) includes a searchable database of performance materials on more than 1000 film and stage productions. The site also contains a 'Resources' section featuring selected essays called 'Shakespeare around the Globe'.

Your library may own a great new database called 'Shakespeare Collections' that offers full-text access to Shakespeare criticism and performance reviews. Check with your library's database page or ask a librarian for assistance. If you don't have access to 'Shakespeare Collections', you can find indexes of performance reviews published in *Shakespeare Bulletin* (www.shakespeare-bulletin.org) or *Shakespeare Newsletter* (www.iona.edu/snl/) directly from their websites.

For those of you who would like to either 'listen in' or participate in the ongoing conversations about Shakespearean topics, check out 'Shaksper: An International Electronic Conference' at (www.shaksper.net/). This is essentially an email discussion list, but it is well organized, edited and moderated, and includes working papers submitted to the list. It's sophisticated, but could be illuminating.

Overview of the Critical Landscape

In 1998, a collection of critical essays on *A Midsummer Night's Dream*, edited by Dorothea Kehler, appeared as a volume in the series Shakespeare Criticism published by Garland.[10] Kehler's text begins with an invaluable 'Bibliographic Survey of the Criticism' that spans almost four centuries of critical response to this play. The text also includes several of the most influential articles on the play from a variety of critical perspectives. Kehler's volume remains the definitive survey of criticism up through the twentieth century, and it is where I would recommend that students turn to get a sense of the critical life of this play. The section of Chapter 1 on the twentieth century (pp. 11–61) offers a crucial overview of the trajectory of criticism that informs all of the essays I discuss in this section.[11]

Since Kehler's book was published, criticism on *Dream* has followed several theoretical threads. In general, the work has clustered around particular elements in the play. New historicist and psychoanalytic approaches have tended to look closely at fairy lore, providing an important cultural context for Shakespeare's deployment of fairies in the play. The Indian boy, who is referred to in the play but is not indicated in the stage directions, serves as the hub of numerous postcolonial analyses, including several that are deeply grounded in history. The mechanicals and their performance of *Pyramus and Thisbe* in Act v serve as material for a number of different essays, including several interpretive approaches. Other exciting areas of research involve appropriations or interpretations of the play that have appeared in popular culture media including film, stage performance, non-traditional theatrical modes and graphic novels. It is important to note that there are many ways in which these three categories intersect with each other, often merging critical modes. The following is a selective overview of the main areas of research done on the play since the turn of the twenty-first century.

Fairies and fairy lore

Dorothea Kehler's chapter in this volume outlines much of the work that new historicist critics have done recently to elucidate early modern beliefs and attitudes about fairies and fairy lore. As this is an important thread of the current scholarship, I add here a few additional articles for your reference. Responding to Wendy Wall – who argues that Robin Goodfellow and his broom resonate not only with beliefs about industrious fairies, but also with the social conventions governing the female domestic sphere[12] – Douglas Bruster suggests that Puck's sweeping also resonated with the masculine duties of the servant, labourer or apprentice.[13] Diane Hunter reframes the conversation about the fairies in *Dream* to further encompass a Minoan/Celtic aspect that she sees as opposing the Athenian/Elizabethan sensibility represented in the play by Theseus and the lovers. For Hunter, the Celtic world is associated with an occult and mysteriously creative aspect of the unconscious that is ultimately represented by the narrative of the play being absorbed by the English national consciousness.[14]

In *Why Shakespeare?*, Catherine Belsey also writes about connections between Shakespeare and early English fairy stories. She argues that *Dream* 'takes its own world of magic seriously without asking its audience to believe in fairies. Instead, its creatures of fantasy have the effect of deconstructing the conventional opposition between fact and fiction, reality and dream'.[15]

The mysterious Indian boy

Ania Loomba, in 2000, pointed out that colonialist discourses associated with trade and travel are present in *Dream*, and that these intersect with discourses of gender and the family. Since then, critics have found various ways to explore and explain the mysterious and sometimes contradictory references – particularly to India – that season the play. Responding directly to Loomba, as well as to earlier work by Margo Hendricks and Allen Dunn,[16] R.W. Desai reminds readers that *Dream* was written and performed roughly 150 years before England colonized India. Desai suggests, therefore, that the relationship between England and India was less exploitative than previously argued. Instead, England was engaged in a competition with Portugal for trading supremacy in India, a struggle eventually resolved in favour of England with the establishment of the East India Trading Company in 1600. Desai provocatively links this competition allegorically with the struggle between Titania and Oberon for the Indian boy.[17] In a similarly historicized piece, Bindu Malieckal connects the Indian boy to the matrilineal Muslims of Malabar (a precolonial name for Kerala).[18]

Because of its references to India, *Dream* has been singled out as illustrative of the complex, postcolonial clash of cultures between East and West. Interestingly, *Dream* has recently been taken up by Indians themselves, in each case engaging with the psychological complexities of the relationship between the former colony and the poet of its colonizer. David Mason, for example, analyses a Sanskrit translation of *Dream* called *Vasantikasvapnam* (translated as *A Dream in Spring*). This version, Mason argues, creates a 'hybrid text' that uses Shakespearean cachet to enhance Sanskrit drama.[19] Similar issues are addressed in performance and through literature. An Indian version of *Dream* – commissioned and produced by the British Council in India, and directed by Tim Supple – celebrated and embraced the exotic. The actors spoke some lines in English and others in Hindi, Bengali, Tamil, Malayalam etc. The choreography and music also pointed to a merging of eastern and western cultural elements. Similarly, in the novel *Eastwords*, by Bangladeshi Kalyan Ray, we get the back-story of Titania's votaress and the birth and later abduction of Puck. This magical tale is told by a narrator who addresses himself directly to Shakespeare, oscillating between indignation and reverence in a manner deeply resonant of an ambivalent postcolonial subjectivity.

Thomas Frosch explains the Indian boy's simultaneous presence and absence (he is referred to, yet he does not, according to Shakespeare's playtext, appear on stage) in psychoanalytic terms. According to Frosch, the narrative structure of the play mirrors a particular trajectory of the psychological transition from childhood to adulthood, and then back to an idealized childhood that is in keeping with the play's 'comic vision'.[20]

Pyramus, Thisbe, and the Wall
Scholars have found much to elucidate by focusing on the play-within-the-play in *Dream*. Alexander Leggatt analyses 'walls' either

as actual walls, represented walls (such as the one played by Snout in *Pyramus and Thisbe*), or as divisions between characters in both *Dream* and *Timon of Athens*. For Leggatt, these partitions vanish, as Snout does once he has his 'part discharged so' (V.i.203), giving place to new unities.[21] Similarly, Stephen Booth discusses several 'image patterns' in the play including an array of 'dog' references.[22] In a detailed analysis that also focuses on *Pyramus and Thisbe*, Peter Happé compares Ovid's version of this myth with three later texts, one of which is Shakespeare's.[23] Using a different approach, Tom Pettitt historicizes the *Pyramus and Thisbe* episode, linking it to Elizabethan household revels, whose function was to strengthen the reciprocal relationship among social degrees. Pettitt suggests that the interlude has a similar function in Shakespeare's play.[24]

Pop culture and performance

One of the more recent lines of scholarship on Shakespeare traces and theorizes its appearance in popular media such as comics and film. Neil Gaiman includes a fascinating rendition of *A Midsummer Night's Dream* in Volume 19 of the graphic novel series *The Sandman*. A group of current articles praise the collaborative work of Gaiman and the artist Charles Vess and explore the intersections between this art form and drama. For example, Kurt Lancaster observes that the divisions between 'high' and 'low' art that some have used to marginalize comics have themselves been applied to Shakespeare at various times. Using Gaiman's *Dream* as an example, Lancaster theorizes the arbitrariness of such divisions.[25] John Pendergast finds Gaiman's comic book is an ideal medium for the expression of a Shakespearean text since both writers seem to view their work as 'a product of the interaction of social conventions and norms with myth'.[26]

A film version of Shakespeare's play directed by Michael Hoffman, which came out in 1999, inspired several articles that have been published in the past few years, primarily discussing the portrayal of Bottom by Kevin Kline. The unconventional decision to give Bottom a shrewish wife, who appears as a character but is not given any lines, elicited a comment by Nicholas Jones, who feels that such additions effectively obscure the theme of transformation that is present in the play.[27] Kline's Bottom is not ultimately transformed by his experience with Titania or with the mechanicals, because he returns in the end to his original existence. Both Jones and Stephen Buhler notice that Hoffman's film erases the gender conflicts that are present in the playtext.[28] Offering another perspective, Frank Riga interprets Hoffman's film positively, viewing his directorial decisions as appropriately giving Bottom's character a serious treatment.[29]

Annotated Bibliography

The following bibliography includes major texts published since 2000. In general, I have concentrated on books or articles that take *Dream* as their main subject, or books that contain a useful chapter that focuses on the play. I have omitted performance reviews, dissertations and notes.

Belsey, Catherine, *Why Shakespeare?* (New York: Palgrave, 2007). This book traces the connections between English fairy stories and Shakespeare's plays. Chapter 5 argues that the supernatural realm in *Dream* 'has the effect of deconstructing the conventional opposition between fact and fiction, reality and dream' (p. 87).

Boehrer, Bruce, 'Economies of Desire in *A Midsummer Night's Dream*', *Shakespeare Studies* 32 (2004), pp. 99–117. According to Boehrer, bestiality and same-sex attachments (both male and female) in *Dream* cohere to represent early modern anxieties about heterosexual bonds and marriage. These 'economies of desire', he argues, 'may be characterized as the competing impulses to embrace and to repudiate alterity' (p. 114). Boehrer concludes that this helps to explain the darker interpretations of the play that have been circulating since Jan Kott's influential chapter from *Shakespeare Our Contemporary*.[30]

Booth, Stephen, 'A Discourse on the Witty Partition of *A Midsummer Night's Dream*', in *Inside Shakespeare: Essays on the Blackfriar's Stage*, ed. Paul Menzer (Selinsgrove, PA: Susquehanna University Press, 2006), pp. 216–22. This article is derived from a conference paper in which, in addition to wryly poking fun at poststructuralist critics, Booth comments on the image patterns in *Dream*. He notices that in addition to repeated references to the moon, the play also includes a pattern of 'dog' references, and also a varied use of the word 'part' and its assortment of meanings.

Bruster, Douglas, *Shakespeare and the Question of Culture: Early Modern Literature and the Cultural Turn* (New York: Palgrave, 2003). Bruster refigures the conclusion that Wendy Wall (referenced below) draws about Puck's sweeping at the close of *Dream*. Whereas Wall finds the sweeping activity to be gendered feminine, Bruster sees it as instead masculine, since it also invokes duties associated with domestic labourers, servants and apprentices.

Buccola, Regina, *Fairies, Fractious Women, and the Old Faith: Fairy Lore in Early Modern British Drama and Culture* (Selinsgrove, PA: Susquehanna University Press, 2006). This book provides much historical and cultural information about fairy lore and its impact on early modern society. While the entire book is of interest in this regard, the first chapter ('The Story Shall Be Changed', pp. 58–82) takes *Dream* as its subject, connecting the fairies with the other female characters in the play. Buccola demonstrates that through this connection, a possibility for female power emerges that coexists with the narrative of female containment.

Buhler, Stephen M., 'Textual and Sexual Anxieties in Michael Hoffman's Film of *A Midsummer Night's Dream*', *Shakespeare Bulletin* 22.3 (2004), pp. 49–61. Buhler takes issue with Hoffman's film version of the play because, as he demonstrates, it erases the complexities about gender and power with which the play engages. Hoffman, according to Buhler, does not seem to wish to offend (and therefore alienate) any audience members, and as a result he erases the elements in the play that question or challenge the establishment of patriarchal authority. This critique raises important questions about the ethics of editing and interpreting a source text.

Burke, Jessica, ' "How Now, Spirit! Whither Wander You?": Diminution: The Shakespearean Misconception and the Tolk-ienian Ideal of Faerie', in *Tolkien and Shakespeare: Essays on Shared Themes and Language*, ed. Janet Brennan Croft (Jefferson, NC: McFarland & Co., 2007), pp. 25–41. As a guiding question, Burke asks: how did fairies become the trivial figures found in Disney movies? She explores the role of Shakespeare's *Dream* in bringing about this 'diminution'.

Burke, Kenneth, 'Why *A Midsummer Night's Dream*?', *Shakespeare Quarterly* 57.3 (2006), pp. 297–308. In an engaging argument, Burke suggests that, as in *Coriolanus*, *Dream* encodes a 'socio-psychotic' relationship between the aristocracy and the working class. Unlike the tragedy, however, Shakespeare's comedy is invested in smoothing over the anxieties associated with this relationship. According to Burke, the class tension represents larger competing cultural tensions between 'new humanism' and 'technologism'. Just as the play is built upon the convergence of three worlds – including the not-quite-anachronistic references to the fairy world – *Dream* presents, in the staging of *Pyramus and Thisbe*, a 'medicinal nostalgic fantasy' that combines and defuses technologism (p. 307). Burke sees the play as 'a fanciful embodiment of the Humanistic attitude' (p. 307).

Clarke, Bruce, 'Paradox and the Form of Metamorphosis: Systems Theory in *A Midsummer Night's Dream*', *Intertexts* 8.2 (2004), pp. 173–87. In an interesting interdisciplinary approach, Clarke argues that at the core of *Dream* is a paradox that parallels Niklas Luhmann's 'Paradox of Observing Systems'. In the play, the 'metamorphic turn-about' of the narrative shifts from '*the transformation of observation* – as when fickle male lovers turn their erotic gaze from one female to the next – to *the observation of transformation*' as characters observe others in the process of transformation (p. 184). Clarke implies that the same formula works when considering the metatheatrics of the play itself.

Corrigan, Alan, 'Jazz, Shakespeare, and Hybridity: A Script Excerpt from *Swingin' the Dream*', *Borrowers and Lenders: The Journal of Shakespeare and Appropriation* 1.1 (2005), online: www.borrowers.uga.edu. Corrigan details the 1939 swing version of Shakespeare's play and includes a thorough discussion of the production concept as well as some information on the reception and an excerpt from the script. The article includes MP3 samples of music inspired by the production (just click on the MP3 icon while you're reading).

Desai, R. W., 'England, the Indian Boy, and the Spice Trade in *A Midsummer Night's Dream*', in *India's Shakespeare*, ed. Poonam Trivedi and Dennis Bartholomeusz (Newark, DE: University of Delaware Press, 2005), pp. 141–57. Responding to earlier work by Margo Hendricks and Allen Dunn, Desai reminds readers that when *A Midsummer Night's Dream* was written and performed, England was involved in a struggle with Portugal over trading supremacy in India. Desai offers strong historical evidence to support the claim that the relationship between India and England represented by the struggle between Oberon and Titania for the Indian boy reflects England's manoeuvrings in regard to trade prior to the establishment of the East India Company in 1600.

Do Rozario, Rebecca-Anne C., 'Just a Little Bit Fey: What's at the Bottom of *The Lord of the Rings* and *A Midsummer Night's Dream*?', in *Tolkien and Shakespeare: Essays on Shared Themes and Language*, ed. Janet Brennan Croft (Jefferson, NC: McFarland & Co., 2007), pp. 42–59. As the title suggests, the author connects the Hobbits in *The Lord of the Rings* with the rude mechanicals in *Dream*. She discovers that both serve as more than mediations between the 'fey' supernatural realm and the natural one; in her analysis, they represent the 'uncanny' possibility of the unknown (p. 56).

Frosch, Thomas R., 'The Missing Child in *A Midsummer Night's Dream*', *American Imago* 64.4 (2008), pp. 485–511. This article takes a psychoanalytic approach to explaining the problem of the Indian boy who, as Frosch's title suggests, does not appear onstage in the play. Frosch interprets the narrative structure of the play as representative of 'psychological development' from a nostalgic vision of childhood, through adulthood and then back to a version of childhood that offers a different 'idealization' of youth. Frosch concludes that the 'comic vision' that closes the play is therefore psychologically fulfilling, with the promise of a new beginning.

Hale, David G., '"Her Indian Boy": Postcolonial Criticism and Performance on Film and Television', *Shakespeare in Southern Africa* 16 (2004), pp. 53–57. Hale discovers that in performance (at least on screen), the staging of the Indian boy does not support the critics'[31] claim that his presence is suggestive of early English imperialism.

Happé, Peter, '*Pyramus and Thisbe*: Rhetoricians and Shakespeare', in *Medieval Texts and Cultures of Northern Europe* (Turnhout: Brepols, 2006), pp. 149–68. A comparison of the *Pyramus and Thisbe* story in three sixteenth-century European texts (one of which is Shakespeare's) with Ovid's text. Happé concludes that each writer pays careful and subtle homage to Ovid.

Hunt, Maurice, 'A Speculative Political Allegory in *A Midsummer Night's Dream*', *Comparative Drama* 34.4 (2000–01), pp. 423–53. Cautiously, but with convincing insistence, Hunt argues that one can locate in *Dream* a veiled allegory involving Elizabeth I's decision to behead her cousin Mary, and her subsequent relationships with Mary's son James, and Essex.

Hunter, Diane, 'Cultural Politics of Fantasy in *A Midsummer Night's Dream*', *PsyArt: A Hyperlink Journal for the Psychological Study of the Arts* (2003), online: www.clas.ufl.edu/ipsa/journal/2003_hunter01.shtml. Hunter argues that the play presents us with two opposing but also similar realms: the Athenian/Elizabethan world (represented by Theseus and the lovers) and a Minoan/Celtic world (represented by the fairies). She argues that as the play contrasts and joins these two realms, it presents an English subjectivity in which the Celtic 'imaginary functions as a creative repository of occulted power and infantile unconscious'. The play, in Hunter's formulation, enacts the process by which the Celtic is absorbed into the English national consciousness.

Jess-Cooke, Carolyn, '"The Promised End" of Cinema: Portraits of Cinematic Apocalypse in 21st Century Shakespearean Cinema',

Literature/Film Quarterly 34.2 (2006), pp. 161–68. A discussion of current cinematic trends applied to Shakespeare's plays as they are 're-imagined' for different purposes for today's audiences. Part of the essay focuses on Cristine Edzard's *Children's Midsummer Night's Dream* (2001) – a film that Jess-Cooke identifies as a 'prequilization' of Shakespeare's play (p. 161). Jess-Cooke argues that this film (along with the several others she discusses) provide an alternate set of beginnings that in turn reorient the narrative of the playtext. She views this process as productive – an effect that holds promise for the future of the cinema.

Jones, Nicholas, 'Bottom's Wife: Gender and Voice in Hoffman's *Dream*', *Literature Film Quarterly* 32.2 (2004), pp. 126–33. Taking Hoffman's *Dream* as his topic, Jones suggests that the director's decisions, specifically related to the addition of the character of Bottom's wife and the operatic score, combine to trap the film in a 'virtual fantasy' that offers no real possibility of fulfillment.

Karimi-Hakak, Mahmood, 'Exiled to Freedom: A Memoir of Censorship in Iran', *The Drama Review* 47.4 (2003), pp. 17–50. This is a first-person account of an Iranian director who suffered his production of *Dream* to be closed by censors, and endured prosecution and exile for 'Raping the Public's Innocence' (p. 17). Not only does Karimi-Hakak provide a fascinating account of the process of getting a production approved under the intense scrutiny of the officials, he carefully reconstructs the aftermath of the play's closure.

Lamb, Mary Ellen, 'Taken by the Fairies: Fairy Practices and the Production of Popular Culture in *A Midsummer Night's Dream*', *Shakespeare Quarterly* 51.3 (2000), pp. 277–312. Lamb argues that the representation of the fairies in *Dream* is both 'profoundly social and ultimately political'. In Shakespeare's hands, the traditional fairies (which she outlines in detail) transform to conform to more courtly and elite standards and tastes. The various fairies in *Dream* constitute a site of struggle between 'high' and 'low' culture as these categories began to emerge from an inclusive 'common culture'.

Lancaster, Kurt, 'Neil Gaiman's "A Midsummer Night's Dream": Shakespeare Integrated into Popular Culture', *Journal of American and Comparative Cultures* 23.3 (2000), pp. 69–78. This essay analyses the presence of Shakespeare in popular culture and argues that in the twentieth century it shifts from being considered 'high art' to something more connected to the popular sphere.

Discussing another genre that oscillates between being considered 'high' and 'low' art – the graphic novel – Lancaster demonstrates that such arbitrary divisions intersect in meaningful ways. He uses Gaiman's *A Midsummer Night's Dream* (volume 19 of the *Sandman* comic book series) to demonstrate these connections. Gaiman's interpretation of Shakespeare, Lancaster argues, constructs a new kind of myth that remains true to Shakespearean themes while engaging popular imaginations. Gaiman's new Shakespearean mythos, Lancaster concludes, reintegrates Shakespeare into popular culture.

Leggatt, Alexander, 'The Disappearing Wall: *A Midsummer Night's Dream and Timon of Athens*', in *Shakespeare and the Mediterranean: The Selected Proceedings of the International Shakespeare Association World Congress, Valencia*, ed. Tom Clayton, Susan Brock and Vicente Fores (Newark, DE: University of Delaware Press, 2001), pp. 194–205. Leggatt focuses on walls – either literal or figurative – as they function in *Dream* and *Timon of Athens*. For Leggatt, the walls disappear – leading to apparent divisions merging together in instructive ways. This article complements Stephen Booth's paper referenced above.

Lewis, Alan, 'Reading Shakespeare's Cupid', *Criticism* 47.2 (2005), pp. 177–213. Merging the methodology of new historicism with that of psychoanalytic criticism, Lewis attempts to historicize Shakespeare's representations of subjectivity by constructing an 'interpretive field' within which Shakespeare represents his masculine subjects in love. The figure of Cupid can be understood as bringing together ideas of desire and love as they manifest and disrupt notions of masculinity.

Loomba, Ania, 'The Great Indian Vanishing Trick – Colonialism, Property, and the Family in *A Midsummer Night's Dream*', in *A Feminist Companion to Shakespeare*, ed. Dympna Callaghan (Oxford: Blackwell, 2000), pp. 163–87. Loomba identifies a gap in the scholarship on *Dream*, which tends to examine the ways in which the play represents and shapes the discourses of gender and the family, but not colonial discourses associated with travel and trade. Focusing on the battle between Titania and Oberon for the Indian boy, Loomba claims that gender and colonialism interrelate in important ways. As the narrative reinforces patriarchy, it also more subtly approves colonialism.

Malieckal, Bindu, 'Muslims, Matriliny, and *A Midsummer Night's Dream*: European Encounters with the Mappilas of Malabar, India', *The Muslim World* 95 (2005), pp. 297–316. Malieckal offers another interpretation of the significance of the Indian boy in Shakespeare's play. The author suggests that the boy might be seen as representative of the Mappilas of Malabar (the precolonial name for Kerala) who are a matrilineal culture. Malieckal's essay, which historicizes Shakespeare's play and places it within a more global framework than many critics do, argues that these overlooked connections between the play and Malabar combine to create a subtext that makes resistance to patriarchal domination possible.

Mason, David V., 'Who is the Indian Shakespeare?: Appropriation of Authority in a Sanskrit *Midsummer Night's Dream*', *New Literary History* 34.4 (2003), pp. 639–58. Mason's article analyses the ways in which a Sanskrit translation of the play called *Vasantikasvapnam* (translated as *A Dream in Spring*) exposes the tensions that arise between the former colonizer and the colonized subject.

Moffatt, Laurel, 'The Woods as Heterotopia in *A Midsummer Night's Dream*', *Studia Neophilologica* 76 (2004), pp. 182–87. This essay offers a reading of the geographical division in *Dream* between Athens and the woods as signalling a Foucauldian 'heterotopia', functioning as a 'counterpoint' to the courtly world of Athens and ultimately serving to bring about what Moffatt views as the 'concord' that ends the play.

Moore, Ann M., '*Monsoon Wedding*: Another *Midsummer Night's Dream*', *Studies in Popular Culture* 27.1 (2004), pp. 19–29. As the title suggests, Moore observes that the Indian-American film *Monsoon Wedding*, directed by Mira Nair, borrows much from Shakespeare's *Dream*. She concedes that the resonances she identifies may not be Nair's intention, but a connection does emerge through thematic and structural comparison.

Paulus, Diane, 'It's All About the Audience', *Contemporary Theatre Review* 16.3 (2006), pp. 334–47. Paulus describes her radical theatrical events: *The Donkey Show* (an adaptation of *Dream* set in a disco to 1970s period music) and *The Karaoke Show* (based on *A Comedy of Errors*). Her shows are constructed to engage audiences in the productions, freeing them to collaborate with the performers. Paulus gives a detailed account of her creative choices, explaining the effects she attempted to create.

Pendergast, John, 'Six Characters in Search of Shakespeare: Neil Gaiman's *Sandman* and Shakespearean Mythos', *Mythlore* 26.3–4 (2008), pp. 185–97. Making a case for comic books as an ideal medium to represent a Shakespearean play, Pendergast analyses Gaiman's *A Midsummer Night's Dream* from the *Sandman* series. He finds (as have other scholars) that the interaction between Gaiman and Shakespeare is particularly productive, because both writers seem to view their work as 'a product of the interaction of social conventions and norms with myth' (p. 190). This essay also discusses Gaiman's representation of the *Tempest* which appears in Volume 75 of *Sandman*.

Pequigney, Joseph, '"What the Age Might Call Sodomy" and Homosexuality in Certain Studies of Shakespeare's Plays', *Intertexts* 8.2 (2004), pp. 117–37. Pequigney mentions *Dream* only briefly in this article in which he identifies a tendency by queer scholars to 'exhibit a deficiency in exegetical skills' that undermines their otherwise important arguments.

Pettitt, Tom, 'Midsummer Metadrama: "Pyramus and Thisbe" and Early English Household Theatre', *Angles on the English-Speaking World* 5 (2005), pp. 31–43. Pettitt's article provides useful information that historicizes the metatheatrical performance of *Pyramus and Thisbe* that appears in the concluding act of *Dream*. He links the entire performance ('presentation, interlude, and masking') to Elizabethan household revels, which functioned historically to reinforce a reciprocity between aristocratic and working classes. By including this episode, Pettitt argues, Shakespeare is himself reinforcing reciprocity between his acting company and his audience.

Purkiss, Diane, *At the Bottom of the Garden: A Dark History of Fairies, Hobgoblins, and Other Troublesome Things* (New York: New York University Press, 2000). This book offers a comprehensive history of fairies from antiquity to contemporary popular culture. A section on 'Early Modern Fairies' (Chapters 3–5) includes a discussion of Shakespeare's use of fairies.

Riga, Frank P., '"Where is that Worthless Dreamer?": Bottom's Fantastic Redemption in Hoffman's *A Midsummer Night's Dream*', *Mythlore* 95/96 (2006), pp. 197–211. Arguing against the trend that interprets Bottom as merely a buffoon or a lewd clown (spearheaded by Jan Kott's criticism and Peter Brook's famous 1970s production), Riga asserts that Bottom is a central figure in the play. He is supported by many scholars who view the scenes with the mechanicals as informing the play and enriching its meaning. Riga praises Michael Hoffman, whose filmed version of *Dream* (1999) 'humanizes' Bottom, and gives him depth and focus. An important (and questionable) part of Riga's evidence involves aspects that the director added to the film, so the argument derives not from the playtext but from a film interpretation that some critics have seen as too liberal.

Sinfield, Alan, *Shakespeare, Authority, Sexuality: Unfinished Busi-*

ness in Cultural Materialism (New York: Routledge, 2006). In Chapter 5 ('Intertextuality and the Limits of Queer Reading in *A Midsummer Night's Dream*'), Sinfield conducts an intertextual reading of the homoerotic relationships in *Dream* and *Two Noble Kinsmen*.

Teague, Fran, 'Swingin' Shakespeare from Harlem to Broadway', *Borrowers and Lenders: The Journal of Shakespeare and Appropriation* 1.1 (2005), online: www.borrowers.uga.edu. Teague discusses two musical versions of Shakespeare's plays: *Play On!*, a 1997 musical production of *Twelfth Night* put on at the Old Globe Theater in San Diego, and *Swingin' the Dream*, a 1939 swing version of *Dream*. Teague's article includes MP3 samples of songs from the shows within the text. Teague evaluates the alterations in *Play On!* between the play and the adaptation, but she does not offer as detailed an analysis of *Swingin' the Dream*, other than documenting its lack of commercial success.

Teague, Fran, 'Beards and Broadway: Shakespeare as Unacknow-ledged Agent', *The Upstart Crow* 25 (2005), pp. 4–15. In this article, Teague deepens her exploration of Shakespeare and musical comedy. She notices that when Shakespeare is evoked by a musical comedy team, it functions to cover up or screen unconventional ('queer') themes expressed by the musicals themselves. Here she returns to her discussion of *Play On!* and *Swingin' the Dream* referred to above.

Traub, Valerie, *The Renaissance of Lesbianism in Early Modern England* (Cambridge: Cambridge University Press, 2002). This important work argues that rather than being invisible, same-sex eroticism between women was instead being represented with increasing frequency in early modern European texts. In Chapters 1 ('Setting the Stage Behind the Seen: Performing Lesbian History') and 4 ('The (In)significance of *Lesbian* Desire') Traub discusses the relationship between Hermia and Helena which is presented as idealized and eroticized in *Dream*, but is ultimately replaced by the heteronormative relationships that conclude the play. Traub essentially concludes that in Shakespeare's presenta-tion, female homoerotic relationships are presented as always in the past, and therefore 'insignificant' in relation to the more immediate ones ultimately sanctioned by the play.

Wall, Wendy, 'Why Does Puck Sweep?: Fairylore, Merry Wives, and Social Struggle', *Shakespeare Quarterly* 52.1 (2001), pp. 67–106. Wall's examination of the function of fairy lore in *Dream* and *The Merry Wives of Windsor* suggests that the presence of the fairies in these plays links domestic ideology with an idea of Englishness and community. The 'class-specific elements of fairylore', she asserts, might 'represent household and national relations' (p. 106). Domesticity is foregrounded by the play and by extension so is the politicized connection between household order and political order that she argues was occupying the collective imagination.

Walsh, William, 'Shakespeare's Lion and Ha Jin's Tiger: The Interplay of Imagination and Reality', *Papers on Language and Literature: A Journal for Scholars and Critics of Language and Literature* 42.4 (2006), pp. 339–59. This essay compares Ha Jin's short story 'A Tiger-Fighter is Hard to Find' (from *The Bridegroom* collection, 2000) with the *Pyramus and Thisbe* episode in *Dream*. Walsh explores the two texts' approach to the relationship between imagination and reality and discusses the effectiveness of using art as a political tool. In Ha Jin's story, the inability of an official in Mao's regime to be convinced that a television show featuring a man who beats a tiger to death is convincing enough to be instructive to communist audiences leads to disastrous consequences when the show responds by getting a real tiger. Walsh notes that this situation is the mirror opposite of that of the mechanicals in *Pyramus and Thisbe*, who worry excessively that their audience's imaginations will too readily transform the characters into the things they represent, so they draw comical attention to their reality as actors. Walsh concludes that while Ha Jin creates a 'fantasy to cover an ugly reality', Shakespeare's play makes the point that imagination enhances the experience of love and possibly also 'the triumph of the virtual over the actual' (p. 358).

Wells, Stanley, *Looking for Sex in Shakespeare* (Cambridge: Cambridge University Press, 2006). In Chapter 1, 'Lewd Interpreters', Wells argues that those who posit that *Dream* is a particularly bawdy play go too far, suggesting instead that the critics are essentially reading their own perversity into the play.

Watts, Cedric, 'Fundamental Editing: In *A Midsummer Night's Dream*, Does "Bottom" Mean "Bum"? And How About "Arse" and "Ass"?', *Anglistica Pisana* 3.1 (2006), pp. 215–22. Watts takes on the controversial task of attempting to prove that 'bottom' referred to the buttocks in sixteenth-century parlance. *OED* attributes this reference to Erasmus Darwin's *Zoonomia*, 1794–96.

Notes

1   In addition to Louis Adrian Montrose, '"Shaping Fantasies": Figurations of Gender and Power in Elizabethan Culture', *Representations* 1.2 (1983), pp. 61–94, feminist scholars like Shirley Nelson Garner, '"Jack shall have Jill: / Nought shall go ill"', *Women's Studies: An Interdisciplinary Journal* 9.1 (1981), pp. 47–63, have made similar arguments.

2   All Shakespeare quotations from William Shakespeare, *A Midsummer Night's Dream*, ed. Peter Holland (Oxford: The Clarendon Press, 1994).

3   See, for example, Kathryn Schwartz, *Tough Love: Amazon Encounters in the English Renaissance* (Durham, NC: Duke University Press, 2000).

4   Robert Lublin, 'Feminist History, Theory, and Practice in the Shakespeare Classroom', *Theatre Topics* 14.2 (2004), pp. 397–410, p. 403.

5   John Wilders, 'Teaching *A Midsummer Night's Dream*', in *Teaching With Shakespeare*, ed. Bruce McIver and Ruth Stevenson (Newark, NJ: University of Delaware Press, 1994), pp. 152–65.

6   Wilders, 'Teaching *A Midsummer Night's Dream*', p. 155.

7   Patricia Parker, '"Teaching and Wordplay: The "Wall" of *A Midsummer Night's Dream*', in *Teaching With Shakespeare*, ed. Bruce McIver and Ruth Stevenson (Newark, NJ: University of Delaware Press, 1994), pp. 205–14.

8   As a starting point for this guide, I used Michael Best and Melanie Lambrick, 'Electronic Shakespeares: Students and the Web', *The Shakespeare Newsletter*, spring (2004), pp. 23–24.

9   Because Wikipedia is a source that anyone might post information to or edit, it could contain misinformation. While you may want to use it as a starting point for further research, you should not cite it as a source, and you should be careful to check all of the information that you take from it by consulting directly the bibliographic material provided in each entry.

10 Dorothea Kehler, ed., *A Midsummer Night's Dream: Critical Essays* (New York: Garland, 1999).

11 See Kehler's essay, 'The Critical Backstory and the State of the Art', in this volume for her more recent survey of criticism on *Dream*.

12 Wendy Wall, 'Why Does Puck Sweep?: Fairylore, Merry Wives, and Social Struggle', *Shakespeare Quarterly* 52.1 (2001), pp. 67–106.

13 Douglas Bruster, *Shakespeare and the Question of Culture: Early Modern Literature and the Cultural Turn* (New York: Palgrave, 2003).

14 Diane Hunter, 'Cultural Politics of Fantasy in *A Midsummer Night's Dream*', *PsyArt: A Hyperlink Journal for the Psychological Study of the Arts* (2003), online: www.clas.ufl.edu/ipsa/journal/2003_hunter01.shtml.

15 Catherine Belsey, *Why Shakespeare?* (New York: Palgrave, 2007), pp. 86–87.

16 Kehler, *A Midsummer Night's Dream: Critical Essays*, p. 45.

17 R. W. Desai, 'England, the Indian Boy, and the Spice Trade in *A Midsummer Night's Dream*', in *India's Shakespeare*, ed. Poonam Trivedi and Dennis Bartholomeusz (Newark, DE: University of Delaware Press, 2005), pp. 141–57.

18 Bindu Malieckal, 'Muslims, Matriliny, and *A Midsummer Night's Dream*: European Encounters with the Mappilas of Malabar, India', *The Muslim World* 95 (2005), pp. 297–316.

19 David Mason, 'Who is the Indian Shakespeare?: Appropriation of Authority in a Sanskrit *Midsummer Night's Dream*', *New Literary History* 34.4 (2003), pp. 639–58.

20 Thomas Frosch, 'The Missing Child in *A Midsummer Night's Dream*', *American Imago* 64.4 (2008), pp. 485–511.

21 Alexander Leggatt, 'The Disappearing Wall: *A Midsummer Night's Dream* and *Timon of Athens*', in *Shakespeare and the Mediterranean: The Selected Proceedings of the International Shakespeare Association World Congress, Valencia*, ed. Tom Clayton, Susan Brock and Vicente Fores (Newark, DE: University of Delaware Press, 2001), pp. 194–205.

22   Steven Booth, 'A Discourse on the Witty Partition of *A Midsummer Night's Dream*', in *Inside Shakespeare: Essays on the Blackfriar's Stage*, ed. Paul Menzer (Selinsgrove, PA: Susquehanna University Press, 2006), pp. 216–22.

23   Peter Happé, '*Pyramus and Thisbe*: Rhetoricians and Shakespeare', in *Medieval Texts and Cultures of Northern Europe* (Turnhout: Brepols, 2006), pp. 149–68.

24   Tom Pettitt, 'Midsummer Metadrama: "Pyramus and Thisbe" and Early English Household Theatre', *Angles on the English-Speaking World* 5 (2005), pp. 31–43.

25   Kurt Lancaster, 'Neil Gaiman's "A Midsummer Night's Dream": Shakespeare Integrated into Popular Culture', *Journal of American and Comparative Cultures* 23.3 (2000), pp. 69–78.

26   John Pendergast, 'Six Characters in Search of Shakespeare: Neil Gaiman's *Sandman* and Shakespearean Mythos', *Mythlore* 26.3–4 (2008), pp. 185–97, p. 190.

27   Nicholas Jones, 'Bottom's Wife: Gender and Voice in Hoffman's *Dream*', *Literature Film Quarterly* 32.2 (2004), pp. 126–33.

28   Stephen Buhler, 'Textual and Sexual Anxieties in Michael Hoffman's Film of *A Midsummer Night's Dream*', *Shakespeare Bulletin* 22.3 (2004), pp. 49–61.

29   Frank Riga, ' "Where is that Worthless Dreamer?": Bottom's Fantastic Redemption in Hoffman's *A Midsummer Night's Dream*', *Mythlore* 95/96 (2006), pp. 197–211.

30   See Kehler, *A Midsummer Night's Dream: Critical Essays*, or Kehler's chapter in this volume for a discussion of Jan Kott's influence on subsequent interpretations of *Dream*.

31   See for example Ania Loomba, 'The Great Indian Vanishing Trick – Colonialism, Property, and the Family in *A Midsummer Night's Dream*', in *A Feminist Companion to Shakespeare*, ed. Dympna Callaghan (Oxford: Blackwell, 2000), pp. 163–87.

Selected Bibliography

Anon., 'Bard's Love Potion Brewed' (*Western Mail*, 14 February 2002), p. 10.

Andrews, Richard, 'A *Midsummer Night's Dream* and Italian Pastoral', in *Transnational Exchange in Early Modern Theatre*, ed. Robert Henke and Eric Nicholson (Aldershot: Ashgate, 2008), pp. 49–62.

Arnold, Jean, Buell, Lawrence *et al.*, 'Forum on Literatures of the Environment', *PMLA* 115 (October 1999), 1089–104.

Aronson, Alex, 'Eros: Sons and Mothers: III', in *Psyche & Symbol in Shakespeare* (Bloomington, IN: Indiana University Press, 1972).

Arthos, John, *Shakespeare's Use of Dream and Vision* (London: Bodley Head Ltd, 1977).

Baker, Susan, 'Chronotope and Repression in A *Midsummer Night's Dream*', in *A Midsummer Night's Dream: Critical Essays*, ed. Dorothea Kehler (New York: Garland, 1998), pp. 345–68.

Barber, C. L., *Shakespeare's Festive Comedy: A Study of Dramatic Form in Relation to Social Custom*, 2nd. edn (Princeton, NJ: Princeton University Press, 1972).

Barkan, Leonard, *The Gods Made Flesh: Metamorphosis and the Pursuit of Paganism* (New Haven, CT: Yale University Press, 1986).

Bate, Jonathan, *Shakespeare and Ovid* (Oxford: The Clarendon Press, 1993).

Baxter, John, '"Growing to a Point": Mimesis in A *Midsummer Night's Dream*', *English Studies in Canada* 22 (1996), pp. 17–33.

Belsey, Catherine, 'Peter Quince's Ballad: Shakespeare, Psychoanalysis, History', *Deutsche Shakespeare–Gesellschaft/Deutsche Shakespeare–Gesellschaft West Jahrbuch* (1994), pp. 65–82.

Bentley, G.E., *The Profession of Dramatist in Shakespeare's Time, 1590–1642* (Princeton, NJ: Princeton University Press, 1971).

Berry, Philippa: 'Nomadic Eros: Remapping Knowledge in A *Midsummer Night's Dream*', in *Forgetting in Early Modern English Literature and Culture: Lethe's Legacies*, ed. Christopher Ivic and Grant Williams, Routledge Studies in Renaissance Literature and Culture (New York: Routledge, 2004), pp. 137–50.

Berry, Ralph, *Shakespeare's Comedies: Explorations in Form* (Princeton, NJ: Princeton University Press, 1972).

Bevington, David, ' "But We Are Spirits of Another Sort": The Dark Side of Love and Magic in A *Midsummer Night's Dream*', *Medieval and Renaissance Studies*, 7 (1975), pp. 80–92.

Bicks, Caroline, *Midwiving Subjects in Shakespeare's England* (Aldershot: Ashgate, 2003).

Bloom, Harold, *Shakespeare: The Invention of the Human* (New York: Riverhead Books, 1998).

Boas, Frederick S., *Shakespere and His Predecessors* (New York: Scribner's, 1896).

Boehrer, Bruce Thomas, 'Bestial Buggery in *A Midsummer Night's Dream*', in *The Production of English Renaissance Culture*, ed. David Lee Miller, Sharon O'Dair and Harold Weber (Ithaca, NY: Cornell University Press, 1994), pp. 123–50. Revised version in *Shakespeare Among the Animals: Nature and Society in the Drama of Early Modern England* (New York: Palgrave, 2002).

Boehrer, Bruce Thomas, 'Economies of Desire in *A Midsummer Night's Dream*', *Shakespeare Studies* 32 (2004), pp. 99–117.

Bogue, Ronald, *Deleuze on Literature* (London: Routledge, 2003).

Bonnard, George A., 'Shakespeare's Purpose in *A Midsummer Night's Dream*', *Shakespeare Jahrbuch* 92 (1956), pp. 268–79.

Booth, Stephen, 'A Discourse on the Witty Partition of *A Midsummer Night's Dream*', in *Inside Shakespeare: Essays on the Blackfriars Stage*, ed. Paul Menzer (Selinsgrove, PA: Susquehanna University Press, 2006), pp. 216–22.

Booth, Stephen, 'Shakespeare in California and Utah', *Shakespeare Quarterly* 28 (1977), pp. 229–44.

Brandes, George, *William Shakespeare*, trans. William Archer, Mary Morison and Diana White (New York: Macmillan, 1924).

Briggs, K. M., *The Anatomy of Puck: An Examination of Fairy Beliefs among Shakespeare's Contemporaries and Successors* (London: Routledge & Kegan Paul, 1959).

Brissenden, Alan, *Shakespeare and the Dance* (Atlantic Highlands, NJ: Humanities Press, 1981).

Bristol, Michael D., *Carnival and Theater: Plebeian Culture and the Structure of Authority in Renaissance England* (New York: Methuen, 1985).

Brook, Peter, *The Empty Space* (New York: Touchstone, 1968).

Brooks, Harold F., 'A Notorious Shakespearian Crux: *Midsummer Night's Dream*, V.i.208', *Notes and Queries* n.s. 17 (1970), pp. 125–27.

Brown, James Neil, ' "A Calendar, A Calendar! Look in the Almanac" ', *Notes and Queries* 225, n.s. 27 (1980), pp. 162–65.

Brown, Jane K., '*Discordia Concors*: On the Order of *A Midsummer Night's Dream*', *Modern Language Quarterly* 48 (1987), pp. 20–41.

Brown, John Russell, *Free Shakespeare* (London: A & C Black, 1974).

Bruster, Douglas, *Shakespeare and the Question of Culture: Early Modern Literature and the Cultural Turn* (New York: Palgrave Macmillan, 2003).

Buccola, Regina, *Fairies, Fractious Women, and the Old Faith: Fairy Lore in Early Modern British Drama and Culture* (Selinsgrove, PA: Susquehanna University Press, 2006).

Buccola, Regina, 'Virgin Fairies and Imperial Whores: The Unstable Ground of Religious Iconography in Thomas Dekker's *The Whore of Babylon*', in *Marian Moments in Early Modern British Drama*, ed. Regina Buccola and Lisa Hopkins (Aldershot: Ashgate, 2007), pp. 141–60.

Bullough, Geoffrey, ed., 'Introduction to *A Midsummer Night's Dream*', in *Narrative and Dramatic Sources of Shakespeare*, vol. 3 (London: Routledge & Kegan Paul, 1957).

Burke, Kenneth, 'Why *A Midsummer Night's Dream*?', *Shakespeare Quarterly* 57 (2006), pp. 294–308.

Byrne, Muriel St Clare, 'The Shakespeare Season at the Old Vic, 1958–59 and Stratford-upon-Avon, 1959', *Shakespeare Quarterly* 10, (1959), pp. 545–67.

Calderwood, James L., *A Midsummer Night's Dream* (New York: Twayne, 1992).

Calderwood, James L., '*A Midsummer Night's Dream*: Art's Illusory Sacrifice' in *Shakespearean Metadrama: The Argument of the Play in 'Titus Andronicus', 'Love's Labour's Lost', 'Romeo and Juliet', 'A Midsummer Night's Dream', and 'Richard II'* (Minneapolis, MN: University of Minnesota Press, 1971).

Callaghan, Dympna C., *Shakespeare Without Women: Representing Gender and Race on the Renaissance Stage* (London: Routledge, 2000).

Carroll, William C., *The Metamorphoses of Shakespearean Comedy* (Princeton, NJ: Princeton University Press, 1985).

Carver, Robert H. F., 'Shakespeare's Bottom and Apuleius' Ass', in *The Protean Ass: The Metamorphoses of Apuleius from Antiquity to the Renaissance* (Oxford: Oxford University Press, 2007), pp. 429–45.

Chambers, E. K., '*A Midsummer Night's Dream*' (1905) repr. in *Shakespeare: A Survey* (London: Sidgwick & Jackson, 1958).

Champion, Larry S., *The Evolution of Shakespeare's Comedy: A Study in Dramatic Perspective* (Cambridge, MA: Harvard University Press, 1970).

Charlton, H. B., '*A Midsummer Night's Dream*' (1933), in *Shakespearian Comedy* (London: Methuen, 1938).

Chesterton, G. K., '*A Midsummer Night's Dream*' (1904) repr. in *The Common Man* (London: Sheed & Ward, 1950).

Clary, Frank Nicholas, '"Imagine No Worse of Them": Hippolyta on the Ritual Threshold in Shakespeare's *A Midsummer Night's Dream*', in *Ceremony and Text in the Renaissance*, ed. Douglas F. Rutledge (Newark, DE: University of Delaware Press, 1996).

Clayton, Thomas, '"Fie what a question's that if thou wert near a lewd interpreter": The Wall Scene in *A Midsummer Night's Dream*', *Shakespeare Studies* 7 (1974), pp. 101–13.

Clayton, Thomas, '"So quick bright things come to confusion"; or, What Else is *A Midsummer Night's Dream* About?', in *Shakespeare: Text and Theater: Essays in Honor of Jay L. Halio*, ed. Lois Potter and Arthur F. Kinney (Newark, DE: University of Delaware Press, 1999), pp. 62–91.

Clayton, Thomas, 'Shakespeare at the Guthrie: *A Midsummer Night's Dream*', *Shakespeare Quarterly* 37 (1986), pp. 229–36.

Clubb, Louise George, 'Pastoral Jazz from the Writ to the Liberty', in *Italian Culture in the Drama of Shakespere and His Contemporaries: Rewriting, Remaking, Refashioning*, ed. Michele Marrapodi (Aldershot: Ashgate, 2007), pp. 15–26.

Cody, Richard, *The Landscape of the Mind: Pastoralism and Platonic Theory in Tasso's 'Aminta' and Shakespeare's Early Comedies* (Oxford: The Clarendon Press, 1969).

Coleridge, Samuel Taylor, 'Notes on the Comedies of Shakespeare: *Midsummer Night's Dream*' (1818), repr. in *Shakespearean Criticism*, ed. Thomas Middleton Raysor, 2nd edn, vol. 1 (New York: Dutton, 1960).

Colthorpe, Marion, 'Queen Elizabeth I and *A Midsummer Night's Dream*', *Notes & Queries* 34.2 (1987), pp. 205–7.

Comtois, M. E., 'The Hardiness of *A Midsummer Night's Dream*', *Theatre Journal* 32 (1980), pp. 305–11.

Conlan, J.P., 'The Fey Beauty of *A Midsummer Night's Dream*: A Shakespearean Comedy in its Courtly Context', *Shakespeare Studies* 32 (2004), pp. 118–72.

Cox, Richard H., 'Shakespeare: Poetic Understanding and Comic Action (A Weaver's Dream)', in *The Artist and Political Vision*, ed. Benjamin R. Barber and Michael J. Gargas McGrath (New Brunswick, NJ: Transaction Books, 1982), pp. 165–92.

Crane, Milton, *Shakespeare's Prose* (Chicago: University of Chicago Press, 1951).

Culler, Jonathan and Lamb, Kevin, eds, *Just Being Difficult?: Academic Writing in the Public Arena* (Stanford, CA: Stanford University Press, 2003).

Davidson, Clifford, '"What Hempen Home-spuns Have We Swagg'ring Here?": Amateur Actors in *A Midsummer Night's Dream* and the Coventry Civic Plays and Pageants', *Shakespeare Studies* 19 (1987), pp. 87–99.

Davies, Stevie, *The Feminine Reclaimed: The Idea of Woman in Shakespeare, Spenser, and Milton* (Lexington, KY: University of Kentucky Press, 1986).

De la Mare, Walter, 'Introduction', in *A Midsummer Night's Dream*, ed. C. Aldred (London: Macmillan, 1935), repr. as '*The Dream*', in *Pleasures & Speculations* (London: Faber & Faber, 1940), pp. 270–305.

Deleuze, Gilles, and von Sacher-Masoch, Leopold, *Masochism: An Interpretation of Coldness and Cruelty: Together with the Entire Text of Venus in Furs* (New York: Braziller, 1971).

Dent, R. W., 'Imagination in *A Midsummer Night's Dream*', *Shakespeare Quarterly* 15.2 (1964), pp. 115–29.

Desai, R. W., 'England, The Indian Boy, and the Spice Trade in *A Midsummer Night's Dream*', in *India's Shakespeare: Translation, Interpretation, and Performance,* ed. Poonam Trivedi and Dennis Bartholomeusz (Newark, DE: University of Delaware Press, 2005), pp. 141–57.

Desmet, Christy, 'Disfiguring Women with Masculine Tropes: A Rhetorical Reading of *A Midsummer Night's Dream*', in *A Midsummer Night's Dream: Critical Essays,* ed. Dorothea Kehler (New York: Garland, 1998), pp. 299–329.

Dobson, Michael, 'Shakespeare Performances in England, 2001', *Shakespeare Survey* 55 (2002), pp. 285–321.

Donaldson, E. Talbot, *The Swan at the Well: Shakespeare Reading Chaucer* (New Haven, CT: Yale University Press, 1985).

Doran, Madeleine, 'Pyramus and Thisbe Once More', in *Essays on Shakespeare and Elizabethan Drama in Honor of Hardin Craig,* ed. Richard Hosley (Columbia, MO: University of Missouri Press, 1962), pp. 149–61.

Dryden, John, 'The Authors Apology for Heroique Poetry; and Poetique Licence', in *The State of Innocence, and Fall of Man: The Complete Works of John Dryden,* ed. Vinton A. Dearing, vol. 12 (Berkeley, CA: University of California Press, 1994), pp. 86–97 .

Dubrow, Heather, *Shakespeare and Domestic Loss: Forms of Deprivation, Mourning, and Recuperation* (Cambridge: Cambridge University Press, 1999).

Dunn, Allen, 'The Indian Boy's Dream Wherein Every Mother's Son Rehearses His Part: Shakespeare's *A Midsummer Night's Dream*', *Shakespeare Studies* 20 (1988), pp. 15–32.

Eagleton, Terry, *William Shakespeare* (Oxford: Blackwell, 1986).

Edwards, Philip, *Shakespeare and the Confines of Art* (London: Methuen, 1968).

Egan, Gabriel, *Green Shakespeare: From Ecopolitics to Ecocriticism* (London: Routledge, 2006).

Ehnenn, Jill, ' "An Attractive Dramatic Exhibition"? Female Friendship, Shakespeare's Women, and Female Performativity in 19th-Century Britain', *Women's Studies: An Interdisciplinary Journal* 26 (1997), pp. 315–41.

Empson, William, 'The Spirits of the "Dream" ', in *Essays on Renaissance Literature,* ed. John Haffenden, vol. 2 (Cambridge: Cambridge University Press, 1994), pp. 170–248.

Evans, Bertrand, *Shakespeare's Comedies* (Oxford: The Clarendon Press, 1960).

Evans, B. Ifor, *The Language of Shakespeare's Plays* (London: Methuen, 1952).

Faber, M. D., 'Hermia's Dream: Royal Road to *A Midsummer Night's Dream*', *Literature and Psychology* 22 (1972), pp. 179–90.

Falk, Florenc, 'Dream and Ritual Process in *A Midsummer Night's Dream*', *Comparative Drama* 14 (1980), pp. 263–79.

Fender, Stephen, *Shakespeare: 'A Midsummer Night's Dream'* (London: Edward Arnold, 1968).

Fisher, Peter F., 'The Argument of *A Midsummer Night's Dream*', *Shakespeare Quarterly* 8 (1957), pp. 307–10.

Folkerth, Wes, *The Sound of Shakespeare* (London: Routledge, 2002).

Forey, Madeleine, ' "Bless thee, Bottom, bless thee! Thou art translated!": Ovid, Golding, and *A Midsummer Night's Dream*', *Modern Language Review* 93 (1998), pp. 321–29.

Frame, Jeffrey D., ' "Now will I to the chink,/To spy ...": Scopophilia as Gender Sport in *A Midsummer Night's Dream*', *Upstart Crow* 19 (1999), pp. 50–61.

Franke, Wolfgang, 'The Logic of *Double Entendre* in *A Midsummer Night's Dream*', *Philological Quarterly* 58 (1979), pp. 282–97.

Freake, Douglas, '*A Midsummer Night's Dream* as a Comic Version of the Theseus

Myth', in *A Midsummer Night's Dream: Critical Essays*, ed. Dorothea Kehler (New York: Garland, 1998), pp. 259–74.

Freedman, Barbara, *Staging the Gaze: Postmodernism, Psycho-analysis, and Shakespearean Comedy* (Ithaca, NY: Cornell University Press, 1991).

Frosch, Thomas R., 'The Missing Child in *A Midsummer Night's Dream*', *American Imago: Psychoanalysis and the Human Sciences* 64 (winter 2007), pp. 485–511.

Frye, Northrop, *A Natural Perspective* (New York: Columbia University Press, 1965).

Furness, Horace Howard, *New Variorum Shakespeare* (New York: Dover, 1895).

Garber, Marjorie B., *Dream in Shakespeare: From Metaphor to Metamorphosis* (New Haven, CT: Yale University Press, 1974).

Garner, Shirley Nelson, '*A Midsummer Night's Dream*: "Jack shall have Jill: / Nought shall go ill" ', *Women's Studies* 9 (1981), pp. 47–63.

Gervinus, G. G., 'Second Period of Shakspeare's Dramatic Poetry: *Midsummer-Night's Dream*', in *Shakespeare Commentaries* (1849), trans. F. E. Bunnètt, rev. edn (1877), repr. New York: AMS Press, 1971, pp. 187–203.

Girard, René, 'Myth and Ritual in Shakespeare: *A Midsummer Night's Dream*', in *Textual Strategies: Perspectives in Post-Structuralist Criticism*, ed. Josué V. Harari (Ithaca, NY: Cornell University Press, 1979), pp. 189–212.

Girard, René, *A Theatre of Envy: William Shakespeare* (Oxford: Oxford University Press, 1991).

Goddard, Harold C., *The Meaning of Shakespeare*, vol. 1 (Chicago: University of Chicago Press, 1951).

Granville–Barker, Harley, 'Preface to *A Midsummer Night's Dream*' (1924), in *More Prefaces to Shakespeare*, ed. Edward M. Moore (Princeton, NJ: Princeton University Press, 1974), pp. 94–134.

Green, Douglas E., 'Preposterous Pleasures: Queer Theories and *A Midsummer Night's Dream*', in *A Midsummer Night's Dream: Critical Essays*, ed. Dorothea Kehler (New York: Garland, 1998), pp. 369–97.

Green, Roger Lancelyn, 'Shakespeare and the Fairies', *Folklore* 73 (1962), pp. 89–103.

Greenfield, Thelma N., '*A Midsummer Night's Dream* and *The Praise of Folly*', *Comparative Literature* 20 (1968), pp. 236–44.

Greenfield, Thelma N., 'Our Nightly Madness: Shakespeare's *Dream* without *The Interpretation of Dreams*', in *A Midsummer Night's Dream: Critical Essays*, ed. Dorothea Kehler (New York: Garland, 1998), pp. 331–44.

Greer, Germaine, 'Love and the Law', in *Politics, Power, and Shakespeare*, ed. Frances McNeely Leonard (Arlington, TX: Texas Humanities Research Center, 1981), pp. 29–45.

Griffiths, Trevor R., ed., *Shakespeare in Production: A Midsummer Night's Dream* (Cambridge: Cambridge University Press, 1996).

Grosz, Elizabeth A., 'Thinking the New: Of Futures Yet Unthought' in *Becomings: Explorations in Time, Memory, and Futures*, ed. by Elizabeth A. Grosz (Ithaca, NY: Cornell University Press, 1999), pp. 15–28.

Hackett, Helen, '*A Midsummer Night's Dream*', in *A Companion to Shakespeare's Works*, ed. Richard Dutton and Jean E. Howard, vol. 3, *The Comedies* (Oxford: Blackwell, 2003), pp. 338–57.

Halio, Jay L., *A Midsummer Night's Dream: A Guide to the Play* (London: Greenwood Press, 2003).

Halio, Jay L., ed., *Shakespeare in Performance: A Midsummer Night's Dream*, 2nd edn. (Manchester: Manchester University Press, 2003).

Hall, Kim F., *Things of Darkness: Economies of Race and Gender in Early Modern England* (Ithaca, NY: Cornell University Press, 1995).

Halliwell-Phillips, James Orchard (1841) *An Introduction to Shakespeare's 'Midsummer Night's Dream'* (London: Folcroft Library Editions, 1974).

Halliwell-Phillips, James Orchard, *Memoranda on the 'Midsummer Night's Dream'* (London: Fleet & Bishop, 1879).

Halliwell-Phillips, James Orchard, ed., *Illustrations of the Fairy Mythology of A Midsummer Night's Dream* (London: Shakespeare Society, 1845).

Hawkes, Terence, *Meaning by Shakespeare* (London: Routledge, 1992).

Hazlitt, William, *Characters of Shakespeare's Plays* (1817) (London: Oxford University Press, 1916), pp. 103–9.

Hendricks, Margo, ' "Obscured by Dreams": Race, Empire, and Shakespeare's *A Midsummer Night's Dream*', *Shakespeare Quarterly* 47 (1996), pp. 37–60.

Herbert, T. Walter, *Oberon's Mazéd World: A Judicious Young Elizabethan Contemplates 'A Midsummer Night's Dream' with a Mind Shaped by the Learning of Christendom Modified by the New Naturalist Philosophy and Excited by the Vision of a Rich, Powerful England* (Baton Rouge, LA: Louisiana State University Press, 1977).

Hinely, Jan Lawson, 'Expounding the Dream: Shaping Fantasies in *A Midsummer Night's Dream*', in *Psychoanalytic Approaches to Literature and Film*, ed. Maurice Charney and Joseph Reppen (Rutherford, NJ: Fairleigh Dickinson University Press, 1987), pp. 120–38.

Hodgdon, Barbara, 'Gaining a Father: The Role of Egeus in the Quarto and the Folio', *Review of English Studies* n.s. 37 (1986), pp. 534–42.

Hodgdon, Barbara, 'Looking for Mr. Shakespeare after "The Revolution": Robert LePage's Intercultural Dream Machine', in *Shakespeare, Theory, and Performance*, ed. James Bulman (London: Routledge, 1996), pp. 68–91.

Holland, Norman N., 'Hermia's Dream', in *Annual of Psychoanalysis* 7 (1979), pp. 369–89, repr. in *Representing Shakespeare: New Psychoanalytic Essays*, ed. Murray M. Schwartz and Coppélia Kahn (Baltimore, MD: Johns Hopkins University Press, 1980).

Hollindale, Peter, *Shakespeare: A Midsummer Night's Dream* (Harmondsworth: Penguin, 1992).

Homan, Sidney R., 'The Single World of *A Midsummer Night's Dream*', *Bucknell Review* 17.1 (1969), pp. 72–84.

Hopkins, Lisa, '*A Midsummer Night's Dream* and Mary Sidney', *English Language Notes* 41.4 (2004), pp. 23–28.

Hopkins, Lisa, *Writing Renaissance Queens: Texts by and about Elizabeth I and Mary, Queen of Scots* (Newark, DE: University of Delaware Press, 2002).

Hopkins, Lisa, *Shakespeare on the Edge: Border-Crossing in the Tragedies and the Henriad* (Aldershot: Ashgate, 2005).

Hopkins, Lisa, 'The Dark Side of the Moon: Semiramis and Titania', in *Goddesses and Queens: The Iconography of Elizabeth I*, ed. Annaliese Connolly and Lisa Hopkins (Manchester: Manchester University Press, 2007), pp. 117–35.

Howard, Jean E, *The Stage and Social Struggle in Early Modern England* (London: Routledge, 1994).

Howard, Skiles, 'Hands, Feet, and Bottoms: Decentering the Cosmic Dance in *A Midsummer Night's Dream*', *Shakespeare Quarterly* 44 (1993), pp. 325–42.

Hudson, H. N., Rev., *Shakespeare: His Life, Art, and Characters* (rev. ed. vol. 1. 1872) (New York: Haskell House, 1970).

Hunt, Maurice, 'A Speculative Political Allegory in *A Midsummer Night's Dream*', *Comparative Drama* 34 (2000–01), pp. 423–53.

Hunt, Maurice, 'The Voices of *A Midsummer Night's Dream*', *Texas Studies in Literature and Language* 34 (1992), pp. 18–38.

Hunter, G. K., *Shakespeare: The Later Comedies* (London: Longmans, Green 1962).

Hunter, William B., 'New Readings of *A Midsummer Night's Dream*', *ANQ* 15 (2002), pp. 3–10.

Hunter, William B., 'Performance and Text: The Evidence of *A Midsummer Night's Dream*', *ANQ* 11 (1998), pp. 7–11.

Huston, J. Dennis, *Shakespeare's Comedies of Play* (New York: Columbia University Press, 1981).

Jacobson, Gerald F., 'A Note on Shakespeare's *Midsummer Night's Dream*', *American Imago* 19 (1962), pp. 21–26.

Kastan, David Scott, *Shakespeare After Theory* (New York: Routledge, 1999).

Kavanagh, James H., 'Shakespeare in Ideology', in *Alternative Shakespeares*, ed. John Drakakis (London: Methuen, 1985), pp. 144–65.

Kehler, Dorothea, '*A Midsummer Night's Dream*: A Bibliographic Survey of the Criticism', in *A Midsummer Night's Dream: Critical Essays*, ed. Dorothea Kehler (New York: Garland, 1998), pp. 3–76.

Kehler, Dorothea, ed., *A Midsummer Night's Dream: Critical Essays* (New York: Garland, 1999).

Kennedy, Judith M., '*A Midsummer Night's Dream* in the 1990s', *Shakespeare International Yearbook* 1 (1999), pp. 287–301. Also titled *Where Are We Now in Shakespearean Studies*, ed. W. R. Elton and John M. Mucciolo (Aldershot: Ashgate, 1999).

Kennedy, Judith M., *Shakespeare: The Critical Tradition: A Midsummer Night's Dream* (London: Athlone, 1999).

Kermode, Frank, 'The Mature Comedies', in *Early Shakespeare*, ed. John Russell Brown and Bernard Harris (London: Edward Arnold, 1961), pp. 211–27.

Knight, G. Wilson, *The Shakespearian Tempest* (Oxford: Oxford University Press, 1932).

Kott, Jan, 'Titania and the Ass's Head', in *A Midsummer Night's Dream: Critical Essays*, ed. Dorothea Kehler (New York: Garland, 1998), pp. 107–25.

Kott, Jan, 'The Bottom Translation', trans. Daniela Miedzyrzecka, in *Assays: Critical Approaches to Medieval and Renaissance Texts*, ed. Peggy A. Knapp and Michael A. Stugrin, vol. 1 (Pittsburgh, PA: University of Pittsburgh Press), pp. 117–49.

Kott, Jan, *Shakespeare Our Contemporary* (New York: Doubleday, 1964).

Krieger, Elliot, *A Marxist Study of Shakespeare's Comedies* (New York: Barnes & Noble, 1979).

Lamb, Mary Ellen, 'Taken by the Fairies: Fairy Practices and the Production of Popular Culture in *A Midsummer Night's Dream*', *Shakespeare Quarterly* 51 (2000), pp. 277–312.

Lamb, Mary Ellen, '*A Midsummer Night's Dream*: The Myth of Theseus and the Minotaur', *Texas Studies in Literature and Language* 21 (1979), pp. 478–91.

Latham, Minor White, *The Elizabethan Fairies: The Fairies of Folklore and the Fairies of Shakespeare* (1930) (New York: Octagon, 1972).

Leggatt, Alexander, *Shakespeare's Comedy of Love*, (London: Methuen, 1974).

Leinwand, Theodore B., ' "I Believe We Must Leave the Killing Out": Deference and Accommodation in *A Midsummer Night's Dream*', *Renaissance Papers 1986*, pp. 11–30.

Long, John H., *Shakespeare's Use of Music: A Study of the Music and Its Performance in the Original Production of Seven Comedies* (Gainesville, FL: University of Florida Press, 1955).

Loomba, Ania, 'The Great Indian Vanishing Trick: Colonialism, Property, and the Family in *A Midsummer Night's Dream*', in *A Feminist Companion to Shakespeare*, ed. Dympna Callaghan (Malden: Blackwell Publishers, 2000), pp. 163–87.

Lull, Janis, 'Textual Theory, Literary Interpretation, and the Last Act of *A Midsummer Night's Dream*', in *A Midsummer Night's Dream: Critical Essays*, ed. Dorothea Kehler (New York: Garland, 1998), pp. 241–58.

Lynch, Kathryn L., 'Baring Bottom: Shakespeare and the Chaucerian Dream Vision', in *Reading Dreams: The Interpretation of Dreams from Chaucer to Shakespeare*, ed. Peter Brown (Oxford: Oxford University Press, 1999), pp. 99–124.

MacKenzie, Agnes Mure, *The Women of Shakespeare's Plays: A Critical Study from the Dramatic and the Psychological Points of View and in Relation to the Development of Shakespeare's Art* (Garden City, NY: Doubleday, Page, 1924).

MacOwan, Michael, 'The Sad Case of Professor Kott', *Drama* 88 (spring, 1968), pp. 30–37.

Maginn, William, *The Shakespeare Papers of the Late William Maginn, LL.D.*, ed. Shelton Mackenzie (New York: Redfield, 1856).

Malone, Edmond, '*The Plays and Poems of William Shakspeare*, vol. 2 (1821) (New York: AMS Press, 1966).

Mansfield, Nick, *Masochism: The Art of Power* (Westport, CT: Praeger, 1997).

Marcus, Mordecai, 'A Midsummer Night's Dream: The Dialectic of Eros-Thanatos', *American Imago* 38.3 (1981), pp. 269–78.

Marowitz, Charles, *Recycling Shakespeare* (New York: Applause/Theatre Books, 1991).

Marshall, David, 'Exchanging Visions: Reading *A Midsummer Night's Dream*', *ELH* 49 (1982), pp. 543–75.

Maslen, R. W. , 'Dream, Freedom of Speech, and the Demonic Affiliations of Robin Goodfellow', *Journal of Northern Renaissance* 1 (2009), online: www.northernrenaissance.org/issues/The–Idea–of–North/1.

Maus, Katharine Eisaman, 'Sorcery and Subjectivity in Early Modern Discourses of Witchcraft', in *Historicism, Psychoanalysis, and Early Modern Culture*, ed. Carla Mazzio and Douglas Trevor (New York: Routledge, 2000), pp. 325–48.

McAlindon, Tom, *Shakespeare Minus Theory* (Aldershot: Ashgate, 2004).

McDonald, Marcia, 'Bottom's Space: Historicizing Comic Theory and Practice in *A Midsummer Night's Dream*', in *Acting Funny: Comic Theory and Practice in Shakespeare's Plays*, ed. Frances Teague (Rutherford, NJ: Fairleigh Dickinson University Press, 1994), pp. 85–108.

McGinn, Colin, *Shakespeare's Philosophy: Discovering the Meaning behind the Plays* (New York: HarperCollins, 2006).

McGuire, Philip C., 'Egeus and the Implications of Silence', in *Shakespeare and the Sense of Performance: Essays in the Tradition of Performance Criticism in Honor of Bernard Beckerman*, ed. Marvin and Ruth Thompson (Newark, DE: University of Delaware Press, 1989), pp. 103–115.

Mikics, David, 'Poetry and Politics in *A Midsummer Night's Dream*', *Raritan* 18.2 (1998), pp. 99–119.

Miller, Donald C., 'Titania and the Changeling', *English Studies* 22 (1940), pp. 66–70.

Miller, Ronald F., '*A Midsummer Night's Dream*: The Fairies, Bottom, and the Mystery of Things', *Shakespeare Quarterly* 26 (1975), pp. 254–68.

Moffatt, Laurel, 'The Woods as Heterotopia in *A Midsummer Night's Dream*', *Studia Neophilologica* 76 (2004), pp. 182–87.

Moisan, Thomas, 'Antique Fables, Fairy Toys: Elisions, Allusion, and Translation in *A Midsummer Night's Dream*', in *A Midsummer Night's Dream: Critical Essays*, ed. Dorothea Kehler (New York: Garland, 1998), pp. 275–98.

Moisan, Thomas, 'Chaucerian *Solempnytee* and the Illusion of Order in Shakespeare's Athens and Verona', *Upstart Crow* 7 (1987), pp. 36–49.

Montrose, Louis Adrian, ' "Shaping Fantasies": Figurations of Gender and Power in Elizabethan Culture', *Representations* 2 (1983), pp. 61–94.

Montrose, Louis Adrian, 'A Kingdom of Shadows', in *The Theatrical City: Culture, Theatre, and Politics in London 1576–1649*, ed. David L. Smith, Richard Strier and David Bevington (Cambridge: Cambridge University Press, 1995), pp. 68–86.

Montrose, Louis Adrian, *The Purpose of Playing: Shakespeare and the Cultural Politics of the Elizabethan Theatre* (Chicago: University of Chicago Press, 1996).

Mousley, Andy, *Renaissance Drama and Contemporary Literary Theory* (New York: St Martin's Press, 2002).

Muir, Kenneth, *Shakespeare's Sources*, vol. 1, *Comedies and Tragedies* (London: Methuen, 1961).

Nemerov, Howard, 'The Marriage of Theseus and Hippolyta', *Kenyon Review* 18 (1956), pp. 633–41.

Nevo, Ruth, *Comic Transformations in Shakespeare* (London: Methuen, 1980).

Normand, Lawrence and Roberts, Gareth, *Witchcraft in Early Modern Scotland: James VI's Demonology and the North Berwick Witches* (Exeter: Exeter University Press, 2000).

Nutt, Alfred, 'The Fairy Mythology of English Literature: Its Origins and Nature', *Folklore* 8 (1897), pp. 29–53.

Nuttall, A. D., 'A Midsummer Night's Dream: Comedy as Apotrope of Myth', Shakespeare Survey 53 (2000), pp. 49–59.

Olson, Paul A., 'A Midsummer Night's Dream and the Meaning of Court Marriage', ELH 24 (1957), pp. 95–119.

Ormerod, David, 'A Midsummer Night's Dream: The Monster in the Labyrinth', Shakespeare Studies 11 (1978), pp. 39–52.

Ovid, Metamorphoses, trans. Arthur Golding, ed. John Frederick Nims (Philadelphia, PA: P. Dry Books, 2000).

Palmer, John, Comic Characters of Shakespeare (London: Macmillan, 1946).

Paré, Ambroise, On Monsters and Marvels, trans. and ed. Janis Pallister (Chicago: University of Chicago Press, 1982).

Parker, Patricia, '(Peter) Quince: Love Potions, Carpenter's Coigns, and Athenian Weddings', Shakespeare Survey 56 (2003), pp. 39–54.

Parker, Patricia, Shakespeare from the Margins: Language, Culture, Context (Chicago: University of Chicago Press, 1996).

Parker, Patricia, 'The Name of Nick Bottom', in Autour du Songe d'une nuit d'été de William Shakespeare, ed. Claire Gheeraert-Graffeuille and Nathalie Vienne-Guerrin (Rouen: Publications de l'Université de Rouen, 2003), pp. 9–29.

Pask, Kevin, 'Engrossing Imagination: A Midsummer Night's Dream', Shakespearean International Yearbook 3 (2003), pp. 172–92.

Paster, Gail Kern and Howard, Skiles, A Midsummer Night's Dream: Texts and Contexts (Boston, MA: Bedford, 1999).

Patterson, Annabel, 'Bottoms Up: Festive Theory in A Midsummer Night's Dream', Renaissance Papers (1988), pp. 25–39.

Pearson, D'Orsay W., 'Male Sovereignty, Harmony and Irony in A Midsummer Night's Dream', Upstart Crow 7 (1987), pp. 24–35.

Pearson, D'Orsay W., '"Unkinde" Theseus: A Study in Renaissance Mythography', English Literary Renaissance 4.2 (1974), pp. 276–98.

Pepys, Samuel, '29 September 1662', in The Diary of Samuel Pepys, ed. Robert Latham and William Matthews, vol. 3 (Berkeley, CA: University of California Press, 1970).

Pettet, E. C., Shakespeare and the Romance Tradition (London: Staples, 1949).

Phialas, Peter G., Shakespeare's Romantic Comedies: The Development of Their Form and Meaning (Chapel Hill, NC: University of North Carolina Press, 1966).

Pinciss, Gerald, Why Shakespeare: An Introduction to the Playwright's Art (London: Continuum, 2005).

Priestley, J. B., The English Comic Characters (London: Bodley Head, 1925).

Prior, Roger, 'The Occasion of A Midsummer Night's Dream', Library Record 17 (2000), pp. 56–64.

Purkiss, Diane, At the Bottom of the Garden: A Dark History of Fairies, Hobgoblins, and Other Troublesome Things (New York: New York University Press, 2000).

Raman, Shankar, Framing 'India': The Colonial Imaginary in Early Modern Culture (Stanford, CA: Stanford University Press, 2002).

Reid, Robert L., 'The Fairy Queen: Gloriana or Titania?', Upstart Crow 13 (1993), pp. 16–32.

Richmond, Hugh M., Shakespeare's Sexual Comedy: A Mirror for Lovers (Indianapolis, IN: Bobbs–Merrill, 1971).

Richmond, Hugh M., 'Shaping a Dream', Shakespeare Studies 17 (1985), pp. 49–60.

Rickert, Edith, 'Political Propaganda and Satire in A Midsummer Night's Dream', Modern Philology 21 (1923–24), pp. 133–54.

Riehle, Wolfgang, 'What's in Lysander's Name?' Notes and Queries 54 (2007), pp. 274–75.

Riemer, A.P., Antic Fables: Patterns of Evasion in Shakespeare's Comedies (New York: St Martin's Press, 1980).

Robinson, James E., 'The Ritual and Rhetoric of A Midsummer Night's Dream', PMLA 83 (1968), pp. 380–91.

Robinson, J. W., 'Palpable Hot Ice: Dramatic Burlesque in *A Midsummer Night's Dream*', *Studies in Philology* 61 (1964), pp. 192–204.

Rose, Mark, *Shakespearean Design* (Cambridge, MA: Belknap Press of Harvard University Press, 1972).

Rudd, Niall, 'Pyramus and Thisbe in Shakespeare and Ovid', in *Shakespeare's Ovid: The Metamorphoses in the Plays and Poems*, ed. A. B. Taylor (Cambridge: Cambridge University Press, 2000), pp. 113–25.

Schalkwyk, David, 'Performance and Imagination', in *Shakespeare, Love and Service* (Cambridge: Cambridge University Press, 2008), pp. 57–79.

Schanzer, Ernest, 'The Central Theme of *A Midsummer Night's Dream*', *University of Toronto Quarterly* 20 (1951), pp. 233–38.

Schanzer, Ernest, 'The Moon and the Fairies in *A Midsummer Night's Dream*', *University of Toronto Quarterly* 24 (1955), pp. 234–46.

Schlegel, August Wilhelm, 'Criticisms on Shakspeare's Comedies', in *A Course of Lectures on Dramatic Art and Literature*, trans. John Black, ed. A. J. W. Morrison, rev. edn (London: Henry G. Bohn, 1846), pp. 379–99.

Schleiner, Winfried, 'Imaginative Sources for Shakespeare's Puck', *Shakespeare Quarterly* 36 (1985), pp. 65–68.

Schneider, Michael, 'Bottom's Dream, the Lion's Roar, and Hostility of Class Difference in *A Midsummer Night's Dream*', in *From the Bard to Broadway*, ed. Karelisa V. Hartigan (Lanham, MD: University Press of America, 1987), pp. 191–212.

Scholar, Richard, *The je-ne-sais-quoi in Early Modern Europe: Encounters with a Certain Something* (Oxford: Oxford University Press, 2005).

Scot, Reginald, *The Discoverie of Witchcraft*, ed. Brinsley Nicholson (Wakefield: E. P. Publishing, 1973).

Schwarz, Kathryn, *Tough Love: Amazon Encounters in the English Renaissance* (Durham, NC: Duke University Press, 2000).

Sewell, Elizabeth, *The Orphic Voice: Poetry and Natural History* (New Haven, CT: Yale University Press, 1960–61).

Shakespeare, William, *A Midsummer Night's Dream*, ed. Harold F. Brooks (Cambridge, MA: Harvard University Press, 1979).

Shakespeare, William, *A Midsummer Night's Dream*, ed. R.A. Foakes (Cambridge: Cambridge University Press, 1984).

Shakespeare, William, *A Midsummer Night's Dream*, ed. Peter Holland (Oxford: Oxford University Press, 1994).

Shakespeare, William, *A Midsummer Night's Dream*, ed. Helen Hackett (Plymouth: Northcote House, 1997).

Shakespeare, William, *A Midsummer Night's Dream*, ed. Burton Raffel (New Haven, CT: Yale University Press, 2005).

Shakespeare, William, *A Midsummer Night's Dream*, ed. Mario DiGangi (New York: Barnes & Noble, 2007).

Sidgwick, Frank, *The Sources and Analogues of 'A Midsummer-Night's Dream'* (London: Chatto & Windus, 1908).

Sidnell, Michael J. 'Semiotic Arts of Theatre', *Semiotica* 168 (2008), pp. 11–43.

Sillars, Stuart, ' "Howsoever, strange and admirable:" *A Midsummer Night's Dream as via stultitiae'*, *Archiv für das Studium der neueren Sprachen und Literaturen* 244 (2007), pp. 27–39.

Sinfield, Alan, 'Cultural Materialism and Intertextuality: The Limits of Queer Reading in *A Midsummer Night's Dream* and *The Two Noble Kinsmen*', *Shakespeare Survey* 56 (2003), pp. 67–78.

Slights, William W. E., 'The Changeling in *A Dream*', *SEL: Studies in English Literature, 1500–1900* 28 (spring 1988), pp. 259–72.

Speaight, Robert, *Shakespeare on Stage* (New York: Little Brown, 1973).

Spenser, Edmund, *The Faerie Queene*, ed. A.C. Hamilton, 2nd edn, rev. (Harlow: Pearson Longman, 2007).

Stansbury, Joan, 'Characterization of the Four Young Lovers in *A Midsummer Night's Dream*', *Shakespeare Survey* 35 (1982), pp. 57–63.

Stern, Tiffany, *Rehearsal from Shakespeare to Sheridan* (Oxford: The Clarendon Press, 2000).

Stern, Tiffany and Palfrey, Simon, *Shakespeare in Parts* (Oxford: Oxford University Press, 2007).

Stott, Andrew,' "The Fondness, the Filthiness": Deformity and Laughter in Early-Modern Comedy', *Upstart Crow* 24 (2004), pp. 15–24.

Stroup, Thomas B., 'Bottom's Name and His Epiphany', *Shakespeare Quarterly* 29 (1978), pp. 79–82.

Styan, J. L., *The Shakespeare Revolution* (Cambridge: Cambridge University Press, 1977).

Sullivan, Garrett A., *Memory and Forgetting in English Renaissance Drama: Shakespeare, Marlowe, Webster* (Cambridge: Cambridge University Press, 2005).

Suzuki, Mihoko, 'The Dismemberment of Hippolytus: Humanist Imitation, Shakespeare's Translation', *Classical and Modern Literature* 10 (1990), pp. 103–12.

Swann, Marjorie, 'The Politics of Fairylore in Early Modern English Literature', *Renaissance Quarterly* 53 (2000), pp. 449–73.

Szskolczai, Arpad, 'Image-magic in *A Midsummer Night's Dream*: Power and Modernity from Weber to Shakespeare', *History of the Human Sciences* 20.4 (2007), pp. 1–26.

Tave, Stuart M., *Lovers, Clowns, and Fairies: An Essay on Comedies* (Chicago: University of Chicago Press, 1993).

Taylor, Anthony Brian, 'Golding's Ovid, Shakespeare's "Small Latin" and the Real Object of Mockery in *Pyramus and Thisbe*', *Shakespeare Survey* 42 (1990), pp. 53–64.

Taylor, Anthony Brian, 'John Gower and "Pyramus and Thisbe" ', *Notes and Queries* 54 (2007), pp. 282–83.

Taylor, Anthony Brian, 'Ovid's Myths and the Unsmooth Course of Love in *A Midsummer Night's Dream*', in *Shakespeare and the Classics*, ed. Charles Martindale and A. B. Taylor (Cambridge: Cambridge University Press, 2004), pp. 49–65.

Taylor, Anthony Brian, ' "When everything seems double": Peter Quince, the Other Playwright in *A Midsummer Night's Dream*', *Shakespeare Survey* 56 (2003), pp. 55–66.

Taylor, Mark, *Shakespeare's Imitations* (Newark, DE: University of Delaware Press, 2002).

Thompson, Ayanna, ed., *Colorblind Shakespeare: New Perspectives on Race and Performance* (New York: Routledge, 2006).

Thomsen, Kerri Lynne, 'Melting Vows: *A Midsummer Night's Dream* and Ovid's *Heroycall Epistles*', *English Language Notes*, 40.4 (2003), pp. 25–33.

Traub, Valerie, 'Setting the Stage behind the Seen: Performing Lesbian History', in *The Queerest Art: Essays on Lesbian and Gay Theater*, ed. Alisa Solomon and Framji Minwalla (New York: New York University Press, 2002), pp. 55–105.

Traub, Valerie, 'The (In)Significance of "Lesbian" Desire in Early Modern England', in *Erotic Politics: Desire on the Renaissance Stage*, ed. Susan Zimmerman (New York: Routledge, 1992), pp. 150–69.

Turner, Frederick, *Shakespeare's Twenty-First Century Economics: The Morality of Love and Money* (Oxford: Oxford University Press, 1999).

Turner, Henry S., *Shakespeare's Double Helix* (London: Continuum, 2007).

Turner, Robert K., Jr, 'Printing Methods and Textual Problems in *A Midsummer Night's Dream* Q1', *Studies in Bibliography* 15 (1962), pp. 33–55.

Ulrici, Hermann, *Shakspeare's Dramatic Art: And His Relation to Calderon and Goethe*, trans. A. J. W. Morrison (London: Chapman Brothers, 1846).

Van Doren, Mark, *Shakespeare* (New York: Henry Holt, 1939).

Vickers, Brian, 'From Clown to Character', in *The Artistry of Shakespeare's Prose* (London: Methuen, 1968), pp. 52–88.

Vyvyan, John, *Shakespeare and Platonic Beauty* (London: Chatto and Windus, 1961).

Wall, Wendy, 'Why Does Puck Sweep?: Fairylore, Merry Wives, and Social Struggle', *Shakespeare Quarterly* 52.1 (2001), pp. 67–106.

Wall, Wendy, *Staging Domesticity: Household Work and English Identity in Early Modern Drama* (Cambridge: Cambridge University Press, 2002).

Warren, Roger, *Text & Performance: 'A Midsummer Night's Dream'* (Basingstoke: Macmillan, 1983).

Watts, Cedric, 'Does Bottom Cuckold Oberon?' in *Henry V, War Criminal? and Other Shakespeare Puzzles,* ed. John Sutherland and Cedric Watts (Oxford: Oxford University Press, 2000), pp. 127–42.

Wedgwood, Julia, 'The *Midsummer Night's Dream*', *Contemporary Review* (April 1890), pp. 580–87, repr. in *Women Reading Shakespeare 1660–1900: An Anthology of Criticism*, ed. Ann Thompson and Sasha Roberts (Manchester: Manchester University Press, 1997).

Weil, Herbert S., 'Comic Structure and Tonal Manipulation in Shakespeare and Some Modern Plays', *Shakespeare Survey* 22 (1969), pp. 27–33.

Weimann, Robert, *Author's Pen and Actor's Voice: Playing and Writing in Shakespeare's Theatre* (Cambridge: Cambridge University Press, 2000).

Weiner, Andrew D., ' "Multiformitie Uniforme": A Midsummer Night's Dream', *ELH* 38 (1971), pp. 329–49.

Wells, Stanley, *Looking for Sex in Shakespeare* (Cambridge: Cambridge University Press, 2004).

Wells, Stanley, 'Translation in *A Midsummer Night's Dream*', in *Translating Life: Studies in Transpositional Aesthetics*, ed. Shirley Chew and Alistair Stead (Liverpool: Liverpool University Press, 1999), pp. 15–32.

Wells, Stanley, Taylor, Gary, *et al.*, *William Shakespeare: The Complete Works*. Oxford Shakespeare, 2nd edn (Oxford: Clarendon Press, 2005).

Welsford, Enid, *The Court Masque: A Study in the Relationship Between Poetry & the Revels* (Cambridge: Cambridge University Press, 1927).

Wiles, David, *Shakespeare's Almanac: 'A Midsummer Night's Dream', Marriage, and the Elizabethan Calendar* (Cambridge: D.S. Brewer, 1993).

Williams, Gary Jay, *Our Moonlight Revels: 'A Midsummer Night's Dream' in the Theatre* (Iowa City, IA: University of Iowa Press, 1997).

Williams, Penry, 'Shakespeare's *A Midsummer Night's Dream*: Social Tensions Contained', in *The Theatrical City: Culture, Theatre and Politics in London 1576–1649*, ed. David L. Smith, Richard Strier and David Bevington (Cambridge: Cambridge University Press, 1995), pp. 55–67.

Wilson, John Dover, 'The Copy for *A Midsummer Night's Dream*', in *A Midsummer-Night's Dream*, ed. Arthur Quiller-Couch and John Dover Wilson (Cambridge: Cambridge University Press, 1924).

Wilson, John Dover, *Shakespeare's Happy Comedies* (London: Faber & Faber, 1962), pp. 184–220.

Wilson, Richard, *Shakespeare in French Theory: King of Shadows* (London: Routledge, 2007).

Witte, Anne E., 'Bottom's Tangled Web: Texts and Textiles in *A Midsummer Night's Dream*', *Cahiers Élisabéthains* 56 (1999), pp. 25–39.

Woodcock, Matthew, *Fairy in The Faerie Queene: Renaissance Elf-Fashioning and Elizabethan Myth-Making* (Aldershot: Ashgate, 2004).

Woodcock, Matthew, 'The Fairy Queen Figure in Elizabethan Entertainments', in *Elizabeth I: Always Her Own Free Woman*, ed. Carole Levin, Debra Barrett-Graves and Jo Eldridge Carney (Aldershot: Ashgate, 2003), pp. 97–118.

Wright, George T., *Shakespeare's Metrical Art* (Berkeley, CA: University of California Press, 1988).

Wyrick, Deborah Baker, 'The Ass Motif in *The Comedy of Errors* and *A Midsummer Night's Dream*', *Shakespeare Quarterly* 33 (1982), pp. 432–48.

Young, David P., *Something of Great Constancy: The Art of 'A Midsummer Night's Dream'* (New Haven, CT: Yale University Press, 1996).

Zimbardo, R. A., 'Regeneration and Reconciliation in *A Midsummer Night's Dream*', *Shakespeare Studies* 6 (1970), pp. 35–50.

Zitner, Sheldon P., 'The Worlds of *A Midsummer Night's Dream*', *South Atlantic Quarterly* 59 (1960), pp. 397–403.

Notes on Contributors

Regina Buccola holds a PhD from the University of Illinois at Chicago. She is an Associate Professor of English and Core Faculty in Women's and Gender Studies at Roosevelt University. Among her publications on issues of gender roles and gendered identity in early modern British drama are *Fairies, Fractious Women and the Old Faith* and, with Lisa Hopkins, the essay collection *Marian Moments in Early Modern British Drama*. She is also a poet, with a recent chapbook entitled *Conjuring*.

Tom Clayton earned his DPhil at Oxford University. He is a Regents Professor of English Language and Literature and chair of the Classical Civilization Program at the University of Minnesota, where he has won awards for both graduate and undergraduate teaching, and chairs the Faculty Senate Committee on Academic Freedom and Tenure. He has published extensively on Shakespeare's plays in performance and as literary works, earlier-seventeenth-century British poetry and a variety of other subjects. His lifelong interest in literature *qua* literature, and his conviction that literature is perennially relevant as a 'criticism of life' survived and even intensified during the 'culture wars', and continue unabated.

Annaliese Connolly is lecturer in English at Sheffield Hallam University. Her publications include 'Peele's *David and Bethsabe*: Reconsidering the Drama of the Long 1590s' and 'Evaluating virginity: *A Midsummer Night's Dream* and the iconography of marriage', in *Goddesses and Queens: The iconography of Elizabeth I*. She is also managing editor of *Early Modern Literary Studies*.

Adrienne Eastwood is an assistant professor of English and Comparative Literature at San Jose State University. She earned her doctorate in 2004 from UCSD, specializing in early modern literature and culture. Dr Eastwood is currently investigating early English wedding poetry and the uses of epithalamic conventions in Shakespearean comedy. Other current research interests include early modern women authors, gender and queer studies and popular representations of Elizabeth I.

Dorothea Kehler is an emeritus professor of English Literature at San Diego State University and a Life Member of Clare Hall, Cambridge University. She is the editor of three anthologies: *'A Midsummer Night's Dream': Critical Essays*; *The Single Woman in Medieval and Early Modern England: Her Life and Representation* (with Laurel Amtower); and *In Another Country: Feminist Perspectives on Renaissance Drama* (with Susan Baker). She has published four editions of *Problems in Literary*

Research: A Guide to Selected Reference Works as well as numerous essays, primarily on Shakespeare and his contemporaries. Her monograph, *Shakespeare's Widows*, was published in July 2009.

Jeremy Lopez is associate professor of English at the University of Toronto and the theatre review editor for *Shakespeare Bulletin*. He is the author of *Theatrical Convention and Audience Response in Early Modern Drama* and a book on *Richard II* in the Palgrave Shakespeare Handbooks series (2009).

Paul Menzer is associate professor and director of the MLitt/MFA in Shakespeare and Performance program at Mary Baldwin College. He is author of *The Hamlets: Cues, Q's, and Remembered Texts* and editor of the collection *Inside Shakespeare: Essays on the Blackfriars Stage*. He has published on performance, text and theatre history in such journals as *Shakespeare Quarterly*, *Renaissance Drama*, *Shakespeare Bulletin* and the *Ben Jonson Journal*. His plays, *Anonymous, The Brats of Clarence* and *Shakespeare on Ice* have appeared on the Blackfriars Stage in Staunton, Virginia, and elsewhere.

Tripthi Pillai is a doctoral candidate in the department of English at Loyola University Chicago, where she is completing her dissertation on feminist engagements with temporality and early modern drama. Her current research includes an analysis of the rhetorical tensions in Renaissance literature between memory and anti-memory as they erupt on the cusps of geographical spaces. She teaches introductory and advanced-level courses on Shakespeare and seventeenth-century drama.

Matthew Woodcock is senior lecturer in Medieval and Renaissance Literature at the University of East Anglia, Norwich. He is the author of *Fairy in The Faerie Queene* and *Henry V: A Reader's Guide to Essential Criticism*. He has co-edited an essay collection on Fulke Greville for the *Sidney Journal*, published articles on Shakespeare, Spenser, Milton and Elizabethan entertainments, and is currently researching a biography of Thomas Churchyard.

Index